Introduction to Assemblies of God Missions

An Independent-Study Textbook

by Ronald A. Iwasko and Willard Teague

Second Edition

**Berean School of the Bible,
a Global University School**

1211 South Glenstone Avenue
Springfield, MO 65804 USA

1-800-443-1083
Fax: (417) 862-0863
E-mail: berean@globaluniversity.edu
Web: www.globaluniversity.edu

Dr. Ronald A. Iwasko, was an ordained minister of the General Council of the Assemblies of God. He graduated from the University of Minnesota with a BS degree in pre-engineering (1957) and an MS degree in civil engineering. After becoming as an Air Force officer and a civil engineer, he and his wife Kathy sensed the Lord's calling to full-time ministry. Dr. Iwasko then completed requirements for an MDiv from Trinity Evangelical Divinity School in 1971 and a DMiss in 1984. The couple pastored in the US and then served as missionaries to Brazil, where Dr. Iwasko spent five years pioneering distance education. He and Kathy returned to Springfield, MO, and he worked sixteen years in the Division of Foreign Missions (later called Assemblies of God World Missions department) as Personnel Director and as Director of Special Ministries. Next, Dr. Iwasko spent seven years at North Central University as Chair of the Cross Cultural Ministries Department and as Director of the Carlson Institute, the distance education program of North Central University. He was President of Global University from 1999 to 2006. The Iwaskos' next ministry involved working with AGWM's Africa's Hope. Following a lifetime of ministerial and missionary accomplishments and a battle with leukemia, Dr. Iwasko went home to be with his Lord in January 2014.

Willard Teague graduated from Southwestern Assemblies of God University in 1966 with a BS degree in Bible and Theology. In 1972, he earned a Specialized Diploma in French Studies from Ecole Lémania in Lausanne, Switzerland. Willard completed requirements for the MA degree from the Assemblies of God Theological Seminary in 1980 and the MDiv degree in 1986. In 1996, Dr. Teague completed a DMin degree at Denver Seminary. He also pastored in Oklahoma and served as an evangelist. His missionary service includes fifteen years with the Ivory Coast field, where he planted churches and established the Bible College in Daloa. Following Ivory Coast ministry, Dr. Teague served as faculty and president at the West Africa Advanced School of Theology in Lomé, Togo, West Africa for twelve years. He continues to serve as an appointed world missionary in the capacity of Dean of the School of Undergraduate Studies at Global University, Springfield, Missouri.

The term *Palestine* is used throughout this course to identify the geographic region generally located between the Sea of Galilee and the Negev desert and west of the Jordan River. Although this term is not an official political label for this area either now or during the first century AD, it is a convenient way to reference a geographic area that is very difficult to name due to its tumultuous political, ethnic, and religious history. This descriptive term has been used since the fifth century BC, even though it was not officially applied as a political designation until the second century AD. It is used for convenience because of its general recognition and does not intend any historical, political, or ethnic implications.

Global University
Springfield, Missouri, USA

PN 02.14.01

ISBN 978-0-7617-1470-5

Printed in the United States of America

Table of Contents

Digital Course Options

This printed independent-study textbook (IST) represents only one of the ways you can study through Global University's Berean School of the Bible (BSB). Global University offers electronic delivery formats that allow you to complete courses without using printed material.

You may choose one or more of these course delivery options with or without the printed IST.

Digital Courses

- <u>Online Courses</u>. Complete your entire ministry training program online with fully interactive learning options.

  You can complete your chapter reviews, unit progress evaluations, and final exam online and receive instant results, even if you use print or other digital study versions.

- <u>Logos Bible Software</u>. Purchase an entire digital library of Bibles and Bible reference titles and the Berean courses specifically created to function inside these digital library environments.

- <u>Electronic courses</u>. Check Global University's website for additional electronic course versions (for e-readers and other devices) and their availability.

Enrollment Policies and Procedures

Enrollment policies and procedures are provided in the most current Berean School of the Bible Academic Catalog. An electronic version of the catalog is available at the Global University website.

Contact Global University for Enrollment Information

Phone: 1-800-443-1083 (9 a.m. to 6 p.m., CST, Monday–Friday)

> **Spanish language representatives are available to discuss enrollment in Spanish courses.**

E-mail: berean@globaluniversity.edu

Web: www.globaluniversity.edu

Fax: 417-862-0863

Mail: 1211 S. Glenstone Ave., Springfield, MO 65804

How to Use Berean Courses

Independent study is one of the most dynamic and rapidly growing educational methods. Although different from traditional classroom study, the goal is the same—to guide you, the student, through a systematic program of study and help you gain new knowledge and skills. Berean courses are independent-study courses. Some students may participate in a Berean study group, where a facilitator enhances the learning experience for a group of Berean students. Other options include studying the courses online and/or purchasing digital study tools made possible through Berean's partnership with Logos Bible Software.

All Berean courses are printed in a comprehensive independent-study textbook (IST). The IST is your teacher, textbook, and study guide in one package. Once you have familiarized yourself with the course components, explained below, you are ready to begin studying. Whether you are studying for personal growth or working toward a diploma, the Berean faculty, advisers, and student service representatives are available to help you get the most out of your Berean program.

General Course Design

- Each course is based on course objectives.
- Each course is composed of several units.
- Each unit is composed of several chapters.
- Each chapter is composed of two or more lessons.
- Each lesson contains one or more lesson objectives.
- Each lesson objective corresponds to specific lesson content.

Course Objectives

Course objectives represent the concepts—or knowledge areas—and perspectives the course will teach you. Review these objectives before you begin studying to have an idea of what to focus on as you study. The course objectives are listed on the course introduction page.

Unit Overview

A unit overview previews each unit's content and outlines the unit development.

Chapter, Lesson Content, Lesson Objectives, and Numbering System

Each *chapter* begins with an introduction and outline. The outline presents the chapter's lesson titles and objectives. Chapters consist of short lessons to allow you to complete one lesson at a time (at one sitting), instead of the entire chapter at one time.

The *lesson content* is based on lesson objectives.

Lesson objectives present the important concepts and perspectives to be studied in the course.

Each chapter, lesson, and objective is uniquely numbered. This numbering system is designed to help you relate the lesson objective to its corresponding lesson content. Chapters are numbered consecutively throughout the course. Lessons are numbered within each chapter with a two-digit decimal number. For example, Lesson 2 in Chapter 3 is numbered 3.2. The first number is the chapter (3), the second number is the lesson (2) within the chapter.

Lesson objectives are tagged with a three-digit decimal number. For example, Chapter 1, Lesson 1, Objective 1 is identified as Objective 1.1.1. Chapter 1, Lesson 2, Objective 3 is Objective 1.2.3. The first number is the chapter, the second is the lesson, and the third is the objective. The numbering system is to assist you in identifying, locating, and organizing each chapter, lesson, and objective.

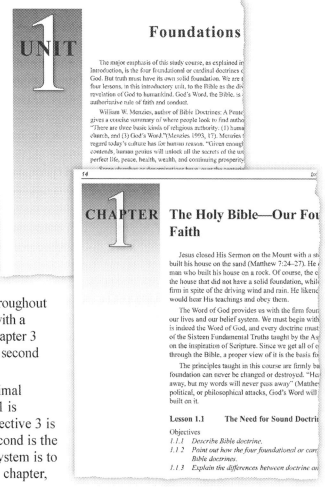

took the place of Hebrew as the langua
Pharisees, Saducees, and **Scribes**—
(small places of worship, study, and s
Jews were ruled by the powerful and h
years under the cultural influence of th
completely (Scroggins 2003, 328).

The Greek Period

The Persian Empire was in power
and Nehemiah rebuilt Jerusalem's wal

 Test Yourself

Circle the letter of the *best* answer.
1. Why are only two chapters of the entire Bibl
devoted to the never-ending eternity?
a) Eternity will be a constant repeat of regular
activity, so no more space is needed.
b) The eternal fate of the wicked should not be
given any more attention
c) Greater details of New Jerusalem would be
meaningless.
d) The purpose of Scripture is to encourage he
living now

2. What happens to the present heaven and eart
make way for new heaven and earth?
a) They are gradually cleansed and changed in

What to Look for in the Margins

Left margins contain numbers for units, chapters, and lessons. In addition, margins contain two learning tools—*lesson objectives with their respective numbers* and *interactive questions* that focus on key principles. Read, understand, and use these two learning tools to study the lesson text.

Interactive questions relate to specific lesson content and specific lesson objectives. Interactive questions, along with lesson objectives, will help you learn the concepts and perspectives that are tested in exam questions. Interactive questions are numbered consecutively within each chapter. Once you understand what the interactive question is asking, search for the answer as you study the lesson's related content section. You can compare your responses to our suggested ones at the back of each chapter.

Lesson objectives present the key concepts. These tips on using lesson objectives will help you master the course content and be prepared for exams:

- Identify the key concept(s) and concept perspectives in the objective.
- Identify and understand what the objective is asking you to do with the key concept(s).
- Think of the objective as an essay test question.
- Read and study the lesson content related to the objective and search for the answer to the "essay test question"—the objective.

Lesson Titles and Subheads

Lesson titles and subheads identify and organize specific lesson content.

Key Words

Key words are presented in **boldface** print and defined in the glossary of this IST; they are words that are used with a specific meaning in the lesson.

Reference Citations

Outside sources are documented using in-text citations in parentheses. These sources are compiled in more detail in the Reference List at the end of the IST.

Test Yourself

The Test Yourself section concludes the chapter with multiple-choice questions based on the lesson objectives, interactive questions, and their supporting lesson content. Test Yourself answer keys are in the Essential Course Materials at the back of this IST.

Glossary and Reference List

A *glossary* (which defines key words) and *reference list* (works cited in each chapter) follow the last chapter of the IST.

Recommended Reading Textbook

An optional textbook is recommended for use with each course. The textbook recommended to accompany this course is listed on the course introduction page. Some courses may provide additional suggested reading lists following the *reference list.*

Essential Course Materials in the back of this IST contain the following:

- Service Learning Requirement (SLR) Assignment and SLR Report Form
- Unit Progress Evaluation (UPE) Instructions and UPEs
- Answer Keys for Test Yourself quizzes and UPEs
- Forms: Round-Tripper (as needed) and Request for a Printed Final Examination (if needed)

Two Requirements to Receive a Course Grade:
To receive a grade for this course, you must:

1. Submit your SLR Report Form. The instructions for the SLR assignment are in the Essential Course Materials at the back of this IST. The report is required, but not graded.

2. You must also take a closed-book final examination. Your course grade is based on the final exam. The Berean School of the Bible grading scale is 90–100 percent, A; 80–89 percent, B; 70–79 percent, C; and 0–69 percent, F.

Checklist of Study Methods

STUDY METHODS	√	If you carefully follow the study methods listed below, you should be able to complete this course successfully. As you complete each chapter, mark a √ in the column for that chapter beside each instruction you followed. Then continue to study the remaining chapters in the same way.																
1. Read the introduction in the Independent-Study Textbook (IST) to learn how to use the IST.																			
2. Study the Table of Contents to familiarize yourself with the course structure and content.																			
CHAPTERS	1	2	3	4	5	6	7	8	9	10	11	12	13	14	15	16	17	18
3. Pace yourself so you will study at least two or three times each week. Plan carefully so you can complete the course within the allowed enrollment period. Complete at least one lesson each study session.																			
4. Read Scripture references in more than one translation of the Bible for better understanding.																			
5. Underline, mark, and write notes in your IST.																			
6. Use a notebook to write additional notes and comments.																			
7. As you work through each chapter, make good use of reference tools, such as a study Bible, a comprehensive concordance, a Bible dictionary, and an English dictionary.																			
8. Complete all interactive questions and learning activities as you go.																			
9. In preparation for the Test Yourself, review the objectives for each lesson in the chapter and your notes and highlights to reinforce the key principles learned in the chapter.																			
10. Discuss with others what you are learning.																			
11. Apply what you have learned in your spiritual life and ministry.																			
UNIT EVALUATIONS																			
Review for each Unit Progress Evaluation by rereading the																			
a. lesson objectives to be sure you can achieve what they state.																			
b. questions you answered incorrectly in Test Yourself.																			
c. lesson material for topics you need to review.																			

Student Planner and Record

This chart is for you to record your personal progress in this course. Be sure to keep it **up to date** for quick reference.

In the boxes below, record the unit number, the date you expect to complete each chapter, the date you *do* complete the chapter, and the date of review.

Unit Number	Chapter Number	Expected Completion Date	Actual Completion Date	Date Reviewed
	1			
	2			
	3			
	4			
	5			
	6			
	7			
	8			
	9			
	10			
	11			
	12			
	13			
	14			
	15			
	16			
	17			
	18			

UNIT EVALUATIONS	Date Completed
Unit Evaluation 1	
Unit Evaluation 2	
Unit Evaluation 3	
Unit Evaluation 4	
Unit Evaluation 5	
Unit Evaluation 6	

WRITTEN ASSIGNMENTS & FINAL EXAM	Date Completed
Service Learning Requirement (SLR) Report	
Final Examination	
SLR report & closed-book final exam materials submitted (The SLR report does not apply to the internship courses.)	

Introduction to
Assemblies of God Missions

The most vital task in our world today is not finding ways to solve the enormous problems facing humanity. These problems include nuclear energy, insufficient and diminishing natural resources, environmental pollution, increasing poverty, and political turmoil. While every Christian should be concerned about these problems, the most pressing need of human society is world evangelism. Global University's motto, "All the Word to all the World," is an indication of the school's emphasis on presenting the gospel "from all nations to all nations." The entire church in every nation must be mobilized for this missionary task.

The Bible clearly declares that the only mediator between God and humanity and the only way of salvation is Christ (Acts 4:12). The consequence of this truth places on each of us an inescapable responsibility to proclaim the gospel to all men and women everywhere.

What exactly are we talking about when we refer to missions? It means communicating the gospel concerning the Lord Jesus Christ to unreached people in all nations. In its technical sense, it refers to evangelism across cultural lines. This course deals with the cross-cultural sense of missions where people are won to Christ, trained as His disciples, and involved in a local church.

Course Description   BMIN261 Introduction to Assemblies of God Missions (5 CEUs)

This is an introductory course in the science of missions. It is a survey of the theology, history, and methods of Christian missions in general and within the Assemblies of God. There is a special emphasis on recent developments, crucial issues, current trends, and missions as they are carried out through national and local churches.

As a supplement to the printed text, a manual titled "The Missions Awareness Team: Checklist for Building Missions in the Local Church" is available as a free PDF download at: http://worldagfellowship.org/wp-content/uploads/2011/08/MANUAL-THE-CHECKLIST1.pdf. This manual demonstrates how to effectively promote missions in the local church. It was authored by missionary Paul Brannan and produced by U.S. Relations, Assemblies of God World Missions, General Council of the Assemblies of God, Springfield, MO.

In addition to using your Bible, we recommend that you also use *Missions in the Age of the Spirit* by John V. York to enhance your learning experience.

Course Objectives

Upon completion of this course, you should be able to

1. Understand what the Bible teaches about missions.

2. Trace the theme of God's mission throughout the Old and New Testaments.

3. Appreciate the role of missions in church history and in the Assemblies of God, both in the United States and in other countries.

4. Explain various methods used in the task of missions.

5. Apply principles of partnership to missions on the local, national, and international levels.

6. Understand the key role of the local church in missions.

7. Identify and examine current trends in modern missions.

8. Appreciate the role of missions in the social and political environment.

BEFORE YOU BEGIN

Successfully completing this course requires that you apply content you study in a ministry activity. The instructions for this Service Learning Requirement (SLR) are found in the Essential Course Materials in the back of this IST. Please take time now to become familiar with these instructions so that you can be planning your SLR activity throughout your study of this course.

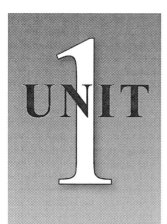

Fundamental Concepts in Missions

A study of the fundamental concepts and the biblical foundations of missions is needed to have a better perspective of what the Holy Spirit has accomplished and is presently doing in the world through the church of the Lord Jesus Christ. Consequently, the first unit of this course covers the basic concepts of missions, the biblical basis of missions in both the Old and New Testaments, and cross-cultural communications.

We need to understand what is meant by the terms *missions* and *missionary*. It is also needful to comprehend the motives and purpose of missions, as well as improper motives that can damage the reputation of the missionary and missions.

Unit 1 establishes the foundation for the entire course. It is the desire of the writers of this course that the reader be inspired to reach out to the nations of the world through giving, praying, and personal going. These are the words of the Lord himself: "All authority in heaven and on earth has been given to me. Therefore go and make disciples of all nations, baptizing them in the name of the Father and of the Son and of the Holy Spirit, and teaching them to obey everything I have commanded you. And surely I am with you always, to the very end of the age" (Matthew 28:18–20). Following Christ to reach all people is at the heart of discipleship and obedience to His command.

Chapter 1　　　The Biblical Perspective

Lessons
1.1　　Missions and the Missionary
1.2　　Motives for Missions
1.3　　Missions in Light of the Second Coming

Chapter 2　　　The Biblical Foundation for Missions

Lessons
2.1　　Missions in the Old Testament
2.2　　Missions in the New Testament

Chapter 3　　　Cross-Cultural Communication

Lesson
3.1　　Worldview and Cultural Barriers

CHAPTER 1

The Biblical Perspective

Foundational to the study of missions is a clear understanding of the terminology and the conceptual basis for missionary activity. Accordingly, the first lesson of Chapter 1 provides a study of the terminology as currently used and as carefully defined by leading missiologists based upon the biblical text. It also includes an examination of the root words for *mission* and *missionary* in both the Greek and Latin languages and as understood by Christ and the apostles. This leads to a study of the ultimate purpose of missions as intended by God. Lesson 2 builds upon these concepts to explore the primary, spiritual, God-given motive for missions and several subordinate motivating factors that flow from it. This is followed by a review of some improper motives that can be destructive. Finally, the third lesson examines the second coming of Christ and its impact on the missionary enterprise. It seeks to answer the question of the relationship of missionary activity to the time of the Lord's return, and it considers the response of the church.

Lesson 1.1   Missions and the Missionary

Objectives
1.1.1   Define the terms missions *and* missionary.
1.1.2   Describe the ultimate purpose of missions as it relates to humanity.

Lesson 1.2   Motives for Missions

Objectives
1.2.1   Identify the primary motive of missions.
1.2.2   Discuss the importance of the Holy Spirit in motivating believers to engage in missions.
1.2.3   Explain what is meant by the sovereignty of God as a motivating factor for missions.
1.2.4   Discuss inappropriate motives for missionary service.

Lesson 1.3   Missions in Light of the Second Coming

Objectives
1.3.1   Examine the imperatives of Matthew 24 as they apply to the Church today.
1.3.2   Evaluate lessons learned from the disciples' confusion over the timing of the "last days."
1.3.3   Discuss Jesus' statement in Matthew 24:14 as it relates to missions efforts and the time of His return.
1.3.4   Identify the four-fold task of the Church.

1.1.1
OBJECTIVE
Define the terms missions
and missionary.

Missions and the Missionary

Missions

Foundational to the study of missions is the understanding of the terminology. Defining *missions* is not as simple as it might first appear. The word has a wide range of meanings depending upon the context. For example, one might speak of diplomatic missions or military missions or inner-city missions. In evangelical church circles, the word is most often associated with the adjective *foreign* or *world*, to mean programs of ministry sent from the United States church to another country. Missions is then associated with geography.

In the truest sense, Christian missions can no longer be tied purely to geographical location. For at its heart, missions is the sending of persons from an existing congregation to address people of other cultures and places beyond the usual influence of the church. The usual purpose of the effort is to bring people to a saving knowledge of Jesus Christ and help them to fervently and completely follow Him.

For administrative purposes, the Assemblies of God USA speaks of World Missions and US Missions. Yet with the effects of globalization today, outreaches to various ethnic and religious populations are to be found both in the United States and around the world. Immigrant ethnic populations in the United States and elsewhere often seek to maintain their cultural identity. Attempts to reach them for Christ surely can be termed missions. Thus, missions may be among Buddhists in Myanmar or Somalis in Minneapolis. In today's globalized world, mission activity can be anywhere.

George Peters gives the following extensive definition of *missions*:

Missions is a specialized term. By it I mean the sending forth of authorized persons beyond the borders of the New Testament church and her immediate gospel influence to proclaim the gospel of Jesus Christ in gospel-destitute areas, to win converts from other faiths or non-faiths to Jesus Christ, and to establish functioning, multiplying local congregations who will bear the fruit of Christianity in that community and to that country. (Peters 1972, 11)

For our purposes in this study, we shall define *missions* as the selecting of certain persons to represent the church to share the claims of Christ across geographical and cultural boundaries so as to win people to Christ and equip them for His service.

In the Christian context, the concept of missions is based on the mission of God himself. From first to last, the Bible reveals God as the great lover of humankind, the Redeemer, the Savior. By both precept and example, God seeks to shepherd the people of His creation into an intimate relationship with himself that they might enjoy the fullness of His presence with them.

Passages such as John 3:16–17 make this clear: "God so loved the world that he gave his one and only Son, that whoever believes in him shall not perish but have eternal life. For God did not send his Son into the world to condemn the world, but to save the world through him." This same thought is echoed by the apostle Paul in Galatians 4:4–5: "When the time had fully come, God sent his Son, born of a woman, born under law, to redeem those under law, that we might receive the full rights of sons."

From these and other passages we note that God initiated the process by sending (mission) His Son, Jesus, with the purpose of redeeming lost humankind so they could enjoy the full benefits of an intimate relationship with himself. Jesus, in turn, continues the mission as He sends forth His followers to do the same: "Jesus said, 'Peace be with you! As the Father has sent me, I am sending you.' And with that he breathed on them and said, 'Receive the Holy Spirit. If you forgive anyone his sins, they are forgiven; if you do not forgive them, they are not forgiven'" (John 20:21–23).

Missionary

The focus of missions is on sending. From this concept, we get the term *missionary*. The word comes from the Latin verb *mitto* (I send). It is the equivalent of the Greek verb of Jesus' day *apostello* (to send someone) from which is derived *apostolos* (one sent, an apostle).

In the New Testament, *apostle* is most frequently associated with the Twelve, but is used of others as well. Paul calls himself an apostle (e.g., Romans 1:1), and even Christ is called "the apostle and high priest whom we confess" (Hebrews 3:1). The term can be used to mean "delegate, envoy, or messenger" (cf 2 Corinthians 8:23, Acts 14:14; Romans 16:7; Galatians 1:19; Philippians 2:25, for example) (Arndt and Gingrich 1957, 99).

J. Herbert Kane states,

In the traditional sense the term *missionary* has been preserved for those who have been called by God to full-time ministry of the Word and prayer (Acts 6:4) and who have crossed geographical and/or cultural boundaries (Acts 22:21) to preach the gospel in those areas of the world where Jesus Christ is largely, if not entirely, unknown (Romans 15:20). (Kane 1986, 28)

The basic idea is that of one specially chosen and sent on a special mission. From this we may conclude that not all Christians are missionaries, just as not all are pastors or evangelists. All are called to witness in word and deed. But not all are specially singled out to be sent forth from the church to cross geographical or cultural boundaries to present the claims of Christ. Today that can include those who use contemporary means of communication to spread those claims abroad, even in areas where they cannot physically go.

We shall define *missionary* as a person called by God and selected by the church to cross socio/cultural and/or geographical boundaries to present the claims of Christ to the unsaved through word and deed, to plant churches, and to train their leaders.

Purpose of Missions

Many means can be used in the missionary endeavor, but the central purpose is ever clear: to win people to Christ and to help disciple them to do the same. The final goal is to get as many as possible from every tribe and tongue to enter into glory and enjoy a relationship with the Triune God forever.

1.1.2
OBJECTIVE
Describe the ultimate purpose of missions as it relates to humanity.

1   What is the two-fold purpose of missions?

The purpose of missions is best illustrated by Christ himself, our supreme example. In Mark's gospel, Christ declares, "Even the Son of Man did not come to be served, but to serve, and to give his life as a ransom for many" (Mark 10:45). In other words, He describes the purpose of His mission as two-fold: to save and to serve. By serving, He did not mean becoming slaves to others. He meant He was sent to fulfill the Father's will by doing for humankind what it could not do for itself (see John 13:1–15). That must be our ultimate purpose as well: to use our abilities in the service of others in ways they cannot do for themselves, resulting in their salvation and growth in Christian maturity.

Whatever means are used to that end, be they preaching, teaching, medical care, community development, or other, the final purpose must be the same. They must not be ends in themselves. We are not called simply to make the world a better place or to make individual lives more satisfactory and fulfilling. Without God through Christ, all the rest is meaningless.

The responsibility of the missionary enterprise is awesome. Perhaps the best biblical expression is found in Ezekiel:

> Son of man, I have made you a watchman for the house of Israel; so hear the word I speak and give them warning from me. When I say to the wicked, "O wicked man, you will surely die," and you do not speak out to dissuade him from his ways, that wicked man will die for his sin, and I will hold you accountable for his blood. (Ezekiel 33:7–8)

Ezekiel was a chosen vessel to fulfill the mission of warning Israel for purposes of securing their redemption. To refuse to carry out that mission was to face serious consequences.

LESSON 1.2

1.2.1
OBJECTIVE
Identify the primary motive of missions.

Motives for Missions

The Primary Motive for Missions: Worship

Missions begins and ends with God. He began the missions enterprise by preparing for and then sending His Son, Jesus. His great desire is to get many to be in His presence forever. As recorded in Hebrews 2:10: "In bringing many sons to glory, it was fitting that God, for whom and through whom everything exists, should make the author of their salvation perfect through suffering."

Missions, then, is not the end of the story. Eternity in God's presence for as many as will heed the call and respond is what missions is all about. Why do we have missions? Because so very many have never heard or, having heard, have not yet responded to the call and are yet to acknowledge the greatness and goodness of our Lord. It is about bringing many sons and daughters to glory.

As John Piper (1993) states: "Missions exists because worship doesn't. Worship is ultimate, not missions, because God is ultimate, not man" (11). That which ought to drive us, and that which is the end goal of our efforts, is the worship of God. He is worthy! Piper continues: "The goal of missions is the gladness of the peoples in the greatness of God. . . . But worship is also the fuel of missions. Passion for God in worship precedes the offer of God in preaching. You cannot commend what you don't cherish" (Piper 1993, 11).

To be overwhelmingly enamored with the greatness and goodness of our God is to be highly motivated and thrilled to proclaim to others who He is. The closer we get to God, the more we will experience His love for us and others, the more we will see His wonderful works, and the more we will be driven to extol His virtues to others. Without that closeness and worship of God, we may go through the motions, but missions will be only a job, not a passion.

The realization of the true identity of Christ as God, the first-hand knowledge of who God is and what He is like, impelled the disciples to spread the good news to others. Jesus told them that to have known Him through experience was also to experientially know the Father (John 14:7–11). They were to be His witnesses—testifying of His true character and works. Witness they did!

Notice the declarations of the Apostles:

The Word became flesh and made his dwelling among us. We have seen his glory, the glory of the One and Only, who came from the Father, full of grace and truth. . . . No one has ever seen God, but God the One and Only, who is at the Father's side, has made him known. (John 1:14, 18)

But Peter and John replied, "Judge for yourselves whether it is right in God's sight to obey you rather than God. For we cannot help speaking about what we have seen and heard." (Acts 4:19–20)

That which was from the beginning, which we have heard, which we have seen with our eyes, which we have looked at and our hands have touched—this we proclaim concerning the Word of life. The life appeared; we have seen it and testify to it, and we proclaim to you the eternal life, which was with the Father and has appeared to us. We proclaim to you what we have seen and heard, so that you also may have fellowship with us. And our fellowship is with the Father and with his Son, Jesus Christ. (1 John 1:1–3)

2   What is the principal motivation for witnessing?

When we intimately know our Lord, we will be motivated to witness. Consider a young couple who fall in love. In short order they are extolling the great attributes of their newfound love to all their friends. Such enthusiasm can be expressed about any new discovery that seems special—from a new job, car, or book to a new principle. How much more One who is altogether lovely, faithful, true, kind, and beneficent! Such ought to be the greatest expressions of joy and delight.

Our greatest motivation for missions is the strong desire to let the world know who God truly is that they might also be glad and rejoice in His presence.

Consider these verses (emphasis added):

Who is like your people Israel—the one nation on earth that God went out to redeem as a people for himself, and **to make a name for himself**, and to perform great and awesome wonders by driving out nations and their gods from before your people, whom you redeemed from Egypt? (2 Samuel 7:23)

He saved them **for his name's sake**, to make his mighty power known. (Psalm 106:8)

Everyone who is called by my name, whom I created **for my glory**, whom I formed and made. (Isaiah 43:7)

Say to the house of Israel, "This is what the Sovereign Lord says: It is not for your sake, O house of Israel, that I am going to do these things, but **for the sake of my holy name**, which you have profaned among the nations where you have gone. I will show the holiness of my great name, which has been profaned among the nations, the name you have profaned among them. Then the nations will know that I am the Lord, declares the Sovereign Lord, when I show myself holy through you before their eyes." (Ezekiel 36:22–23)

The earth will be filled with the knowledge of **the glory of the Lord**, as the waters cover the sea. (Habakkuk 2:14)

Let your light shine before men, that they may see your good deeds and **praise your Father in heaven**. (Matthew 5:16)

From him and through him and to him are all things. **To him be the glory** forever! Amen. (Romans 11:36)

If anyone speaks, he should do it as one speaking the very words of God. If anyone serves, he should do it with the strength God provides, **so that in all things God may be praised** through Jesus Christ. To him be the glory and the power for ever and ever. Amen. (1 Peter 4:11)

A quick review of these verses, and many like them, might lead one to conclude God has an ego problem. Nothing could be farther from the truth. God needs absolutely nothing from us. He is totally self-sufficient and fully content within himself. Why then this emphasis on protecting His name, of getting glory from humanity?

To glorify God is to acknowledge who He is in all His being. To worship Him is to declare He is the one true God, full of mercy and righteousness, all knowing, all powerful, ever faithful and true. His name is His reputation, the symbol of who He is.

Here is the key: To acknowledge God's greatness through our worship and all that we do is to encourage others to trust Him and commit their lives to Him, believing He intends their highest good. To fail to glorify and worship Him is to deny who He is and, de facto, be a discourager to those who might be inclined to seek Him. To profane His name is to openly declare He is not worthy to be trusted. This is serious indeed!

This principle is clearly stated in Hebrews 11:6: "Without faith it is impossible to please God, because anyone who comes to him must believe that he exists and that he rewards those who earnestly seek him."

To have faith means to trust. If people are to come to trust God, they must believe He really is God and is the great benefactor of those who commit their lives to Him. For that to happen depends in large measure upon the faithful witness in word and deed of His followers.

3 Explain how the metaphor of marriage relates to missions.

The Bible frequently uses the metaphor of marriage to picture the relationship of Christ to believers. In North American culture, the period of courtship during engagement is intended to allow the couple to get to know each other to the point of willingness to trust each other in a formal commitment for the rest of their lives on earth. God wants us, and those we influence, to get to know Him to the point of full commitment of all we are and to have into a covenantal relationship with Him for all eternity.

Therefore, the primary motivating force behind our missionary endeavors is that all would come to worship God and to acknowledge His goodness and greatness, that all might come to faith in Him forever.

Subordinate Motives for Missions

The labeling of these motives as "subordinate" does not mean they are unimportant or insignificant. It simply means they flow out of the primary motive of seeking to lead others to worship the Lord.

1.2.2
OBJECTIVE

Discuss the importance of the Holy Spirit in motivating believers to engage in missions.

The Holy Spirit's Work in the Believer

As the third member of the Trinity, the Holy Spirit is at work in believers to reveal to them the greatness and goodness of the Lord. Jesus explained to the disciples what the Spirit would do in and through them (see John 14–16). He told them the Spirit would come as a Counselor to be with them forever (John 14:16). As a result, they would know the reality of Jesus' identity as part of the Godhead. The Spirit would teach them all they needed to know and would restore to their memories all Jesus had taught them (14:26). He would testify about Christ (15:26). He would guide them into all truth and disclose to them what was yet to come (16:13). In all, He would glorify Christ (16:14).

After His resurrection, Jesus instructed His followers to wait for the special "clothing" of the Holy Spirit (Luke 24:49). Again, just before His ascension into heaven, He told the apostles they would receive power (enablement) after the Holy Spirit came upon them, and they would be His witnesses (testifiers) throughout the world (Acts 1:8).

The coming of the Holy Spirit upon the disciples is recorded in Acts 2:1–11. They had been meeting in an upper room, devoting themselves to prayer, not venturing into the streets to witness about what they had seen and heard. But on the Day of Pentecost, empowered and emboldened by the Spirit, they began "declaring the wonders of God" in many languages miraculously given to them by the Spirit (Acts 2:11). From then on, Acts records many supernatural activities of these empowered believers as demonstrations of the reality of God and His great authority, power, and loving-kindness. They were determined that all should glorify God. They had come to know Him in His fullness, and were enabled to declare that with boldness to everyone around, regardless of the response (cf. Acts 4:19–20).

Like those early followers of Christ, we are also instructed to seek the empowering of the Spirit that we would have the courage, the words, and the supernatural gifts to reveal God's glory. It must be His glory we seek, not ours. We are not to draw attention to ourselves, but to point to Christ. We must declare God's greatness, not our own.

The level of authenticity in our witness will depend upon our closeness to the Lord through meditation, prayer, and experiencing Him in real-life situations. As Piper said, "Passion for God in worship precedes the offer of God in preaching. You cannot commend what you don't cherish" (Piper 1993, 11).

God's Sovereignty

1.2.3
OBJECTIVE
Explain what is meant by the sovereignty of God as a motivating factor for missions.

4   What is implied in God's sovereignty?

God is not only great and good, but also is in charge. Before entering heaven, Jesus declared His supreme authority and gave to His followers the Great Commission (Matthew 28:18–20). Wherever they went, they were to make disciples, leading people to a public confession of their faith by water baptism, and then teaching them to put into practice all Christ had taught them.

Mark's Gospel also records Jesus' command to "go into all the world and preach the good news to all creation. Whoever believes and is baptized will be saved, but whoever does not believe will be condemned" (Mark 16:15–16). These were not options, but commands to be obeyed. Neither have they been rescinded. The scriptures demonstrate that the understanding of the early church was that it applied to all (Acts 8:4–5; 9:15; 13:1–3).

One of the great truths of God is that He has ownership of our lives through creation and redemption. When He calls us to a task of His choosing, we are to obey. When the early apostles heard His call, they followed Him (cf. Matthew 4:18–22; 9:9). Saul of Tarsus was determined to serve God in a way totally against God's will. He suddenly found himself arrested by the Lord and turned completely around to obedience (Acts 9:1–20). One of the motives behind missions is obedience to the Lord's call and command.

Compassion for Unbelievers

The realization of the greatness and goodness of God carries with it the urgent desire for others to experience His blessing in their lives. To know the God who loves without limit is to long for the unloved to know Him. To know God as the Great Physician is to long for the sick to receive His healing power. To those who mourn the loss of loved ones, the believer's heart of compassion longs for them to feel God's comfort. For those wandering aimlessly in life without purpose and fulfillment, the great Shepherd is available if they would but know Him. Jesus set the example:

Jesus went through all the towns and villages, teach
preaching the good news of the kingdom and healin
sickness. When he saw the crowds, he had compass
were harassed and helpless, like sheep without a sh
disciples, "The harvest is plentiful but the workers
the harvest, therefore, to send out workers into his
twelve disciples to him and gave them authority to
heal every disease and sickness. (Matthew 9:35–10.1)

Not only out of His heart of compassion did Jesus take action to meet the needs of the hurting; He began to multiply His workforce to do the same. His primary motivation was neither the glory of God nor the revelation of His own deity. Rather He focused on the desperate needs of humanity around Him. Other passages affirm His first concern that all should glorify God, but here He acts out of His own deep compassion.

This should assure us that God wants to show compassion to the helpless and hurting. Such may not only bring health and hope, but point to a loving God who cares about the daily, personal needs of humanity. In the end it is their personal relationship to the Godhead through Jesus Christ that can bring eternal life and final release from suffering. Still, effectiveness as a missionary depends on having compassion for the hurting and hopeless in their everyday living. They are people, not bodiless souls.

Inappropriate Motives for Missions

To Make a Name for Oneself

1.2.4
OBJECTIVE
Discuss inappropriate motives for missionary service.

Traditionally in evangelical and Pentecostal circles, missionaries have been looked upon with admiration and respect. They have gone to the ends of the earth, forsaking family and friends and financial reward to serve Christ. However, as missionaries have engaged in the deputation process, their focus has sometimes changed from God's purposes to obtaining material goods and finances. It is a subtle, but real, temptation to change from being the giver to being the receiver, to take advantage of the missionary role for personal gain.

The temptation can be even greater upon return from the field, especially if the assignment has taken one to more remote and mysterious places where sharing the gospel is considered especially difficult. Those from such places are often paraded before admiring congregations as heroes, as God's elite. Such honor may well be deserved, but it tempts missionaries to embellish stories and to give reports that exaggerate experiences in order to gain greater praise.

Believers observing such a scenario may begin to aspire to such a position themselves in order to gain attention and recognition. This is no substitute for the calling of God. Following Christ's example, we are called to serve, not be served (Mark 10:45). The apostle Paul was not called to a position of prestige and influence, but to suffer for Christ's sake (Acts 9:15–16).

The Lord reminds us that He calls us to do His work on earth, but He will share His glory with no one:

I, the Lord, have called you in righteousness; I will take hold of your hand. I will keep you and will make you to be a covenant for the people and a light for the Gentiles, to open eyes that are blind, to free captives from prison and to release from the dungeon those who sit in darkness. I am the Lord; that is my name! I will not give my glory to another or my praise to idols. (Isaiah 42:6–8)

An example of this is Herod, who accepted a crowd's praise and failed to give God the glory. He was struck with an illness from which he died (Acts 12:21–23).

To Build a Personal Kingdom

This motivation is much like the first in that it centers on gaining praise and power. But the focus is more on receiving accolades from those we serve. Such is the image of those who referred to as "great white father." No matter the color of the skin, the idea is that of one who seeks to dominate, control, or be in a position of importance and power. This is especially tempting to those who represent substantial monetary resources to a destitute national church. It may be a means to control, but not to partnership in the gospel.

We must never forget that the Lord is in charge and that He will not share His glory. He has sent us, not to be served, but to serve others and point them to Him.

To Escape

Some pursue missions as an escape. One path is to escape the guilt of committed sin. Rather than accept God's gracious forgiveness for confessed sin, they seek to atone for their own failures by serving the Lord in missions. Perhaps this will gain them favor, they think, or at least make up for what they have done. The motive is not God's glory, but clearing their consciences.

A similar escape is from the power of some sinful behavior, some addictive practice. By going to the mission field, they think God will somehow protect them from themselves and build a hedge around them. This is a tragic mistake, for we take with us who we are. Such issues must be dealt with before pursuing any sort of ministry, at home or abroad.

Escape may also be sought from a difficult situation or relationship. But withdrawal from a difficult problem neither solves it nor brings closure to the one who withdraws. Sooner or later, the issue must be dealt with, or it will continue to fester in the mind and spirit and will affect other relationships. The mission field has sufficient difficult issues to deal with; taking an unresolved one to the field is a recipe for disaster.

To Gain Favor with God

Those raised in the North American culture may find this a particularly subtle, but real, temptation. Though generalizations are risky, most of us are shaped to daily prioritize work. Substituting work for worship is easy, filling a false need to "prove" ourselves worthy of His grace. Grace is "unmerited favor," not something to be earned or that *can* be earned. We do His bidding to please Him as a thanksgiving for what has already been done on our behalf.

5   How might a Christian guard against having inappropriate motives for missions?

LESSON 1.3

Missions in Light of the Second Coming

The Certainty of Christ's Return

Jesus' first coming to earth was to point the way to the Father and then to die for the sins of the world. Those who believe on Him will enjoy the blessing of eternal life with God. Yet that is not the end of the story. Both Jesus' testimony and the early church's expectation indicate the certainty of Jesus' return to earth (Matthew 16:27; 24:3–51; Mark 8:38; 13:26; Luke 21:27; Acts 1:11; 1 Corinthians 15:23; 1 Thessalonians 1:10; 2 Thessalonians 1:7, 10; James 5:7; 1 Peter 1:13; 1 John 2:28, et al).

Just prior to His crucifixion, Jesus spoke of the judgment that would come upon those Jews who had refused to accept Him.

> O Jerusalem, Jerusalem, you who kill the prophets and stone those sent to you, how often I have longed to gather your children together, as a hen gathers her chicks under her wings, but you were not willing. Look, your house is left to you desolate. For I tell you, you will not see me again until you say, "Blessed is he who comes in the name of the Lord." (Matthew 23:37–39)

1.3.1
OBJECTIVE
Examine the imperatives of Matthew 24 as they apply to the Church today.

The last phrase is a quote from Psalm 118:26, that great Psalm of praise for the entry of God's representative into Jerusalem. While the disciples were admiring the beauty of the temple and other buildings, Jesus told them it all would be destroyed (Matthew 24:1–2). They immediately wanted to know when this would happen, what would be the sign of His coming and the end of the age (Matthew 24:3). Jesus launched into a long discussion of events that would occur prior to His return to earth. Quite apart from these details and their application, two key elements that apply to us today, stand out from His response to them.

First, only the Father—not even Jesus—knows the time of Jesus' return (Matthew 24:36). Since that time, many have tried to discover when that is. Various schemes have been tried, including the search of Bible passages and combinations of dates and numbers to arrive at some conclusion, all to no avail.

6 How did the early church view Christ's return?

The early church apparently thought Jesus' return was imminent. The apostles, at first, seemed fixed on Jerusalem, reluctant to leave lest He return while they were elsewhere. The writers of the New Testament believed the end was near (Romans 13:11–12; 1 Thessalonians 2:19; 3:13; James 5:7–8; 1 Peter 4:7). The nearness of Jesus' return prompted them to lead holy lives and to be about His business lest He return and find them lacking.

Second, amidst the details of the end time described by Jesus in Matthew 24, His clear imperative was to be ready for His return. They were to guard against being misled (4), endure till the end (13), be on alert (42), and be ready (44). The same theme continues in Matthew 25:13 in a series of parables illustrating the need to be prepared for His coming. The passages cited in the previous paragraph also record the writers' repetition of Christ's admonition to be ready.

Just before Jesus ascended into heaven, the apostles once again raised the question of timing. He had instructed them to wait in Jerusalem until they were empowered by the Holy Spirit. They wanted to know if that would be the time He restored the kingdom to Israel. His reply is instructive to us as well: "It is not for you to know the times or dates the Father has set by His own authority" (Acts 1:7). In other words, it was none of their business. They were to carry out His plan of witnessing everywhere. His return date was up to the Father.

The Meaning of the "Last Days"

1.3.2
OBJECTIVE
Evaluate lessons learned from the disciples' confusion over the timing of the "last days."

Do the events of this twenty-first century suggest we are living in the last days? An examination of the perspectives of Jesus' day will help us. The Jewish understanding in that era was that after the Creation, the eons were divided into two major periods: the present age and the last days in which the Messiah would appear, judge the wicked, and usher in His righteous reign (Isaiah 2:2–4; Hosea 3:5; Micah 4:1). (See Cullman 1950, 81.)

For example, Joel prophesied that "afterward," God would pour out His Spirit upon all people (Joel 2:28–29). On the Day of Pentecost, Peter quoted from Joel's prophecy, translating "afterward" as "in the last days" (Acts 2:17). This is significant, for he was saying that the "last days" had already arrived! Jesus had inferred as much earlier, as recorded in Mark 1:15: "The time has come," he said. "The kingdom of God is near. Repent and believe the good news!" The Kingdom promised for the last days had now come, for the King had come.

The disciples slowly came to understand that the Messiah had come, though they did not fully comprehend what that meant (Mark 8:27–33). This confused Jesus' followers, for if Jesus was the Messiah and was ushering in the "last days," where was the judgment and His reign as king? What they could not then understand was there were two comings of the King—His first as the suffering servant and His second as the reigning King of kings. The Church now lives in that "time between the times." That is, since the death and resurrection of Christ, the Church has been living in the "last days." The decisive battle was won at Calvary, but "Victory Day" has yet to be realized in all its fullness when Christ will come again in all His glory (Cullman 1950, 84).

The struggle of the disciples in Jesus' day should instruct us. While we eagerly await the Lord's return, we must be cautious of in attributing any period in the Church's journey as marking the end of the age. To attempt to discern the date of the Lord's return or to think we can somehow determine it is at the least unwise, and at the worst, dangerous.

The history of the church shows it has faced persecution throughout the centuries. At many periods it could have been said that surely the end was imminent. No matter what the world events, whether our Lord returns tomorrow or a hundred or thousand years from now, we are to be ready for His return at any moment and be about the urgent task of proclaiming Him to all people.

Controversy Affecting World Missions

1.3.3
OBJECTIVE

Discuss Jesus' statement in Matthew 24:14 as it relates to missions efforts and the time of His return.

Conflict has arisen over Jesus' statement, "This gospel of the kingdom will be preached in the whole world as a testimony to all nations, and then the end will come" (Matthew 24:14). Some declare it improper to promote the missionary enterprise by suggesting that declaring the gospel throughout the world will, in itself, trigger the Lord's return.

Their concern is justified. Jesus himself said that the time of His return is in the Father's hands, not even His own. If that is true of Jesus, surely it is even truer of us; we cannot force God's hand. Further, to "be ready at all times for His return" clearly shows that the time of the Lord's return will not be determined by the actions of the Church. Just when can it be said that the gospel has been preached in the whole world? Does that mean geographical territory or all the inhabitants of the earth?

On the other hand, Jesus' statement in Matthew 24:14 does show we are to continue to take the Good News to all people, knowing He could return at any time. We do not determine that time, but we must be about His business until He says it is enough. Our responsibility is to preach the gospel everywhere.

Another stumbling block to some is the apostle Peter's statement:

Since all these things are to be destroyed in this way, what sort of people ought you to be in holy conduct and godliness, looking for and hastening the coming of the day of God, because of which the heavens will be destroyed by burning, and the elements will melt with intense heat! (2 Peter 3:11–12, NASU)

What does it mean to "hasten the coming day of the Lord"? Does this suggest that the Church, through its missionary enterprise, can somehow shorten the wait for the Lord's return? The meaning of this phrase is not clearly understood or agreed upon by many scholars. However, the context of these verses should help us.

Peter is not speaking of missionary activity as hastening the coming of the Lord. In fact, verse 10 states, "The day of the Lord will come like a thief" (2 Peter 3:10). One does not determine the day a thief will appear. Further, as Peter urges in verses 11 and 14, the issue is that of personal conduct. Each is urged to be found holy and blameless at the time of Christ's appearing.

Peter's statement may be a veiled reference to the days of the Exodus when the refusal of the Israelites to obey the Lord delayed entry into the Promised Land for forty years. If anything, it should remind us that doing the Lord's missionary work does not allow us to neglect issues of character.

The Missionary Duty of the Church

The period of time between Christ's first and second coming (the Parousia) is the age of the Church, the time of service before the Lord returns and evangelistic tasks are ended. Harry Boer reminds us of our duty:

> The Church lives between the first and second coming of Christ. She is conscious of being the uniting element between the two events, and she must express herself in terms of the consciousness. The Church is an interim phenomenon and her characteristic activity in the interim period is missionary activity. Judging by the Pentecost account we may say that both Church and missions are creations of the Holy Spirit and are both taken up as essential elements in the divine plan for the world. (Boer 1961, 62)

1.3.4
OBJECTIVE
Identify the four-fold task of the Church.

The Church has a four-fold task: (1) adoration: to worship the Lord; (2) edification: to build up one another in the faith; (3) evangelization: to share the gospel with the world that they might be saved; and (4) compassion: to be a people who demonstrate God's love and compassion for all the world. After the Parousia (Christ's second coming) tasks related to evangelism will no longer be needed. The supreme task of the Church in the "time between the times" must be to win as many as possible to Christ before the end of the present age.

Jesus instructed the disciples to be His witnesses (testifiers) "in Jerusalem, and in all Judea and Samaria, and to the ends of the earth" (Acts 1:8). The geographical extent of their witness was to the entire inhabited world. The Great Commission of Matthew 28:18–20 showed this responsibility was "to the very end of the age" (Matthew 28:20). Jesus' command was, "Go into all the world and preach the good news to all creation" (Mark 16:15).

The task of the Church is to proclaim the person and work of Christ in all places, to all peoples, until the end of time. No place is to be ignored, no person young or old, rich or poor, is to be overlooked, no arbitrary stopping to say we have gone far enough. All this is to be undertaken until the end of the age.

Test Yourself

Circle the letter of the *best* answer.

1. Missions involves the selecting of missionaries to
a) share Christ within the western cultural perspective.
b) establish diplomatic relationships between the United States church and foreign church plants.
c) work primarily in humanitarian efforts overseas.
d) share Christ across geographical and cultural boundaries.

2. The focus of missions is on
a) a particular person.
b) sending.
c) a geographical area.
d) cultural boundaries.

3. The ultimate purpose of missions is to
a) save and to serve others as they grow in Christian maturity.
b) make the world a better place to live.
c) make the lives of individuals more satisfactory and fulfilling.
d) develop community.

4. The primary motive of missions is the
a) salvation of humankind.
b) worship of God.
c) reaching of nations.
d) geographical expansion of the Church.

5. The Holy Spirit is primarily at work in believers to
a) empower them with the gifts of the Spirit.
b) make them great evangelists.
c) enlighten them of the greatness and goodness of the Christ.
d) give them wisdom.

6. God's sovereignty primarily refers to His
a) all-sufficiency.
b) supreme authority.
c) creative powers.
d) knowledge of all things.

7. Jesus' primary motivation for ministry to the multitudes was
a) the glory of God.
b) the revelation of His own deity.
c) their desperate needs.
d) to show His power to His disciples.

8. Jews understood the eons were divided into the
a) present age and the last days when the Messiah would appear.
b) age before the Flood and the days of the prophets.
c) days of the prophets and the appearing of the Messiah.
d) kings and the prophets.

9. When Jesus said, "This gospel . . . will be preached in the whole world . . . and then the end will come," He meant
a) the missionary enterprise would hasten His coming.
b) His return would be determined by the actions of the Church.
c) we are to continue taking the Good News to all people, knowing He may return at any time.
d) a definite geographical expansion of the gospel would signal His return.

10. Judging by the Pentecost account, we could say the Church and missions are creations of
a) history.
b) the institutional church.
c) the Holy Spirit.
d) the apostles.

Responses to Interactive Questions
Chapter 1

Some of these responses may include information that is supplemental to the IST. These questions are intended to produce reflective thinking beyond the course content and your responses may vary from these examples.

1 What is the two-fold purpose of missions?

Answer: To save and to serve

2 What is the principal motivation for witnessing?

Answer: Our greatest motivation for missions is the overwhelming desire to let the world know who God is that they might also be glad and rejoice in His presence.

3 Explain how the metaphor of marriage relates to missions.

Answer: Just as marriage involves deep commitment, God wants us and those we influence to get to know Him to the point of full commitment for all eternity.

4 What is implied in God's sovereignty?

Answer: God is not only great and good but also in charge.

5 How might a Christian guard against having inappropriate motives for missions?

Answer: The Christian must remain focused on the mission to serve God by serving others; this commitment involves an awareness of self-sacrifice.

6 How did the early church view Christ's return?

Answer: The early church apparently thought Jesus' return was imminent, and this prompted them to lead holy lives and be about His business lest He return and find them lacking.

CHAPTER 2

The Biblical Foundation for Missions

The missionary message runs throughout the Old and New Testaments. It began in the Garden of Eden when Christ said to the serpent and Eve, "I will put enmity between you and the woman, and between your offspring and hers; he will crush your head, and you will strike his heel" (Genesis 3:15). The offspring of the woman is a theme found from Genesis through the book of Revelation. The offspring would be none other than Christ. This mission of God ends in the words of a loud voice from the throne of God: "Now the dwelling of God is with men, and he will live with them. They will be his people, and God himself will be with them and be their God. He will wipe every tear from their eyes. There will be no more death or mourning or crying or pain, for the old order of things has passed away" (Revelation 21:3–4).

Lesson 2.1   Missions in the Old Testament

Objectives
2.1.1 *Identify in the Pentateuch God's mission for all believers.*
2.1.2 *Describe the worldwide extent of God's mission as expressed in the Psalms and prophetic books.*
2.1.3 *Discuss how Isaiah depicts God and His relationship to all the nations of the earth.*

Lesson 2.2   Missions in the New Testament

Objectives
2.2.1 *Identify the missionary theme of the New Testament.*
2.2.2 *Examine the expansion of the gospel in the book of Acts.*
2.2.3 *Discuss the apostle Paul's call to the Gentiles.*
2.2.4 *Explain the missions message of the book of Revelation.*

LESSON

2.1

2.1.1
OBJECTIVE
Identify in the Pentateuch God's mission for all believers.

Missions in the Old Testament

God's Mission in the Pentateuch

The root of Christian missions is found in the Old Testament. Genesis 3:15 presents the intention of God to save humankind: "I will put enmity between you and the woman, and between your offspring and hers; he will crush your head, and you will strike his heel." The mention of Eve's offspring is the first prophecy of the coming of a Savior to redeem humanity. God's mission begins in the Garden of Eden and will end in the city of God at the end of time. This is the theme or motif that runs throughout the Bible.

God's covenant with Noah also had a universal message for all people (Genesis 9:1, 8–9). Genesis 10 presents a table of the nations which indicated all people belong to God and He is the God of the human race.

The narrative of Genesis moves quickly to the central message of Scripture—God's mission to save humanity. Genesis 1–11 is "the preface to the entire Bible and the foundation upon which the rest of revelation is built" (Peters 1972, 87). The call of Abram to leave his country for a land the Lord God would show him had a far-reaching purpose: that "all peoples of the earth will be blessed" through him (Genesis 12:3). The offspring of Eve is again in focus through this covenant with Abram. This underscores the fact that Abram's call from God was not out of personal favoritism or with the intention to establish a local religion. This call originated in the God of glory and was intended for the welfare of all humanity.

The story of the beginning of human civilization moves quickly to the formation of the twelve tribes of Israel and the more than four hundred years spent in Egypt before the exodus from that land. From the offspring of Eve and Abram, God was forming a priest-nation whose purpose was to represent God to the nations of the world and bring glory to His name. Ezekiel 36:23 speaks of Israel's intended ministry among the nations: "I will show the holiness of my great name, which has been profaned among the nations, the name you have profaned among them. Then the nations will know that I am the Lord, declares the Sovereign Lord, when I show myself holy through you before their eyes."

The Israelites were reminded that they were not "superior by birth or history to the nations" (Glasser 1989, 52). Ezekiel 16:3 says this about the Israelites: "Your ancestry and birth were in the land of the Canaanites; your father was an Amorite and your mother a Hittite."

Foreigners living in Israel had the right to enjoy status with the Israelites in observing the Passover (Exodus 12:48; Numbers 9:14). They were not to be oppressed (Exodus 22:21), and their offerings were to be accepted (Numbers 15:14). In addition, they were to receive righteous judgment from judges in the land (Deuteronomy 1:16). This meant the foreigner shared in the covenant of God with Israel (Deuteronomy 29:11) and was to be instructed in the Law (Deuteronomy 31:12). This indicates the revelation and faith of Israel were not closed to the nations (Peters 1972, 114).

2.1.2
OBJECTIVE
Describe the worldwide extent of God's mission as expressed in the Psalms and prophetic books.

God's Mission in the Historical Books and Psalms

Missions in the Davidic Age

Most of the statements about God's mission in the historical books and the wisdom literature of the Old Testament are found in the Psalms and the dedication of Solomon's temple. Seventy-three psalms are assigned to David and twenty-four ascribed to Asaph and the sons of Korah. Approximately 175 references are made to the nations, with many expressing the hope of salvation for the people of the world. At least seven entire psalms express the missionary message (2, 33, 66, 67, 72, 117, 145). One profitable exercise is to read through the Psalms and underline all passages referring to the nations of the earth.

We note the words of Psalm 67:1–7:

> May God be gracious to us and bless us and make his face shine upon us, that your ways may be known on earth, your salvation among all nations. May the peoples praise you, O God; may all the peoples praise you. May the nations be glad and sing for joy, for you rule the peoples justly and guide the nations of the earth. May the peoples praise you, O God; may all the peoples praise you. Then the land will yield its harvest, and God, our God, will bless us. God will bless us, and all the ends of the earth will fear him.

Psalm 2 is like Psalm 110 in that it refers to the installation of the king in Zion. It is, therefore, a royal psalm of coronation. It is frequently cited in the New Testament as proof of Jesus' claim to be the Messiah of Israel (Matthew 3:17; Acts 13:33; Hebrews 1:5; 5:5). This King goes beyond the kingship of David to worldwide dominion (verse 8). The "Son" in verse 7 is Jesus Christ himself. The promise of worldwide dominion also appears in another royal psalm—Psalm 72. Psalm 2:8 says, "Ask of me, and I will make the nations your inheritance, the ends of the earth your possession" (Boyles 1999, 46, 47).

Parts of other psalms express this theme. One is Psalm 86:9–10, "All the nations you have made will come and worship before you, O Lord; they will bring glory to your name. For you are great and do marvelous deeds." The universal message of missions is consistent in the Psalms.

Missions in the Prophetic Books

Habakkuk

1   How does the universal principle given in Habakkuk relate to you?

Some believe Habakkuk was primarily concerned with suffering in the face of the powers of evil. However, this is not the major theme of this book. The primary theme of the book deals with God's purpose fulfilled in the world. It is concerned with God's covenant with Abraham to establish a new community and the blessing his posterity would bring to all families of the earth. It is about how God keeps His promises to Israel, and through His people, to the whole world.

A universal principle of justification is stated in Habakkuk 2:4: "The righteous will live by his faith." This theme is developed by Paul in the Epistle to the Romans (1:17) and in the Epistle to the Galatians (3:11). The book also declares a universal knowledge of the glory of the Lord: "The earth will be filled with the knowledge of the glory of the Lord" (Habakkuk 2:14). Isaiah makes a similar statement (11:9). One of God's purposes is to fill all the earth with the knowledge of His glory (Achtemeier 1986, 50). A clear declaration of universal worship is found in Habakkuk 2:20: "The Lord is in his holy temple; let all the earth be silent before him." The whole earth is subject to God's will, and God is working out His purpose.

Joel

The prophet Joel declares God's prophetic word in the third part of his book, and this word applies to "all people" (2:28). Joel mentions seven nations and twice refers to "all nations" (3:9; 11–12). The prophecy about the pouring out of the Spirit is part of the first sermon recorded in Christian history in Acts 2:17–18. Joel 2:28–29 prophesied of the power the believer would receive to propagate the gospel to the ends of the earth (Acts 1:8). Paul uses the word "all" from

Joel to include the Gentiles in the receiving of the good news (Romans 10:13) (Limburg 1988, 72). All nations share in the reception of the gifts of the Spirit. The Acts narrative includes an invitation to go in the power of the Spirit, taking the gospel message to the ends of the earth.

Jonah

The prophet Jonah was sent by God to preach repentance to the Gentile city of Nineveh, the capital of the Assyrian empire. The writing of this book had at least two purposes: "(1) to demonstrate to Israel and the nations the magnitude and breadth of God's saving mercy and activity through the preaching of repentance, (2) to show through Jonah's experience how far Israel had fallen from its original missionary calling to be a light of redemption to those who dwell in darkness (Genesis 12:1–3; Isaiah 42:6–7)" (Stamps 1992, 1326–1327). God's attitude toward the nations is expressed in chapter 4 and verse 11, "But Nineveh has more than a hundred and twenty thousand people who cannot tell their right hand from their left, and many cattle as well. Should I not be concerned about that great city?"

Isaiah

The prophet Isaiah, in the first section of his book (chapters 1 through 39), speaks not only to Judah but to the nations of the world. He warns the nations of the judgments of God to come (chapters 10, 13 through 23). God's sovereignty over all the nations of the earth is expressed in the specific judgment pronounced against Assyria (chapters 36–37). There are not only warnings of judgment against the nations, but there is the promise of blessing. Isaiah 2:2 says, "In the last days the mountain of the Lord's temple will be established as chief among the mountains; it will be raised above the hills, and all nations will stream to it." This prophecy of the conversion of Gentiles is an important part of Old Testament prophecy in general (Isaiah 40; 45; Jeremiah 3:17; Amos 9:12). It also refers to God's promise that all people on earth would be blessed through Abraham's seed (Genesis 12:3) (Horton 2000, 62).

It has been said that the climax of all Old Testament prophecy is found in the second part of the book of Isaiah (chapters 40 through 66) (Peters 1972 123). Isaiah 40:5 declares: "The glory of the Lord will be revealed, and all mankind together will see it." This revelation will take place in the presence of all humankind, thus underlining the universal significance of the event. The verse lays the foundation for God's strategies for the world that follow in this section of Isaiah (Hubbard 1987, 81). This truth points out the fact that Israel exists for the nations and its true meaning is only in its mission to the world.

The God-appointed mission for Israel and the Messiah is articulated in chapter 42 and verse 6: "I, the Lord, have called you in righteousness; I will take hold of your hand. I will keep you and will make you to be a covenant for the people and a light for the Gentiles." This passage indicates that the covenant of salvation was intended for both Jews and Gentiles.

The last twenty-six chapters of Isaiah speak frequently of the "servant" of God. The primary responsibility of this "servant" was to be a witness (43:10, 12) and to serve as a messenger (42:19). This directive indicates Israel's mission to the nations of the world to declare the truth of God in the midst of polytheistic and idolatrous nations. Israel was to declare that God is the only true God (44:6). One of the great missionary passages in Isaiah is found in chapter 45 and verses 22 and 23: "Turn to me and be saved, all you ends of the earth; for I am God, and there is no other. By myself I have sworn, my mouth has uttered in all integrity a word that will not be revoked: Before me every knee will bow; by me every tongue will swear."

2.1.3
OBJECTIVE
Discuss how Isaiah depicts God and His relationship to all the nations of the earth.

2 What was the primary purpose of the "servant" in Isaiah?

In chapter 55, Jesus is depicted as the Davidic King who fulfills the promises made by God to David. This passage speaks of the nations coming to Him as the "commander of the peoples" (55:4) and indicates all the people of the world. Here is a reminder of Jesus' words in Matthew 28:18—"All authority in heaven and on earth has been given to me" (Horton 2000, 402).

The suffering servant portrays both Israel and the Messiah. Chapter 53 is a great portrait of the suffering of Christ as He gave himself in an atoning sacrifice for the whole world. Both Israel as the servant of God and Christ as the Messiah and servant of the Father only find their complete meaning in a worldwide service to all humanity.

The universality of salvation and missions is found throughout the Old Testament. God's intention for the salvation of humankind is first announced in the Garden of Eden in the promise of the seed or posterity of Eve. God's mission is particularly evident in the call, life, and ministry of Israel that serves as a witness to the nations. In this way, the Old Testament is a missionary book, and Israel is a missionary people.

LESSON 2.2

2.2.1
OBJECTIVE

Identify the missionary theme of the New Testament.

3   List the three events that illustrate missions in Jesus' ministry.

Missions in the New Testament

The missionary theme of the New Testament is quite easy to identify. All of the books of the New Testament were written by missionaries, and the epistles were written to churches founded by missionary endeavors. All four of the Gospels and the book of Acts declare the missionary mandate. The history of the church as presented in the book of Acts is one of missionary activity and connects the missionary mandate with the coming of the Holy Spirit (Steyne 1992, 261).

Jesus Christ is, of course, the central person in the New Testament, and three events in His earthly ministry illustrate His emphasis on missions. These include His sending of the Twelve (Matthew 10; Mark 6:7–13; Luke 9:1–16), His sending of the seventy-two (Luke 10:1–24), and His commission to the disciples (John 20:21). The culminating event of the post-resurrection presence of the Lord was His giving of the Great Commission (Matthew 28:18–20; Luke 24:44–49; Acts 1:8) (Hedlund 1985, 152).

God's Mission in the Gospels

The Gospel of Matthew

The Gospel of Matthew was written primarily to a Jewish audience. Nevertheless, some passages include Gentiles in God's promises. One such passage is 8:11, in which Christ speaks of the great faith of the Roman centurion: "I say to you that many will come from the east and the west, and will take their places at the feast with Abraham, Isaac and Jacob in the kingdom of heaven."

Chapter 15 records Christ's commendation of the great faith of a Canaanite woman whose daughter was demon possessed. He grants her request for the deliverance of her daughter (15:21–28).

Matthew records another statement of Christ in which He declares the kingdom will be taken from Israel and given to another people (21:43).

Matthew 24:14 clearly indicates Matthew's understanding of the worldwide task of the Church—a commission that includes all people. Between Jesus' resurrection and His rapture of the Church, the gospel will be preached to all nations. The passages declare that before the close of the age, all nations will be confronted with the Good News of the gospel of salvation. Matthew closes his gospel with what has been termed "The Great Commission" (28:18–20).

The Gospel of Mark

4 Identify the element Mark adds to the Great Commission that is absent in the other gospels.

Mark's gospel gives special emphasis to Jesus' miracles, indicating He is Lord over all. It appears the supernatural nature of Christ is the central theme of Mark, and he probably wrote from Rome with a Gentile audience in mind (Elwell and Yarbrough 1998, 89, 90). In Mark, miraculous signs from the Holy Spirit were required to proclaim the gospel effectively. He adds an element to the Great Commission not found in the other gospels: "These signs will accompany those who believe: In my name they will drive out demons; they will speak in new tongues; they will pick up snakes with their hands; and when they drink deadly poison, it will not hurt them at all; they will place their hands on sick people, and they will get well" (16:17–18). Some believe this passage is a later addition to the text. However, the book of Acts records many such miracles occurring during the expansion of the Church. The Great Commission in the book of Mark preceded this miraculous ministry of believers: "Go into all the world and preach the good news to all creation" (16:15).

The Gospel of Luke

At the beginning of his gospel, Luke stresses the universal nature of the Good News by tracing the ancestry of Jesus. Matthew's genealogy of Christ goes back to David and Abraham, but Luke's goes back to the beginning of the human race—to Adam (3:38). The writer wants a certain Theophilus to understand that faith in Christ is based on historical fact. Luke was not a Jew. He was a well-educated Gentile and physician who traveled with the apostle Paul (Colossians 4:14; 2 Timothy 4:11).

The book of Luke includes a clear statement about the universal nature of the gospel in 24:47: "Repentance and forgiveness of sins will be preached in his name to all nations, beginning at Jerusalem."

The Gospel of John

John 20:31 states that one of the main purposes of this gospel is that the readers might believe Jesus is the Christ. A greater statement of missionary purpose cannot be made. The universality of salvation is stated several times, beginning with 3:16: "God so loved the world that he gave his one and only Son, that whoever believes in him shall not perish but have eternal life." John also states that Jesus is the "Lamb of God, who takes away the sin of the world" (1:29). In 8:12, Jesus is portrayed as the "light of the world," and in 1:9 as "the true light that gives light to every man." In 10:16, Jesus states He has "other sheep that are not of this sheep pen." From these statements comes the necessity of missions, and this theme culminates in Jesus' charge to the disciples: "As the Father has sent me, I am sending you" (20:21).

All the synoptic gospels demonstrate a missionary purpose by testifying of Jesus Christ, His life, His purpose, and the redemption He brought for humankind. Christ himself gave the mandate to disciple all nations.

The Acts of the Apostles

2.2.2
OBJECTIVE

Examine the expansion of the gospel in the book of Acts.

5 What is the purpose of the book of Acts as it relates to missions?

The presence of people from many nations on the Day of Pentecost and the fact that they heard the disciples praising God in their languages reveals the Church was born in a universal way (Acts 2:6–8). Jesus had instructed the disciples to await the induement of power before launching a missionary enterprise to the ends of the earth. From the time of this experience, believers began to obey the Great Commission. The book of Acts is a record of missionary activity. Shortly after the Holy Spirit fell on the Day of Pentecost, Peter said Joel's prophecy was fulfilled by this event: "Afterward, I will pour out my Spirit on all people" (Joel 2:28).

The missionary expansion of the Church continues in Acts with the ministry of Philip in Samaria, followed by the baptism of the Ethiopian eunuch, an official of the Ethiopian court. Then the conversion of Paul, the great missionary to the Gentiles, is recorded in Acts 9:11–20. Following is Peter's preparation for ministry, which sends him to the house of Cornelius, a Roman centurion and Gentile (Acts 10). Chapter 11 records the ministry in Antioch to Greeks (11:20). The apostles in Jerusalem sent Barnabas to verify the news from Antioch that Gentiles were accepting the gospel. When Barnabas arrived in Antioch, he "saw the evidence of the grace of God" (11:23).

One significant event in Antioch was the sending of Paul and Barnabas on their first missionary journey (13:2, 4). The Jerusalem council was held and a letter sent to the Gentiles about the requirements of observing Jewish tradition and law (15:24–29).

The book of Acts records the Spirit's directing Paul to Macedonia (Acts 16:6) and eventually his arrival in Rome (28:14). By this time, the Church had left the context of Judaism and was present in the world at large.

2.2.3
OBJECTIVE
Discuss the apostle Paul's call to the Gentiles.

God's Mission in Paul's Writings

Paul acknowledged that God had called him for a specific purpose—to take the gospel to the Gentiles (Romans 1:5), for he believed Christ died for all humanity (Romans 5:18; 1 Timothy 2:4). Thus, Paul wrote that the gospel "is the power of God for the salvation of everyone who believes" (Romans 1:16), and "everyone who calls on the name of the Lord will be saved" (Romans 10:13).

With great energy Paul preached in synagogues, the marketplaces, and wherever the opportunity to preach was made available to him. As an equally prolific writer, he wrote of universal sin and of the universal mission of Christ: "Just as the result of one trespass was condemnation for all men, so also the result of one act of righteousness was justification that brings life for all men" (Romans 5:18). He emphasized this truth again in his writing to Timothy: "This is good, and pleases God our Savior, who wants all men to be saved and to come to a knowledge of the truth. For there is one God and one mediator between God and men, the man Christ Jesus, who gave himself as a ransom for all men" (1 Timothy 2:3–6).

Paul introduces several missionary thoughts in the Epistle to the Romans. First, the universe is God's creation. It is ruled by Him and is responsible to Him (Romans 1:18–32). Second, humankind descended from Adam through whom sin entered the human race (Romans 5:12–21). Third, Christ provided salvation for the entire human race by identifying with them and becoming a sacrifice for their sins (Romans 5:12–21). Fourth, Christ is the only means of salvation for humankind (Romans 3:21–30). Fifth, Paul closes his Epistle to the Romans with a statement about the revelation of a mystery was hidden in the past but now revealed through Christ. He states that the purpose of this revelation was "that all nations might believe and obey him" (Romans 16:26).

Missions in Revelation

OBJECTIVE
Explain the missions message of the book of Revelation.

The book of Revelation also has a great message for world missions. Its theme is the victory of the Church over evil and Satan. In the first part of the book is a message for seven Gentile churches (Revelation 2,3). One of the great missiological passages is found in Revelation 5:9–10: "You are worthy to take the scroll and to open its seals, because you were slain, and with your blood you purchased men for God from every tribe and language and people and nation. You have made them to be a kingdom and priests to serve our God, and they will reign on the earth." John wrote the book of Revelation to call the Church to proclaim the story of redemption through Christ and to face the inevitable struggle against the forces of evil. One clear theme is to announce the final victory of the church in spite of the way things appear in world events (Steyne 1992, 281).

Test Yourself

Circle the letter of the *best* answer.

1. The table of nations in Genesis 10 indicates
a) the languages of the earth were diversified.
b) all people belong to God.
c) unity is the strength of the nations.
d) the three sons of Noah were not united.

2. The purpose of Abram's call was
a) the establishing of Israel as a nation.
b) a reward for his righteous living in the land of Ur.
c) so God could give him the promised land.
d) intended for the welfare of all humanity.

3. In the Pentateuch, the foreigner living in Israel
a) was commanded to live separately from God's people.
b) was to share in the covenant of God with Israel.
c) was not to share in the observance of the Passover with Israel.
d) could not expect his offspring to be accepted by the nation.

4. Most of the statements about God's mission in the historical books and wisdom literature are found in the
a) Psalms.
b) Proverbs.
c) book of Job.
d) Song of Solomon.

5. The major theme of the book of Habakkuk is
a) suffering in the face of the powers of evil.
b) the restoration of Israel.
c) God's keeping His promises to Israel, and through them, to the whole world.
d) God's covenant with Abraham.

6. The climax of Old Testament prophecy is found in the
a) Psalms.
b) first part of the book of Isaiah.
c) second part of the book of Isaiah.
d) second chapter of the book of Joel.

7. The New Testament books were written by
a) apostles of the Lord.
b) writers of Jewish descent.
c) missionaries.
d) people who had walked with the Lord.

8. Jesus' ancestry is traced back to Adam in the Gospel of
a) Luke.
b) John.
c) Matthew.
d) Mark.

9. According to Paul, God called him to
a) take the gospel to the Jews.
b) proclaim Christ in the marketplaces.
c) take the gospel to the Gentiles.
d) abolish Jewish customs.

10. The world missions message of Revelation is seen in the
a) messages to the seven churches.
b) theme of the Church's victory over evil and Satan.
c) struggle between good and evil.
d) fall of the Antichrist.

Responses to Interactive Questions
Chapter 2

Some of these responses may include information that is supplemental to the IST. These questions are intended to produce reflective thinking beyond the course content and your responses may vary from these examples.

1 How does the universal principle given in Habakkuk relate to you?

Personal answer

2 What was the primary purpose of the "servant" in Isaiah?

Answer: The primary responsibility of the "servant" was to be a witness (43:10,12) and to serve as a messenger (42:19).

3 List the three events that illustrate missions in Jesus' ministry.

Answer: Jesus' sending of the Twelve (Matthew 10; Mark 6:7–13; Luke 9:1–16); His sending of the seventy (Luke 10:1–24); and His commission to the disciples (John 20:21)

4 Identify the element Mark adds to the Great Commission that is absent in the other gospels.

Answer: Mark's gospel gives special emphasis to Jesus' miracles, indicating that He is Lord over all.

5 What is the purpose of the book of Acts as it relates to missions?

Answer: The book of Acts chronicles missionary activities that ranged from individual extensions of ministry to the physical and spiritual expansion of the church.

Cross-Cultural Communication

We are called to communicate the gospel in a clear and understanding way. To do this, we must study cross-cultural communication with the different ethnic groups in our neighborhoods and cities, as well as in other lands we may serve. In the United States, there is a wave of immigration unparalleled in the history of the nation. More than 13 percent of the population is foreign born, and one child in four is born to an immigrant. These immigrants come from around the world and speak at least 380 languages (Cross Cultural Communications 2003).

Lesson 3.1   Worldview and Cultural Barriers

Objectives

3.1.1   Identify how cultural differences affect communication of the gospel.

3.1.2   Describe how body language can differ between cultures.

3.1.1
OBJECTIVE
Identify how cultural differences affect communication of the gospel.

Worldview and Cultural Barriers

In a meeting of business people from both North and Latin America in Houston, Texas, the Latins complained the North Americans seemed distant and lacked personal warmth. On the other hand, the North Americans complained about the too personal and presumptuous behavior of the Latins. The reason for the discomfort of both groups had to do with non-verbal communication. North Americans typically prefer to stand about five feet apart when conversing with one another, while Latins tend to get closer. As a Latin would draw close to a North American, the North American would retreat, which seemed to the Latin an indication of aloofness and lack of personal warmth.

Paul Hiebert defines *worldview* as "the basic assumptions about reality which lie behind the beliefs and behavior of a culture" (Hiebert 1985, 44). These assumptions are unconscious and taken for granted. People rarely examine their views of the world, but use them to explain reality.

Acts 14:8–18 is an example of a conflicting worldview in the ministry of Paul and Barnabas in Lystra. They were probably surprised by how the healing of a lame man would be perceived by the citizens of this city. Luke records the story in this way:

> In Lystra there sat a man crippled in his feet, who was lame from birth and had never walked. He listened to Paul as he was speaking. Paul looked directly at him, saw that he had faith to be healed and called out, Stand up on your feet! At that, the man jumped up and began to walk. When the crowd saw what Paul had done, they shouted in the Lycaonian language, "The gods have come down to us in human form!"

The apostle Paul and Barnabas knew this miracle had been performed by God, but the people thought the miracle had come from Zeus and Hermes. Charles Kraft notes that "such worldview differences frequently result in misunderstandings of the messages brought by people from other societies" (Kraft 1996, 51).

Paul also demonstrated in his speech in Athens (Acts 17) that it is possible to quote positively from local poets and local expressions of religion, thus engaging with the culture in order to preach Jesus and the resurrection.

Some Jews in the first century thought the Gentiles had to observe Jewish culture and customs in order to be saved. The first council of the church rejected that notion (Acts 15). The gospel had come from within the context of Jewish culture, but it was not confined to that particular culture.

1 How does the gospel affect culture?

The gospel is a revelation from God, and it must be communicated by means of human cultures without losing its divine character. It must be taught and expressed through the languages, symbols, and rituals of the cultures of the world. This is called *contextualization.* This does not mean the truth is relative and changes from one culture to another. Many things in all cultures are judged by Scripture and must be changed, while other cultural symbols are wholesome and do not change when the gospel arrives.

One cultural symbol in Africa that western missionaries misunderstood was the use of drums. Missionaries stationed in Africa condemned the use of drums since they had been previously used for witchcraft. The missionaries wanted to impose musical instruments from the West, for those seemed more "Christian" to them. However, with time and under local leadership, drums were restored to the African Christians and used for worship. This was also true for dance among African Christians.

On the other hand, polygamy was not negotiable, for the Bible is clear that monogamy is the Scriptural ideal. Paul made it clear to both Timothy and Titus that a leader in the church must be the husband of one wife (1 Timothy 3:2; Titus 1:6). This biblical principle judges any culture and demands conformity to it. Hesselgrave notes:

> The gospel cannot be held captive by western civilization and be true to its divine calling. Western theology is mostly rationalistic or preoccupied with the intellectual issues about faith and reason, and it is greatly influenced by western philosophies. It is also to a large extent in conformity to a secular worldview and individualism. (Hesselgrave 1991, 204)

This means a truly indigenous gospel must affirm the positive values of the culture where it is being announced, but at the same time challenge values expressing evil. Evils in society include slavery, apartheid, oppression, and exploitation.

Worldview differences are the reason for many of the problems we face as we attempt to preach the gospel to other cultures. The gospel must change people at the deepest possible level, and this refers to their worldviews or basic assumptions. This is also the reason we must examine our own culture to determine if our assumptions come from our Christian commitment or from our culture.

The gospel through the work of the Spirit must be the transforming agent in the lives of people in any culture. It must transform and possess a culture. J. H. Bavinck describes this in the following way:

> Within the framework of the non-Christian life, customs and practices serve idolatrous tendencies and drive a person away from God. The Christian life takes them in hand and turns them in an entirely different direction. Even though in external form there is much that resembles past practices; in reality everything has become new, the old has in essence passed away and the new has come. Christ takes the life of a people in his hands, he renews and reestablishes the distorted and deteriorated; he fills each thing, each word, and each practice with a new meaning and gives it a new direction. (Bavinck 1969, 179)

Padilla asserts that the "church has only two alternatives in its confrontation with the world: either it adapts itself to the world and betrays the Gospel, or it responds to the Gospel and enters into conflict with the world" (Padilla 1985, 53).

2   How does language express a people's way of life?

Language is one of the greatest barriers to cross-cultural communication, and languages are always complex. It is said that linguists "have not discovered a single primitive or simple language . . . and dictionaries have been produced for so-called languages containing 40– to 60,000 different entries" (Kraft 1996, 242). The language of a particular society applies to their situations and expresses their way of life. For instance, in West African languages, the word *snow* does not exist, but there are many expressions describing snow among the Eskimos. In the same way, the Arabic language has many words for *camels*. In the United States, particularly in the Southwest, there are many expressions about horses because of the importance of the horse in the past. One such expression is that you do not change horses in the middle of a stream. This means that once you have begun to do something, continue until you have completed it. Knowing the expressions and proverbs of a given people and understanding context are vital to effective Christian communication.

Languages are also unique in that no two are exactly the same. There are differences in structure or grammar. Some languages are oriented toward movement while others emphasize states of being. This also means that words, phrases, and even non-verbal communication can convey different meanings.

3.12
OBJECTIVE
*Describe how body
language can differ
between cultures.*

One example of this is in interpreting Luke 18:13, where the tax collector beat his breast and cried out to God to have mercy on him as a sinner. The beating of the breast was a sign of humility in Israel. However, in Ivory Coast, West Africa, it is a sign of confidence and belligerence.

Body language says a lot and is interpreted differently in various cultures of the world. While westerners signal "no" by shaking their heads sideways, many people from other countries raise their chins. Another example of cultural distinction is in eye contact. Many westerners engage in eye contact, and when it is not reciprocated, viewed this as a sign of evasiveness. However, in many areas of Africa and Asia, averted eyes are a sign of respect.

Thus, words and gestures must be contextualized for effective communication to occur. The form of a message serves to encode its meaning. Understanding the message has to do with the receiver decoding it so the reception matches the sender's intent. Hiebert notes that we are so focused on sending a message we do not hear the responses of our listeners (Hiebert 1985, 164). Therefore, to ensure that the message is received, the sender must pay attention to the recipient.

As we communicate, we must also be aware that individuals from different cultures are more likely to have different frames of reference. Cultures where there is collective identity—such as communal or village settings—tend to be sensitive to relationship building. This is typical of Third World cultures. However, individualistic cultures typical of western societies tend to de-emphasize personal relationships. Communication in these societies is direct and explicit (Cohen 1991, 20). It is important that we communicate in such a way that people do not misunderstand our message and fail to receive the gospel. The sender is responsible to ensure the message is understood.

Communication includes more than the use of words. How words are conveyed is often more important than what is said. The tone or pitch of the voice, or gestures or pauses by which feelings are revealed, may reinforce or contradict what is being said. These secondary messages, or paramessages, determine whether one is speaking with irony, sarcasm, or humor. They can tell us what the speaker thinks of the one listening. For example, silence is interpreted differently according to the particular culture. It may impart a negative reaction, affirmation, or evasion. In North America, one may interpret silence as disinterest or even hostility.

In 2 Corinthians 10:10, Paul writes that some said, "His letters are weighty and forceful, but in person he is unimpressive and his speaking amounts to nothing." He insisted his message was not different whether he was present or absent, but that he could speak with the same authority he used to write (Hesselgrave 1991, 438). May this be true of us as we present the message of the gospel.

 **Test Yourself**

Circle the letter of the *best* answer.

1. Worldviews are
a) consciously held and defended.
b) unconscious and taken for granted.
c) often examined by the people of a particular culture.
d) sophisticated assumptions about reality.

2. In the biblical case of Paul and Barnabas in Lystra, the
a) priest of Hermes wanted to put them on trial.
b) people wanted to prepare a feast.
c) people thought the miracle came from Zeus and Hermes.
d) city clerk called for an assembly.

3. Teaching the gospel through the language, symbols, and rituals of cultures is called
a) worldview.
b) contextualization.
c) synchronism.
d) revelation.

4. At the first council of the church in Acts 15,
a) the observance of Jewish customs was approved.
b) it was decided that Jewish customs need not be observed for a person to be saved.
c) observance of Jewish customs was left up to the Gentile leaders.
d) Jewish customs were condemned.

5. Contextualization refers to
a) the distortion of the truth.
b) teaching that makes the truth relative.
c) truth that is expressed through the language, symbols, and rituals of the cultures of the world.
d) the truth that all cultural symbols are wholesome.

6. Western theology is
a) mostly preoccupied with emotional issues.
b) mostly rationalistic.
c) hostile to western philosophies.
d) not in conformity to a secular worldview.

7. When we say the gospel must possess a culture, we mean it
a) adopts the practices of a culture.
b) rejects the practices of a culture.
c) turns a culture in a different direction.
d) no longer resembles the past.

8. As one of the greatest barriers to cross-cultural communication, languages are
a) always complex.
b) sometimes primitive or simple.
c) often primitive in illiterate societies.
d) only moderately complex.

9. Luke's account of the tax collector beating his breast is an example of
a) a different structure in language.
b) a generally understood gesture in all cultures.
c) non-verbal communication as a sign of humility in a particular culture.
d) non-verbal communication as a sign of humility everywhere.

10. Cultures where there is collective identity tend to
a) be direct.
b) de-emphasize the personal relationships.
c) be secretive.
d) be indirect.

Responses to Interactive Questions
Chapter 3

Some of these responses may include information that is supplemental to the IST. These questions are intended to produce reflective thinking beyond the course content and your responses may vary from these examples.

1   How does the gospel affect culture?

Answer: A truly indigenous gospel must affirm the positive values of the culture where it is being announced, but at the same time it must also challenge those values which express evil. The gospel must change people at the deepest possible level—in their worldview and their basic assumptions. We also must examine our own culture to determine if our assumptions come from a Christian commitment or from our culture.

2   How does language express a people's way of life?

Answer: The language of a particular society applies to their situations and expresses their way of life.

UNIT PROGRESS EVALUATION 1

Now that you have finished Unit 1, review the lessons in preparation for Unit Progress Evaluation 1. You will find it in Essential Course Materials at the back of this IST. Answer all of the questions without referring to your course materials, Bible, or notes. When you have completed the UPE, check your answers with the answer key provided in Essential Course Materials. Review any items you may have answered incorrectly. Then you may proceed with your study of Unit 2. (Although UPE scores do not count as part of your final course grade, they indicate how well you learned the material and how well you may perform on the closed-book final examination.)

The History of Missions

Both a general history of missions and the development of Assemblies of God World Missions are the topic of this unit. History is never pure fact. A fact or event requires analysis and interpretation, and the analysis and interpretation always has a sense of incompleteness, depending on what else the historian associates with that particular fact or event. Historians usually have vast materials at hand, and they select the more appropriate material. An example of this is found in the Gospels. They are not biographies. The writers, under the influence of the Holy Spirit, selected only what contributed to their objectives. Each has its stated purpose. When Luke wrote Acts, he was very selective. Many things were omitted that many of us would like to know. For example, one important figure, Titus, is not even mentioned. What happened to Peter? Many of the speeches in Acts are abridged. It is rather certain that Paul did not speak for only two or three minutes in Athens (Acts 17:22–31).

This brief chapter on missions history demands careful selection of persons, doctrines, or events to allow one to examine how methods, notable persons, and doctrines influence in the expansion of the Church. This is true for both the general history of missions and the history of the Assemblies of God.

General History of Missions

Learning involves change of knowledge and attitudes. A famous saying states that if we ignore history, we are condemned to repeat its mistakes. The history covered in this lesson deals with the expansion of the faith across cross-cultural barriers and the factors involved in that expansion.

The study of history assists us in the area of bias and prejudices. An example of this is the consultation in Greenlake, Wisconsin, on church–missions relationships, conducted by the American Baptist Convention in 1946. Several hundred people gathered to talk as though the problem had originated in the past twenty-five or thirty years. There was no investigating a history in working with church–missions problems. No one referred to Edinburgh in 1910, Jerusalem in 1928, Madras in 1938, or the volumes which existed on church–missions relationships (Covell, 1993). Christians' roots go far beyond our own evangelical and Pentecostal movements; we need to be aware of how history and the insights from the past can shed light on our present time.

Lesson 4.1   AD 40 to AD 950

Objectives

4.1.1   Identify reasons for the rapid growth of the Church in the Roman Empire.
4.1.2   Describe the reign of Charlemagne.

Lesson 4.2   AD 700 to AD 1600

Objectives

4.2.1   Give reasons for the weakness of the Church in the Middle East and
*   North Africa at the beginning of the eighth century.*
4.2.2   Describe the Franciscan and Dominican missionary orders.

Lesson 4.3   AD 1500 to AD 1800

Objectives

4.3.1   Discuss Luther's response to four Catholic concerns.
4.3.2   Describe the beginning of missions through Pietism and the Moravians.

Lesson 4.4   AD 1858 to the Present

Objectives

4.4.1   Name some important events around the year 1858.
4.4.2   Cite one of the primary reasons for the establishment of the Assemblies
*   of God.*

4.1.1
OBJECTIVE
*Identify reasons for the
rapid growth of the Church
in the Roman Empire.*

1   List two factors
contributing to the rapid
growth of the Church in the
Roman Empire.

AD 40 to AD 950

The Conversion of the Roman Empire (AD 40–AD 400)

During the first four hundred years after Christ's ascension, the Christian message penetrated all of the Roman Empire and became its state religion in AD 391. The Christian faith had reached outside the empire, from Ireland to India and from Ethiopia to Armenia. Let us examine some of the reasons for this rapid growth of the Church in the Roman Empire.

First, the Christian message was able to penetrate the cities of the empire. Greek-speaking communities existed in most of the major cities, and Hellenistic ideas and culture were dominant. This connection gave believers easy access to medieval centers of civilization. The Graeco-Roman world was a network of cities. A faith within them tended to penetrate connecting towns and countryside.

Second, Christianity quickly escaped its Jewish connection. Once the break was made with the original Jewish womb, Christianity attracted many people who would not have been attracted to a Jewish religion.

Third, widespread missionary tours were being made, some unquestionably not recorded in the book of Acts. Paul writes in Romans 15:20: "It has always been my ambition to preach the gospel where Christ was not known, so that I would not be building on someone else's foundation." Peter mentions Christians in Pontus, Cappadocia, Asia, and Bithynia (1 Peter 1:1), and no biblical account records when these people found Christ. This is an example of the activity of other apostles and evangelists during the first century.

Fourth, after the apostles, other notable persons were mightily used by the Holy Spirit to win converts. One example is Gregory, called the wonder-worker, who had a powerful ministry of signs and miracles in Cappadocia. "Tradition says that when he became bishop there were only seventeen Christians in the city, but that when he died thirty years later there were only seventeen pagans" (Neill 1986, 47). Another notable person was Gregory the Illuminator of Armenia. He was known for his powerful gift of teaching. From the start, Gregory used the language and thoughts of Armenia to preach and teach the gospel. Later, a new alphabet would be invented, and the New Testament would be translated into Armenian (Neill 1986, 48). This clearly indicates the development of an **indigenous** work.

Fifth, a central church organization served as a unifying factor in a diversified culture. Does this not suggest the need for a strong urban center that serves as the focal point of our work in any area or nation where we are serving Christ?

Sixth, the most dominant force in the spread of Christianity was the ordinary Christian. It must be stressed that the chief agents in the expansion of Christianity appear not to have been those who made it a profession, but men and women who earned their livelihood in some purely secular manner and spoke of their faith to those they met. Edward Gibben notes that every convert considered it a sacred duty to spread his or her faith (Gibben 1945, 385).

Conversion of the Barbarians (AD 400–950)

In a historical overview of this period, one must consider political and religious divisions. Successive waves of barbarians entered the Roman Empire. The imperial armies were first defeated at Adrianople by the Goths in 378, and Emperor Valens was killed in that battle (Cairns 1981, 127). In AD 410, Rome was sacked by Alaric and the Goths. A kingdom was established by the Goths in South Gaul and Spain (Latourette 1975a, 95). In the fifth and sixth centuries, the Ostrogoths, the Vandals, the Burgundians, the Franks, the Lombards, the Angles, the Saxons, and the Huns came. And in the seventh to the ninth centuries, there were movements into the empire by the Bulgars, Agars, and the Slavic peoples.

2   Identify factors leading to the conversion of the Goths.

All these people came into contact with Christianity, and many were converted. The missionary credited with the conversion of the Goths was Ulfilas (AD 311–383), the son of a Gothic father and mother from Cappadocia. He worked for forty years with the Gothic race. He reduced the Gothic language to writing and translated the New Testament into their language. He influenced the widespread evangelization of this people (Neill 1986, 48, 49).

The Kingdom of the Franks

In the fifth century, some of the Franks took over northern Gaul and the lower section of the Rhine Valley. The first leader of this embryonic state was Childeric. He was not a Christian, but was friendly to the Roman political leaders. Clovis, son of Childeric, took the throne in AD 481 and gradually made himself ruler over all of Gaul. Clovis accepted Christ and was baptized in AD 496. Without the use of force, most of his followers eventually followed him in the profession of Christianity. It is said that the conversion of this king was the single most important event in the spread of the faith among the non-Roman people in the northwestern part of the continent of Europe (Neill 1986, 272).

The Holy Roman Empire

4.1.2
OBJECTIVE
*Describe the reign of
Charlemagne.*

The accession of Charles the Great, better known as Charlemagne, to the throne marked the advent of what is known as the Carolingian Empire. From AD 771 to AD 800, Charles the Great utilized fifty military campaigns to bring all of what we know as France, more than half of modern Germany, and northern Italy under his control (Cairns 1981, 185). He was crowned emperor of the Holy Roman Empire in AD 800. Unfortunately, his primary method of getting people to convert to Christianity was by the use of the sword. This was carried out primarily among the Saxons (Latourette 1975a, 350). Latourette (1975b) sums up the results as follows: "The narrative is a repetition, with variations, of campaigns resulting in outward submission and followed by the peaceful efforts of missionaries, of revolts, of fresh campaigns, of more or less sullen acquiescence, of fresh revolts, and of eventual victory" (103).

Stephen Neill (1986) lists some of the Christian rules imposed by Charlemagne:

Anyone who kills a bishop, priest, or a deacon, shall be put to death. Anyone who burns the body of a dead person, as is the pagan fashion, shall be put to death. Any unbaptized Saxon who attempts to hide himself among his own people and refuses to accept baptism shall be put to death. Anyone who plots with the pagans against the Christians shall be put to death. (68, 69)

Although the Saxons eventually accepted Christianity, there was obviously little individual depth or spiritual commitment to the faith. It simply became a part of their culture.

Celtic Missionary Expansion

3   What is an immigrant missionary?

One of the brightest areas of missionary expansion during this period came from the Celtic people. Two Irish monasteries served as the primary training centers for the Celtic missionaries. One was Iona and the other Lindisfarne, off the coasts of Scotland and eastern Britain. McNeill, who is one of the historians of the Celtic movement, made this statement: "For three hundred years the light of Ireland flamed, shedding its rays upon Scotland, England and the Continent" (McNeill 1974, 175). They stressed the use of the Bible and obedience to it in their personal lives. Wherever they went, they established schools to train people in the Bible. They also practiced adult baptism, and strongly emphasized prayer and God's ability to answer, even by miracles, prayer offered in faith. A number of areas in Central and Northern Europe received the gospel from these Celtic missionaries (*National Geographic* 1977, 582–632). They were immigrant missionaries, meaning they became a part of the people and culture where they ministered. The work they established quickly became indigenous.

4.2.1
OBJECTIVE
Give reasons for the weakness of the Church in the Middle East and North Africa at the beginning of the eighth century.

4   How did Ramon Lull attempt to reach Muslims?

AD 700 to AD 1600

Islam and the Crusades

For much of the period between AD 700 to AD 1600, Islam swept most of Christianity from the Middle East and North Africa. The church had been embroiled in political conflict with church authorities in Europe. There were problems with deviant doctrines about Christ, His humanity and divinity, and, in general, the Bible had not been proclaimed in the languages of the native people. Consequently, Islam confronted a weak and divided church. The military conquests of Islam took place particularly between AD 638 and AD 846. Ultimately, Constantinople, headquarters of the Byzantine Roman/Greek Empire, fell in 1453.

The spread of Christianity by military conquest is a sad part of the history of the Church. This was particularly true of the crusades against the Muslim people of North Africa and the Middle East. Rather than preaching the gospel of love, European powers carried out violent military campaigns against the Muslims. In the midst of this, Ramon Lull, one of the greatest missionaries in the history of the church, became an active influence. This scholar felt three things were necessary for the evangelization of the Muslims: fluency in Arabic; writing a book presenting the truths of Christianity demonstrated by sound reasoning; and willingness to be a faithful and courageous witness to the Muslims (Neill 1986, 115–117). Although Lull failed to win Muslims to the Lord, he stimulated an interest in a better approach to Islam and left a model of love, learning, and zeal.

Missionary Orders of Outreach (AD 1200–1600)

4.2.2
OBJECTIVE
Describe the Franciscan and Dominican missionary orders.

Both the Franciscans and Dominicans arose in the ferment of early thirteenth century Europe. This was the time of new universities, new cathedrals, and new commercial ventures by Italian merchants to Asia. It was also a time of religious revival. The personal nature of the Christian faith had impressed itself on many. In its intellectual dimensions, it inspired certain scholars, such as William of Ockham and Bonaventura. It caused others to seek new lifestyles. Among these was Giovanni Bernerdone, called Francesco, or more popularly Saint Francis of Assisi. He was inspired by verses, such as those found in Matthew 10:7–10:

> As you go preach this message: the kingdom of heaven is near. Heal the sick, raise the dead, cleanse those who have leprosy, drive out demons. Freely you have received, freely give. Do not take along any gold, or silver, or copper in

your belts. Take no bag for the journey or extra tunic or sandals, or a staff. For the worker is worth his keep.

Following the admonition of this passage, he advocated simplicity and poverty for the end of personal character, preaching, and meeting the needs of the sick and the poor. His Order was recognized by Pope Innocent III in 1210, and by 1220 the Order had attracted five thousand members. Sacrificially, they lived in poverty to proclaim the gospel.

The Dominicans were founded by Dominic (1170–1221). The Order was devoted to the conversion of heretics through preaching, and its Order had as its official title the "Order of Preachers." It had a genuine missionary impulse as did the Franciscans (Neill 1986, 99). The Dominicans came almost entirely from the aristocracy of society while the Franciscans were recruited primarily from the poor (Latourette 1975a, 437). "Both were intensely missionary and by widely flung enterprises in Europe, Asia, and Africa sought to bring nominal Christians to a deeper faith and to win non-Christians" (Latourette 1975a, 439).

At the end of the fifteenth century, despite much missionary activity, particularly toward the East, Christianity was still largely the faith of Europe. Stephen Neill gives the following reasons for the limited expansion beyond Europe:

> The first and the most obvious is the great distances that had to be covered, and the difficulties of travel. Missionaries remained unvisited for years on end. When reinforcements could be sent, it was by no means certain that they would ever reach their destination. The loss of life was high, both through the violence of the barbarous tribes and through the natural hazards of travel in unknown regions and of exposure to unfamiliar climates. Conversion of the Turkish tribes seems to have been fairly easy; but lapse to Islam or to some other form of religion was equally easy and frequent; there was little permanence and stability in the Christianity of these regions. . . the tragic unsettlement of the times, and the recurrent calamities caused by one invasion of the barbarians after another." (Neill 1986, 112–113)

4.3.1
OBJECTIVE

Discuss Luther's response to four Catholic concerns.

AD 1500 to AD 1800

The Early Protestant Efforts

On October 31, 1517, Martin Luther posted ninety-five propositions for theological debate on the door of the Church in Wittenberg, Germany. He contested abuses in the doctrine of the Roman Catholic Church. Bruce Shelley writes that Luther gave new answers to four basic Catholic concerns:

> To the question how is a person saved, Luther replied: not by works but by faith alone. To the question where does religious authority lie, he answered: not in the visible institution called the Roman Church, but in the Word of God found in the Bible. To the question—what is the church?—he responded: the whole community of Christian believers, since all are priests before God. And to the question—what is the essence of Christian living?—he replied: serving God in any useful calling, whether ordained or lay. To this day any classical description of Protestantism must echo those central truths. (Shelley 1982, 264)

However, Luther and the other reformers did not immediately understand the mission mandate to take the Gospel to all the world. David Bosch pointed out that "the Reformers were indifferent, if not hostile, to mission" (Bosch 1991, 243). There was simply little thought for missions. In fact, until 1648 when the Peace of Westphalia was signed, the Protestants were struggling for their lives and greatly divided in their beliefs (Neill 1986, 187).

The European entry into worldwide missions began with a movement called Pietism under Philipp Jakob Spener (1635–1705), a Lutheran pastor in Frankfurt, Germany. He organized Bible studies and prayer meetings in homes where he taught personal holiness (Cairns 1981, 381). Nicolaus Ludwig, Count of Zinzendorf (1700–1760), grew up in the Pietist atmosphere. He founded a village on his land called Herrnhut, where he received persecuted refugees from Bohemia and Moravia. Zinzendorf had a passion for spreading the Christian faith throughout the world. This group of refugees was known as the Moravians. Missionaries from this group went to various parts of the world (Latourette 1975b, 897). They were generally masons, carpenters, and bakers who lived on the mission field by using and teaching their vocation. At the same time, they spread the gospel and founded churches. They witnessed as a total community—to be a Moravian was to be a missionary.

Another great personality during this period was William Carey from England. He was called the "Father of Modern Missions." Carey sailed for India in 1793, where he established a residence in Serampore, which is located about twenty miles from Calcutta. He learned the Bengali language. During a thirty-year period, he translated the entire Bible into six languages while the New Testament was translated into twenty-three other languages. The gospel was preached extensively. He and his colleagues also gave themselves to the study of the culture, and one of Carey's colleagues, William Ward, wrote a book on the customs of the Hindus. Carey was also credited with being a founder of prose literature in Bengali. He and his colleagues founded a school for the training of native brethren for the ministry (Covell 1993).

4.3.2
OBJECTIVE
Describe the beginning of missions through Pietism and the Moravians.

5   How did the Moravian missionaries make a living in foreign lands?

4.4.1
OBJECTIVE
Name some important events around the year 1858.

AD 1858 to the Present

The Second Wave of Protestant Missions

The year 1858 was a turning point. The war between China and a number of European powers ended with a series of treaties signed by the warring factions. This gave foreigners permission to travel inside China and guaranteed that Christianity would be tolerated (Covell 1977, 94). A second evangelical awakening began in America about this time. This rebirth was characterized by a high level of involvement and prayer of laymen. Missionary agencies came from this awakening. The Bible school movement also arose. There was the development of cooperative missionary conferences, such as the Missionary Conference in New York in 1900, where there were 162 mission boards represented with an attendance of more than 175,000 people (Covell 1993).

In 1858 the first missionary of modern times entered Japan. In 1857, David Livingstone published his Missionary Travels and Researches in South Africa (Neill 1986, 275). This gave a new impetus to work in Africa and led to the work of the university missions to Central Africa, as well as to the work of many other groups. The work in China is an example of the expansion of Christianity during this period. In 1853, there were only 350 Christians in the land. By 1889, the number was approaching forty thousand. In 1858, twenty mission agencies with eighty-one missionaries were operating in the country. By 1889, there were forty-one mission agencies with about thirteen hundred missionaries.

Missions and Pentecost, 1914 to the Present

John Ryland of England made the following statement to William Carey about winning the heathen: "Young man, sit down. You are an enthusiast. When God pleases to convert the heathen, he'll do it without consulting you or me. Besides, there must first be another Pentecostal gift of tongues" (Covell 1993). Although William Carey did go to India, and the modern era of missions was launched, the words of Ryland were to a great extent prophetic in view of the dynamic thrust of missions in the twentieth century after the renewal of Pentecost. The nineteenth century had seen a great expansion of Christianity, and statistics reveal that by 1910 there were 21,307 missionaries serving in various parts of the world (Beaver 1968, 115). However, the twentieth century would see a far greater expansion of Christianity under the power and anointing of the Holy Spirit.

4.4.2
OBJECTIVE

Cite one of the primary reasons for the establishment of the Assemblies of God.

6   What role did missions play in the founding of the Assemblies of God?

Some consideration of the growth and methods of the Assemblies of God World Missions program gives us insights into the impact of Pentecostalism in world missions. Vinson Synan stated that the "history of the Assemblies of God is in large part the story of the entire Pentecostal movement, not only in the United States, but also around the world" (Synan 1987, 15). In 1914, the founders also promoted the organization of this new movement because of the need for a central foreign missions agency (Synan 1987, 19). Five years later, the Foreign Missions Department was established (McGee 1986, 89).

One of the most important methods of Assemblies of God missions was the adherence to a policy of establishing **indigenous churches** that would be self-supporting, self-governing, and self-propagating. This meant great attention would be given to the founding of Bible institutes for the training of indigenous leaders. Preaching the gospel was primary in the missionaries' efforts, and they expected and saw signs of miracles and healings follow their ministries. There was also attention given to the relieving of physical suffering. One of the great examples of this holistic approach to ministry was the orphanage founded in Egypt by Lillian Trasher (McGee 1986, 97–99).

The success of the Assemblies of God World Missions program is reflected in the statistics for December 31, 2004. At that time, there were 52,534,858 members and adherents worldwide. There were also 869 Bible institutes and colleges with 47,628 students, and 1,131 extension training programs with 45,869 students. For those in leadership, the statistics gave 109,463 national ministers and 100,367 lay leaders serving in 181,590 churches of 74,653 preaching points (Assemblies of God World Missions 2004).

In *Christianity Today*, Grant McClung reported 580 million Pentecostal adherents in the world, growing by nineteen million per year and 54,000 per day. He also gave the statistics of David Barrett and Todd Johnson:

1.   Pentecostals comprise 3 major streams and 59 diverse categories of worldwide Christianity.

2.   Pentecostals can be found within all 150 non-charismatic Christian traditions.

3. Pentecostals come from 9,000 ethnolinguistic cultures and speak 8,000 languages.

4. Pentecostalism is more urban than rural, more female than male, more Majority World* (66%) than Western world (34%), more poor (87%) than affluent (13%), more family-related than individualist, and more young than old.

5. Pentecostals are an active presence in 80% of the world's 3,300 largest metropolises. (McClung 2006)

McClung further writes this:

> From the inception of the Pentecostal Movement, our mission has always been missions. Indeed, Pentecostalism cannot be understood apart from its self-identity as a missionary movement raised up by God to evangelize the world in the last days. As we prepare to step into our second century, we must decide whether we will continue to be distinguished by missions in the future. (2006)

Test Yourself

Circle the letter of the *best* answer.

1. Christianity penetrated the Roman Empire in the first
a) two hundred years.
b) three hundred years.
c) four hundred years.
d) five hundred years.

2. One reason for the rapid spread of Christianity in the Roman Empire was
a) its Jewish connection.
b) a diversified church organization developed.
c) the development of a professional clergy.
d) the Christian message was able to penetrate the cities.

3. The political situation of the empire during the conversion of the barbarians
a) was one of relative stability and peace.
b) was marked by successive waves of barbarians into the Roman Empire.
c) saw a temporary upsurge in Roman military conquests and might.
d) saw the establishment of Constantinople as the capital of the empire.

4. The missionary responsible for the conversion of the Goths was
a) Gregory, the wonder-worker.
b) Gregory the Illuminator.
c) Clovis.
d) Ulfilas.

5. The primary method for conversion by Charles the Great was
a) to send missionaries.
b) by the sword.
c) through literature.
d) through translation into indigenous languages.

6. The Celtic missionaries
a) were known as men of zeal but little education.
b) stressed church tradition.
c) were immigrant missionaries.
d) worked primarily in Asia.

7. The founder of the Franciscan Order was
a) William of Ockham.
b) Bonaventura.
c) Boniface.
d) Giovanni Bernerdone.

8. The founder of the Pietist movement in Germany was
a) Philipp Jakob Spener.
b) Nocolaus Ludwig.
c) Melancthon.
d) Zinzendorf.

9. The year of the second wave of Protestant missions was
a) 1797.
b) 1812.
c) 1858.
d) 1901.

10. A key motive for the establishment of the Assemblies of God was
a) to provide ministerial credentials to ministers.
b) the need for a central foreign missions agency.
c) the need to form a Pentecostal denomination.
d) the need to provide formal theological education.

Responses to Interactive Questions
Chapter 4

Some of these responses may include information that is supplemental to the IST. These questions are intended to produce reflective thinking beyond the course content and your responses may vary from these examples.

1 List two factors contributing to the rapid growth of the Church in the Roman Empire.

Answer: Two of the following answers should be given:

1. The Christian message was able to penetrate the cities of the empire.
2. Christianity quickly escaped its Jewish connection.
3. Widespread missionary tours were being made.
4. After the apostles, other notable persons were mightily used by the Holy Spirit to win converts.
5. A central church organization developed and served as a unifying factor in a diversified culture.
6. The most dominant force in the spread of Christianity was the ordinary Christian.

2 Identify factors leading to the conversion of the Goths.

Answer: (1) The work of Ulfilas (AD 311–383), son of a Gothic father and mother from Cappadocia; (2) the translation of the New Testament into their language

3 What is an immigrant missionary?

Answer: An immigrant missionary became a part of the people and culture where he or she ministered.

4 How did Ramon Lull attempt to reach Muslims?

Answer: Lull felt that three things were necessary for the evangelization of the Muslim: good knowledge of Arabic; the writing of a book presenting the truths of Christianity demonstrated by sound reasoning; willingness to be a faithful and courageous witness to Muslims.

5 How did the Moravian missionaries make a living in foreign lands?

Answer: They were generally masons, carpenters, and bakers who lived on the mission field by using and teaching their vocation.

6 What role did missions play in the founding of the Assemblies of God?

Answer: The need for a central foreign missions agency prompted the founders to organize the Assemblies of God.

History of World Missions in the Assemblies of God

Note: For a more complete discussion, see the Berean School of the Bible course BTHE142 Assemblies of God History, Missions, and Governance.

Any discussion of the history of the Assemblies of God USA must inevitably include the history of its missionary efforts. In large measure, the burden and dedication of the early Pentecostal movement to take the full gospel around the world was what led to the formation of the General Council of the Assemblies of God USA. From its beginning, the cause of worldwide missions has been woven into the fabric of the movement. The lost must be found and brought to Christ, and the found must be led into the fullness of the Holy Spirit to continue the process. The Great Commission must be fulfilled.

This chapter presents key developments in the history of Assemblies of God missions at home and abroad. It goes beyond the bare facts to reveal the development of the missions perspectives and principles as they emerged through the years. The foundations laid from the early years set the stage for the development of one of the greatest missionary movements of this day. The future of the movement will depend upon how well they are understood, implemented, and adapted to meet new challenges.

Lesson 5.1   Missions at the End of the Nineteenth Century

Objectives

5.1.1   *Examine the general attitude toward protestant missions in the United States and its impact on the early Pentecostals.*

5.1.2   *State three prominent characteristics of the early Pentecostal missionary movement.*

Lesson 5.2   The Early Years, 1901–1926

Objective

5.2.1   *Describe how the missionary cause affected the call for organization of the Pentecostal churches in 1914.*

Lesson 5.3   The Maturing Years, 1927–1953

Objectives

5.3.1   *Discuss the new emphasis in mission leadership articulated by Noel Perkin.*

5.3.2   *Outline the requirements for missionary candidacy that arose from the 1933 General Council.*

5.3.3   *List the two basic changes in the missionary outreach of the Assemblies due to World War II.*

Lesson 5.4   Preparation, Development, and Growth, 1954 and Beyond

Objectives

5.4.1   *Identify how major changes in administration impacted missions in the 1950s.*

5.4.2   *Discuss the factors that led to the formation of Home Missions.*

5.1.1
OBJECTIVE

Examine the general attitude toward protestant missions in the United States and its impact on the early Pentecostals.

Missions at the End of the Nineteenth Century

To fully understand the missionary impetus of the early Pentecostal movement, one must refer to the events leading up to it. The years 1792–1910, while technically greater than one hundred years, were dubbed by the great mission historian Kenneth Latourette as the "Great Century" (Latourette 1941: IV, 1–8). This was the era of the greatest geographical expansion of Christianity up to that time. This growth was spawned by missionary movements of the period, enabled in large part by the explorers, commercial enterprises, and colonial conquests that paved the way for missionary travel and protection. The industrial revolution produced wealth among Christendom not previously known, making missions ventures viable.

The middle of the century saw the development of four types of missions: denominational, interdenominational, faith missions, and independent missions. James Hudson Taylor formed the first faith mission, the China Inland Mission in 1865. That spawned similar missions, such as the North Africa Mission, the Christian and Missionary Alliance, the Sudan Interior Mission, and the Africa Inland Mission. These later missions were separate from denominational boards and called "faith" missions because they depended on faith for their support, not denominational backing (Terry, 1998a, 214–215). The missionaries were not guaranteed support, but were urged to trust God. This became the stance of the early Pentecostal movement as well.

The end of the century saw a great missionary movement in the United States grow out of revivals of the day. D. L. Moody, A. T. Pierson, John R. Mott, Robert Wilder, and others were instrumental in forming and promoting student missions organizations, like the Student Volunteer Movement about which Kane reports:

> It began in the 1880s. Its inception and much of its early success were due to the missionary vision of Robert P. Wilder, a graduate of Princeton University; the spiritual power of D. L. Moody, the greatest evangelist of the nineteenth century; and the organizing genius of John R. Mott, then a student at Cornell University. It all began in the summer of 1886 when one hundred university and seminary students at Moody's conference grounds at Mount Hermon, Massachusetts, signed the Princeton Pledge, which read: "I purpose, God willing, to become a foreign missionary." . . . In no time at all the movement spread to colleges and universities all over the United States and Canada and even to foreign countries. The watchword of the movement, coined by Wilder, was: "The evangelization of the world in this generation." (Kane 1986, 103)

Bible institutes also grew in this era. Schools, such as the Missionary Training Institute in New York, the Chicago (Moody) Bible Institute, and the Boston Missionary Training School, taught a premillennial eschatology that was concerned that Christ's imminent return might cut short the opportunity to reach the lost. Among their purposes was the commitment to prepare men and women for foreign service (McGee 1986, 27). Thus, when the Pentecostal revival came, it entered an atmosphere of great interest and motivation for the foreign missions effort. That revival had a profound effect on the movement.

The year 1901 saw the beginning of the great Pentecostal revival, starting in Topeka, Kansas, and spreading in the United States and abroad. Many of these new Pentecostal believers were forced out of their home churches, such as the Christian and Missionary Alliance, and carried with them the incentive for missions, now highly motivated by the power of the Spirit. Some had been trained in the Bible institutes.

1   Why was there a sense
of urgency among early
Pentecostals concerning
missions?

5.1.2
OBJECTIVE
*State three prominent
characteristics of the early
Pentecostal missionary
movement.*

The new experience produced a sense of urgency. Since the prophecy of Joel 2:28–29 was interpreted by Peter on the Day of Pentecost to mean they were now in the "last days," these new Pentecostals concluded the Lord's coming was at hand, the day was far spent, and night was near. This called for world evangelization; the gospel must be preached to every creature.

Some went to the foreign field believing that through the "tongues" experience God was supernaturally giving them the language of the people they were to reach. In reality, this did not happen, and many were disillusioned (McGee 1986, 44–45).

McGee notes three important characteristics of the missionary movement that sprang from the Pentecostal revival: 1) the prominent role of women, 2) the unique sense of being led by the Spirit for overseas ministry, and 3) the concept of living by faith (McGee 1986, 46).

First, single women went to the foreign field on their own, believing God had called them and would help them. He did, and several women pioneered important works. One of the best known was Lillian Trasher who founded the great orphanage in Assiout, Egypt, in 1911. Many others must also be counted as female heroes of the faith.

Secondly, the early Pentecostals felt strongly that there should be a definite sense of call for one to become a missionary. Their heightened sense of dependence on the Holy Spirit in all aspects of their spiritual journey contributed to this emphasis. They patterned this after the Scriptures and their own experience. They saw the sense of personal call in Jesus' selection of the Twelve. While many had followed Jesus voluntarily, He selected those who became His apostles ("sent ones"). They were especially called to be with Him, and to preach with the authority, and to cast out demons (Mark 3:13–15). Later, as recorded in Acts, the Holy Spirit is recorded as doing the calling (Acts 13:1–4). Believers did not select themselves.

The importance of a sense of call to missionary service continues today. While there may be other factors influencing one toward missionary service, there must be a settled sense that God is behind it. The missionaries will be tested many times by the world, the flesh, and the devil to question how and why they came to be missionaries. To know a definite call by the Spirit gives much needed stability and renewal of purpose at those moments.

The third characteristic of the early Pentecostal missionaries was their commitment to live by faith. Undoubtedly, they were influenced by the faith mission movement of the period, but they also ascribed to Bible passages like Matthew 10:5–10. They saw that the apostle Paul and his companions lived and ministered with a simple and frugal lifestyle. Besides, if Jesus were coming soon, why accumulate much of this world's goods?

Those early days were marked by much zeal, but often equal inadequacies. Those who went abroad thinking the Holy Spirit had given them the language of the people of their calling were brought up short. Many went with meager financial support and suffered for it. Too often these pioneers went with little sense of any Spirit-led strategy so a small village might have several missionary couples, while larger, more strategic sites were neglected. Sadly, charlatans also who took advantage of the zeal among the churches for missionary outreach. These pseudo-missionaries sought to line their own pockets through false or exaggerated stories of great exploits. Something had to be done. Change was definitely needed.

The Early Years, 1901–1926

The year 1914 marked the formation of the Assemblies of God as a united fellowship. Several Pentecostal churches of varying names believed uniting to be of great benefit. In that first General Council five purposes for their assembly were identified, including these:

Second—Again we come together that we [may] know how to conserve the work, that we may all build up and not tear down, both in home and foreign lands. Third—We come together for another reason, that we may get a better understanding of the needs of each foreign field and may know how to place our money in such a way that one mission or missionary shall not suffer, while another not any more worthy, lives in luxuries. Also that we may discourage wasting money on those who are here and there accomplishing nothing, and may concentrate our support on those who mean business for our King. (Blumhofer 1989a, 201–202)

The process of forming the General Council of the Assemblies of God in 1914 raised the important issue of the relationship between the Council and the churches that came under its umbrella. Was this to be a cooperative fellowship or a move to centralized government? The delegates were assured that the purpose was not to legislate laws of government, nor to usurp authority over the various churches, nor deprive them of their Scriptural and local rights and privileges. Unfortunately, the debate and tension between central control and church rights continues to this day.

This issue carried over to the relationship between the missionaries and the foreign missions leadership of the Council. Some veteran missionaries, already on the field prior to 1914, struggled with their relationship to the foreign missions office of the Council. Even today, the tension between private and corporate vision continues. Later, we will consider development of the infrastructure of the foreign missions office and compare the results of each approach.

A second General Council convened in Chicago at the Stone Church in November, 1914 with special emphasis on the foreign missions program. Lemuel C. Hall presented a resolution by which the delegates committed themselves to "the greatest evangelism the world has ever known" (Blumhofer 1989a, 288). This has been the watch cry of the Assemblies' foreign missions outreach ever since.

At first, funds for missionaries were channeled through the publishing house. That soon became too burdensome as the number of missionaries increased. In 1919, the General Council created a missionary department supervised by the Executive Presbytery, and elected J. Roswell Flower as its first Missionary Secretary. The prevailing sentiment was that Pentecostal missionaries had a holy calling, beyond that of non-Pentecostals. They were not to spend their efforts on building up charitable institutions, hospitals, and schools. They were to be witnesses throughout the earth. Flower's leadership had an impact in two major ways beyond the handling of the finances. First, he sought to insure the missionaries selected were like Paul and Barnabas, not John Mark who turned back. Second, he sought to establish a basic budget for support of the individual missionaries, an attempt to insure they could both survive and minister (Blumhofer 1989a, 292–294).

The importance of these first years in establishing the basis of the missionary outreach of the Assemblies cannot be overstated. From that time forward, the methodology and infrastructure were refined, but the basic purpose and philosophy have remained largely intact.

5.3.1
OBJECTIVE

*Discuss the new emphasis
in mission leadership
articulated by Noel Perkin.*

2   What emphasis did
Noel Perkin view as key to
advancing missions?

5.3.2
OBJECTIVE

*Outline the requirements
for missionary candidacy
that arose from the 1933
General Council.*

The Maturing Years, 1927–1953

In 1927 the leadership of the foreign missions department was given to Noel Perkin, who inherited the mandate of the 1925 General Council:

> To extend the knowledge of Christ throughout the world, by utilizing the service of the church, with a view to establishing self-supporting native churches in each field. To promote an interest in foreign missions by approved methods in the home churches.

The impact of this mandate was not lost on Perkin, who stated:

> This meant moving away from somewhat unrelated efforts of individual missionaries in favor of a concentrated effort on the part of a united Assemblies of God fellowship working through its established channel, the Missionary Department, with the missionaries cooperating to effect world evangelization. (Blumhofer 1989a, 299)

Convictions concerning doctrine and practice naturally produced tension between Pentecostals and non-Pentecostals. Some missionaries fellowshipped with their non-Pentecostal neighbors, but by and large, the conviction among the leadership was that they needed to work alone, producing their own literature. Perkin recognized that the Assemblies could best use its resources by concentrating in areas where evangelical missionaries were not already at work (Blumhofer 1989a, 301).

Other accomplishments under Perkin's leadership included the careful selection of missionary candidates and the emphasis on prayer as the key to advance. He was troubled by the dependence of the work on women missionaries, and urged that more men and married couples seek appointment. He strongly encouraged the churches to support missionary endeavors, but still only about thirty percent of the adherents did so, a problem that tends to persist even today, though to a lesser extent.

In 1931, the first Missionary Manual was published. Only twenty-eight pages in length, it was undoubtedly the most significant publication of the Missionary Department to that point. It included the reason for being, a brief history of the Pentecostal movement, and a listing of departmental policies. General Council policies that affected foreign missions were also included (McGee 1986, 136).

Two aspects of the missions philosophy and responsibility to that date were articulated. The department served basically as a distribution center for funds and information, for promoting missionary interests in the local churches, and for the examining of missionary candidates and assisting them with certain legal procedures. The second was the affirmation of the belief that missionaries should follow the leading of the Lord in carrying out their work, unhindered by the department or the General Council. It was not until the mid-1940s that more direct supervision of overseas activities was applied (McGee 1986, 137). The impact of that change will be shown later.

In 1933, the General Council made important decisions regarding missionary candidacy. Prospective missionaries had to have proven ministries in their district and be physically, mentally, and spiritually fit before being endorsed. If healing was needed, they were encouraged to "pray through" until divine healing came. They were urged to trust God for their finances, while the local churches were responsible to provide consistent and adequate support (McGee 1986, 138–139).

For a time, it was common practice to provide financial support for national preachers, a practice that contradicted the indigenous principle of national churches supporting themselves. In practice, it caused division among the national brethren due to some being supported from abroad and others struggling to continue in the ministry. Terms like *coconut* were sometimes attributed to those receiving mission support. This meant they were "brown on the outside, but white on the inside," sold out to the white man for money. The temptation to provide direct support to the "poor national brethren" can be strong, but all too often it causes more problems than it solves. It caused such friction among the national pastors in Egypt that the practice was stopped (McGee 1986, 139).

Important objectives included winning converts to Christ and establishing assemblies, followed by the establishment of Bible institutes to train national pastors. In so doing, the missionary was to serve the emerging church. The Missionary Manual stated that neither attitudes of "racial superiority [nor] control of finances entitle him to exercise lordship over their Assemblies. As soon as the native converts manifest spiritual gifts of ministry, they should be encouraged to take responsibility." Therefore, missionaries should never think of their place of ministry as fixed (McGee 1986, 140–141).

By 1927, Perkin realized the need for greater supervision. He was particularly concerned that distribution of missionary personnel did not match the need for areas in which the church was rapidly growing. Too much was left to individual initiative. Still, some missionaries reached out to the unevangelized regions, sometimes at great personal risk. In spite of the hardships, great reports came of miracles of healing, deliverance, and other signs and wonders among revivals.

World War II had a revolutionary effect on missionary effort. The immediate impact was the sense of urgency to win the lost. Perhaps these were indeed the "last days" before Christ's return. As the war progressed, many missionaries—especially from the large number deployed in the Far East—had to return to the States or found themselves cut off from communication and support. While Latin America seemed a good alternative for missionary endeavor, the strong opposition of the Roman Catholic Church discouraged many from going there.

Noel Perkin's leadership had produced a growing unity of philosophy and practice among the missionaries. The determination to establish indigenous churches was largely succeeding. The department itself had grown in numbers of staff and efficiency. As the war continued, time and effort were given to considering what new strategy should be developed for post-war deployment. Perkin's fifteen years at the helm had earned him the title of Mr. Missions and great respect among his peers.

OBJECTIVE

List the two basic changes in the missionary outreach of the Assemblies due to World War II.

3 What were the important changes in missions produced by World War II?

Strategic Planning

World War II produced two significant changes in the Assemblies' foreign missions enterprise. Because many fields previously occupied overseas were no longer accessible, Latin America became the focus of outreach. Second, plans had to be drawn as to what should be done following the war. Strategic planning now became a part of missions practice.

The result was a significant three-day conference at Central Bible Institute in April 1943. Fifty-eight missionaries, representing eighteen countries, offered their advice. The outcome was six strategic goals:

1. The call for regional missionary administrators (field secretaries)
2. The recruitment of five hundred new missionaries
3. The call for advisory committees of ministers and missionaries
4. Additional missionary training

5. A call for the organization of regional missions conventions in the United States

6. An effort to raise $5 million to support the program after the war (McGee 1986, 166–168)

In 1953, the mission leadership added four additional goals:

1. To focus more evangelistic efforts on the large cities

2. To aid the sick, hungry, and homeless as resources permitted

3. To strengthen ties among Pentecostal churches around the world

4. To increase efforts to take the gospel to unevangelized regions

A full-orbed Pentecostal missiology was taking shape. Through it all the underlying motivation for missions remained the same as from the first: to fulfill Christ's commission to evangelize the world before His second coming (McGee 1986, 168–169).

Preparation, Development, and Growth, 1954 and Beyond

The 1950s marked a significant turning point in the growth of the international mission enterprise abroad. The chart below shows growth in the number of constituents from 1943–2003. The effect of the move toward more centralized control of missionary assignments had already begun to produce growth from 138,000 in 1943 to 575,000 ten years later (AGWM statistics, 2005).

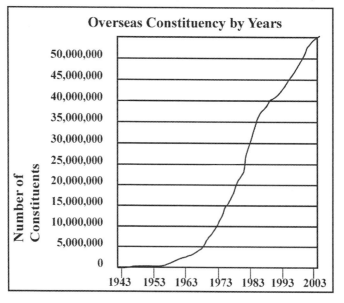

Figure 5.1

OBJECTIVE

Identify how major changes in administration impacted missions in the 1950s.

A Foreign Missions Summit in 1954 led to the decision of the 1955 General Council in session to establish a Foreign Missions Board. At the General Council in 1957, the Board was expanded to include six pastors representing their regions, and a like number of laymen as an Advisory Board. In 1959, the top leader of foreign missions was granted the title *Assistant General Superintendent*, making him equal with all other department heads (McGee 1986, 174-175).

These structural changes gave the foreign mission leadership the authority and infrastructure to carry out the strategy already formulated. By 1959, the number of constituents had grown to 985,000 and then to 1,393,000 by 1960. The value of a coordinated and cooperative program, led by those with the perspective of the whole world scene, had proved itself.

This lesson must not be forgotten, since the tendency of some today is to develop local, church-based foreign mission outreaches independent of the established world mission program of the General Council. The inadequacies and counter productivity of such programs had already been established in 1914 and proven through experience.

The Hogan Years

The 1959, the General Council elected J. Philip Hogan as Executive Director of Foreign Missions, succeeding Noel Perkin. That same council also saw the retirement of J. Roswell Flower and the departure of Ralph Riggs as General Superintendent, who was succeeded by Thomas Zimmerman. This signaled major changes in the leadership of the Assemblies, a pivotal point in the history of the movement (McGee 1989, 42–43).

Hogan and his wife had been missionaries to China, but were forced to leave the mainland because of the Communist takeover in 1949. He continued to minister in Taiwan until mid-1950 and then joined his family in Springfield, Missouri. For a time he promoted missions on behalf of the department and eventually headed the Promotions Division until his election in 1959 (McGee 1989, 44–48).

The Hogan years were marked by a determined and consistent focus on three statements of purpose: evangelization of the spiritually lost, church planting as God's strategy for building the kingdom of God, and training of church leadership to ensure sound doctrine and practice. To do so, he carefully selected staff of high quality and commitment to the principles he espoused. Included among those principles was the insistence on developing indigenous national churches, the elimination of a colonialist approach, and the establishment of a worldwide fellowship of autonomous national Pentecostal churches with which the foreign mission division would work in partnership. The ensuing growth of the overseas national churches proved he was right.

4 What institution was established under Hogan to coordinate and communicate missions strategy?

The worldwide mission outreach Hogan envisioned required massive prayer and financial support. Accordingly, he sought to mobilize the United States constituency to support the missions effort by establishing a quality program of communication and fundraising, an effort that proved highly successful (McGee 1989, 50–51).

To bring consistency, effectiveness, and efficiency to the outreach, great emphasis was placed on an annual school of missions for veteran missionaries during their year of deputation between typical four-year field assignments, and for the incoming missionary candidates. Besides prayer and worship, considerable time was given to discussions of strategy, policies, and procedures (McGee 1989, 97–100).

Hogan also wanted to ensure proper training of national church leadership. If the church was to grow, it would require leaders who were well grounded in the Bible and theology, as well as appropriate pastoral leadership. Accordingly, many Bible schools were established abroad. Included in that period was the establishment of the International Correspondence Institute, later known as ICI, to produce consistency in distance education curricula and avoid duplication of effort in the development of such programs abroad. [ICI was later subsumed under Global University when the latter was formed in 1999.] (McGee 1989, 67–70, 173–176).

Further development of the foreign missions programs of the Assemblies under Hogan's leadership included the establishment of area directors to represent the continent-focused field directors by coordinating the work in several countries and providing pastoral care to the missionaries. He also recognized the value of specialized ministries to support the works around the world with their areas of expertise. Those included ICI, the Center for Ministry to Muslims, Life Publishers, HealthCare, International Media Ministries, Child Care International, and others.

While individual missionaries had engaged in programs of ministry to the poor, sick, and hungry as well as to refugees and orphans, such works were not given much emphasis as valid and vital strategies lest efforts of evangelization be dampened. Hogan, a voracious reader and student of missiology, formally recognized those efforts as a kind of pre-evangelism besides the practical service rendered (McGee 1989, 249–254).

Decade of Harvest

Another significant development was the inspiration to designate the decade of the nineties as a Decade of Harvest, a special emphasis on evangelism and church planting. Accordingly, in 1988, the first Decade of Harvest Conference was held in Springfield, Missouri, with church leaders from forty nations. They dedicated themselves to work and pray "until we witness the evangelization of the entire world." Worldwide church growth in those countries has proved they fully intended to do just that. In 1989, there were 16,414,392 members and adherents, but by 1999 the number was virtually doubled.

Loren Triplett, veteran missionary to Latin America, succeeded Hogan in 1989. His tenure was largely devoted to carrying forward the legacy of the Hogan years and prior. The basic philosophies and strategies continued: the personal call of God to persons to serve as missionaries abroad; faith promise offerings; missionary deputation for prayer and financial support; indigenous church principles, partnership in missions with missionaries of other national Pentecostal churches; world evangelism and church planting; the training of national church leaders; and specialized ministries to complement and support the principal efforts.

World events opened the door for even greater outreach than before. In 1989, the Berlin wall came down, and the opportunity to take the gospel directly to the Eastern Bloc countries followed. Accordingly, missionaries began to enter those countries with primary emphasis on training national leadership since it was apparent that some of the existing national churches had drifted into a variety of theological positions not held by mainstream Pentecostals.

5   How did the *10/40 window* concept change missions?

The cause of the unreached in the world was highlighted by Luis Bush at the Lausanne II Congress on World Evangelization in 1989. He coined the phrase *10/40 window* to designate the region from West Africa through Asia between the tenth and fortieth parallels. This area contained much of the great Muslim, Hindu, and Buddhist blocs, largely untouched by Christianity (*Perspectives* 1991, D–40–43).

Though somewhat arbitrary, the 10/40 window did much to raise the awareness of mission organizations to address this great need. Accordingly, the Division of Foreign Missions doubled its efforts to reach these areas and others. A heightened focus on reaching Muslim populations was part of that response. Outreach into other so-called restricted access countries also accelerated.

Triplett was succeeded at his retirement in 1997 by John Bueno, another veteran missionary to Latin America. He was well-known for his successful

pastorates in El Salvador and for his establishment of Latin Am
Care, a school program for the poor and disenfranchised. Like his
Bueno continued the long-held missiological principles established th
years. His years have been marked by continued rapid growth of the ove
constituency, so that by 2004, the number had grown to 49,755,763.

Due to the great geographical and demographic growth of the outreach, Bueno
subdivided two of the existing mission fields (now called regions) to form the
Northern Asia Region and the Europe region. This meant there were now six regions
instead of four. The separation of Europe from Eurasia was pragmatic. The previous
extent of the Eurasia Region extended from all of Europe, North Africa, the Middle
East, the former Soviet bloc, and Southern Asia. So it was with Northern Asia
from the Asia-Pacific Region. With the huge difference in territories and cultural
differences, it seemed wise to make the outreach efforts more manageable.

During this period, the name was changed from the *Division of Foreign
Missions* to *Assemblies of God World Missions* (AGWM). Its purpose is
characterized by four words representing the basic building blocks of the foreign
outreach: *reaching*, *planting*, *training*, and *touching*. These, in turn, represented
evangelism, church planting, leadership training, compassion ministries.

What the future holds is in God's hands. However, all indications at present
are that AGWM will continue to focus on these elements of strategy. The basic
difference is likely to be in the specific strategies employed to accomplish them.
The greatest challenges are most likely to come from any attempt to make
significant inroads into the non-Christian world religions. Part of the answer will
have to come from partnerships with other national Pentecostal and evangelical
churches wherever possible.

The question for the Assemblies of God USA is whether there will be the
personnel, prayerful, and sacrificial response of this and future generations to
share the gospel throughout this globalized world in the twenty-first century. In
part this will depend on the determination of the churches of the fellowship to
follow the lead of early pioneers. They joined in common cause for the sake of
effectiveness and the most efficient use of personnel and financial resources to
the glory of God alone. May it be so again.

Home Missions

5.4.2
OBJECTIVE
*Discuss the factors that led
to the formation of Home
Missions.*

The call for the meeting in Hot Springs, Arkansas, in 1914 was in large
measure due to the recognition of the need for world evangelization. Foreign
missions needs were foremost, but the needs in the United States were also
recognized. To that end, in 1919, the General Council established a missionary
department to handle pioneer evangelism in the United States as well as foreign
missions. Most of the responsibility at home was laid upon the various districts
to "press this work . . . of carrying the Pentecostal Message to the neglected
districts of this country" (Blumhofer 1989a, 334).

The missionary department did undertake to help in certain areas. Notably,
missionaries were appointed to work with the hearing impaired and also
in neglected areas, such as in the Kentucky District, where several female
missionaries were instrumental in carrying on the work (Lyon 1992, 13–16).

A Home Missions committee was appointed in 1920 and, at its urging, saw the
establishment of a separate Home Missions Fund. By 1937, it was obvious that the
administration of both home and foreign missionary work was too much for one
department. That year the General Council established a new Home Missions and

ucation Department. The emphasis was on church planting and overseeing Bible titutes. Fred Vogler was named head of the department and served with both ion and vigor until his retirement in 1954 (Lyon 1992, 10–12, 26–29).

In the ensuing years, much emphasis was placed on church planting. But soon er specialized ministries evolved to the Native Americans, prisoners, Jewish ple, the hearing impaired, armed forces, Civilian Conservation Corps, and ska. The foreign-speaking populations were also the focus of the specialized istries section. During World War II, the military outreach spawned a small, idenominational devotional periodical called *Reveille* that was highly acclaimed and welcomed by the government and the servicemen alike (Lyon 1992, 36, 37, 80).

In 1959, David Wilkerson formally established Teen-Age Evangelism. The following year, he was granted Home Missions appointment for his program that was subsequently placed under the Prison Department. Later, the name was changed to Teen Challenge as centers were established across the nation to minister to drug and alcohol addicts and troubled teens. The program has received both national and international acclaim for its effectiveness in using biblical principles to redeem and restore troubled men and women.

For some eight years, the ministry to college youth was part of the Youth Department of the General Council. In 1987, the Council in session placed the program under the Home Missions Division to allow for missionary appointment to that ministry. Through the leadership of Dennis Gaylor, the program has rapidly grown under the title *Chi Alpha*. At first its focus was to provide a safe harbor for Assemblies of God college students who found their faith sharply attacked on secular campuses. However, through the years, the program has expanded to reach out to all college youth in order to lead them to Christ and disciple them in their subsequent walk with the Lord.

In 1971, the name of the Home Missions Department was changed to the *Division of Home Missions*, and more recently to *Assemblies of God US Missions* (AGUSM), which better reflects the true nature of the division.

Shortly after taking office as the leader of the division in 1992, Charles Hackett expressed great concern for the lack of training for inner-city ministry. Accordingly, he established urban Bible institutes to be organized in thirty-nine key cities across America. These have become successful in training workers within their own cultural environment.

A further development is the establishment of training centers among Native Americans. The Assemblies of God has maintained an outreach to the many tribes almost from the beginning, evangelizing and planting churches among them. However, much of the leadership, until recently, was in the hands of missionaries. Now the Native American Fellowship has emphasized the training of Native American leaders through centers within their own tribal environs.

In recent years an ever-increasing emphasis has been placed on ministering to the many concentrations of immigrants to the United States In contrast to immigrations of the turn of the last century, these populations tend to retain their language and cultural practices. A partnership has been formed between Global University and the Intercultural Ministries Department of AGUSM because of much of the university's materials already being in many of these languages and its expertise in working with foreign cultures.

Through it all, AGUSM has continued its emphasis on evangelism, discipleship, church planting, and specialized ministries working in partnership with the districts.

Test Yourself

Circle the letter of the *best* answer.

1. Faith missions of the nineteenth century were so called because they
a) had limited denominational backing.
b) were only partially guaranteed their support.
c) depended on faith for their support.
d) were poorly organized.

2. A characteristic of the missionary movement springing from Pentecostal revival was
a) a new intellectual approach to missions.
b) the prominent role of women.
c) more personal choice as to mission field.
d) a carefully organized missions agency.

3. The second General Council of the Assemblies of God emphasized
a) church organization.
b) doctrinal purity.
c) the foreign missions program.
d) establishing Bible schools.

4. One of J. Roswell Flower's areas of impact was
a) establishing individual budgets for missionaries.
b) listing qualifications for missionary selection.
c) establishing educational requirements for missionaries.
d) emphasizing prayer.

5. Noel Perkin's leadership encouraged
a) missionaries to work independently of the churches.
b) greater supervision of missionary personnel.
c) female missionaries to take the lead.
d) tension concerning doctrine and practice.

6. To coordinate and communicate missions strategy, J. Philip Hogan established
a) an elite task force.
b) Teen Challenge.
c) an annual school of missions.
d) a medical initiative that treated AIDS patients.

7. If the church was to grow, national leaders must
a) emphasize commitment to the local church.
b) hire qualified staff to assist them.
c) be grounded in the Bible and theology.
d) receive continual support from founding missionaries.

8. The *10/40 window* is a phrase describing
a) the region from Western Europe through the former Soviet Union.
b) an area limited to Asia.
c) a region from West Africa through Asia.
d) areas limited to Muslim populations.

9. The primary function of the Home Missions department was to
a) keep missionaries closer to home.
b) reach the neglected areas of the United States
c) minister on secular college campuses.
d) establish urban recreational centers.

10. Shortly after taking office in 1992, Charles Hackett determined to establish
a) a global Teen Challenge.
b) the Master's Commission.
c) urban Bible training centers.
d) Chi Alpha.

Responses to Interactive Questions
Chapter 5

Some of these responses may include information that is supplemental to the IST. These questions are intended to produce reflective thinking beyond the course content and your responses may vary from these examples.

1   Why was there a sense of urgency among early Pentecostals concerning missions?

Answer: The new experience produced a sense of urgency because it indicated they were living in the "last days" as the Lord's coming was at hand. This called for world evangelization; the gospel must be preached to every creature.

2   What emphasis did Noel Perkin view as key to advancing missions?

Answer: The careful selection of missionary candidates and prayer

3   What were the important changes in missions produced by World War II?

Answer: First, Latin America became the focus of outreach. Second, plans had to be drawn as to what should be done following the war.

4   What institution was established under Hogan to coordinate and communicate missions strategy?

Answer: To bring consistency, effectiveness, and efficiency to the outreach, emphasis was placed on an annual school of missions for veteran missionaries during their year of deputation between typical four-year field assignments. The school also catered to incoming missionary candidates.

5   How did the *10/40 window* concept change missions?

Answer: The Division of Foreign Missions redoubled its efforts to reach the unreached both in that area and others. A heightened focus on reaching Muslim populations was part of that response. Outreach into other so-called restricted access countries also accelerated.

UNIT PROGRESS EVALUATION 2

Now that you have finished Unit 2, review the lessons in preparation for Unit Progress Evaluation 2. You will find it in the Essential Course Materials section at the back of this IST. Answer all of the questions without referring to your course materials, Bible, or notes. When you have completed the UPE, check your answers with the answer key provided in the Essential Course Materials section, and review any items you may have answered incorrectly. Then you may proceed with your study of Unit 3. (Although UPE scores do not count as part of your final course grade, they indicate how well you learned the material and how well you may perform on the closed-book final examination.)

UNIT 3

The Twenty-First Century in Missions

Missions methodology today still has some of the traditional elements of the past, but there are many new approaches and trends in this age of technology and new media. This unit examines the essential role and presence of the Holy Spirit in missionary deployment and strategy in general. The four cardinal facets of the philosophy of missions of Assemblies of God World Missions are discussed as are the traditional views of indigenous principles, with the addition of two modern aspects: self-theologizing and self-missionizing.

Missionary Deployment and the Holy Spirit

How, then, can they call on the one they have not believed in? And how can they believe in the one of whom they have not heard? And how can they hear without someone preaching to them? And how can they preach unless they are sent? As it is written, "How beautiful are the feet of those who bring good news!" (Romans 10:14–15)

The passage above represents a divine principle of sending laborers into the harvest field to proclaim the good news. This chapter addresses answers to several questions. Why is missionary presence important on the fields of the world? How are missionaries selected, appointed, and deployed? How are missionaries and their ministries supported?

For missionary work to be effective, the empowerment of the Holy Spirit is necessary. Intercessory prayer is needed on the part of those who send, and the guidance and equipping of the Holy Spirit are crucial for the work on any field. The work cannot be accomplished by the wisdom and physical might of humanity, for "our struggle is not against flesh and blood, but against the rulers, against the authorities, against the powers of this dark world and against the spiritual forces of evil in the heavenly realms" (Ephesians 6:12).

Lesson 6.1   Missionary Deployment

Objectives
6.1.1   Explain the importance of calling in missions outreach.
6.1.2   Identify important factors in determining a candidate's fitness for missionary service.
6.1.3   Justify the deputation approach for missionary support.

Lesson 6.2   The Power of the Holy Spirit

Objectives
6.2.1   Explain the primary purpose of the baptism in the Holy Spirit.
6.2.2   Discuss three reasons for prayer, and analyze the Spirit's work in our lives.

6.1.1
OBJECTIVE

*Explain the
importance of calling
in missions outreach.*

Missionary Deployment

The Importance of "Calling"

When Jesus began His ministry on earth, He called and discipled people. The Twelve became the pioneers, the flag bearers of the Kingdom. The choosing of those leaders was so important Jesus spent all night in prayer before calling them (Luke 6:12–13). God's method of reaching the world is through people, not through angels or even the Bible alone. While He may use a variety of means to gain attention and plant the seeds of redemption in the minds of the lost, in the end His chosen people are called upon to explain and demonstrate the truth. If that were not the case, God would not have sent His Son to live as one of us. Jesus is called "apostle" (Hebrews 3:1), which, in Greek, means "sent one" and is translated from the Latin as "missionary."

While some people may believe that a look at the spiritual, physical, and material needs in the world, coupled with the ability to respond to those needs, ought to be enough to cause someone to choose to go to the mission field, it is vital that missionaries know they are called by God. This calling may be through a growing burden, a special dream or vision, a sermon, or something else. But there must be a settled sense of God's direction.

The biblical pattern is clear. From Abraham to the apostle Paul and others, the Bible reveals God as the initiator, calling those He desires for special service (see Genesis 12:1–3, 45:4–8; Exodus 3:1–10; 1 Samuel 3:1–21; 16:1–13; Jeremiah 1:4–10; Ezekiel 1:1–3; Luke 1:13–17, 30–35; 6:12–16; Acts 9:1–18; 13:1–3). It is reasonable to assume that since God knows everything about everyone, He is in the best position to make the appropriate choice.

There can be no doubt of God's concern in the matter. He wants the right people in the right place at the right time, and He knows the times we live in. He also knows the enemy of our souls will do everything possible to convince missionaries they do not belong in the ministry or in a particular place of service. At such moments, a missionary's conviction that God did the calling and the placing will help him or her stand strong against the devil's schemes.

6.1.2
OBJECTIVE

*Identify important
factors in determining
a candidate's fitness for
missionary service.*

Qualifications for Missionary Service

As previously stated, the one chosen must be the right person, for the right place, at the right time. Some factors are obvious, such as age, physical fitness, and general health. The next issue concerns the sense of divine call to missionary service. Does the candidate know he or she is called and how is that demonstrated? By what means has that conviction come, and how is it being played out in life? If God is truly behind this, then how do we judge by other factors? This is not an easy decision but one that must be made prayerfully and wisely. Even if the call is genuine, is this the right time in the life of this person, or is further personal and professional growth in order?

A person's sense of call needs to be borne out by other evidence. What is the candidate's level of Christian maturity? What ministry experience is there, and how successful has that been? Does the person's church and denomination endorse the candidate? If there is a professed burden for a certain people group, is there evidence of deepening knowledge and even ministry among them in this country where possible?

What is the person's level of education and training? What does this person know about missionary ministry and cultural factors that must be faced? Is there sound evidence of spiritual and emotional stability? What evidence is there of spiritual gifts and practical abilities? What about interpersonal relationships and a sense of servanthood?

If the person is unmarried, what is his or her feeling about going to the field unmarried? If married, are both partners fully committed to the vision? If there are children, how many are there and of what ages? This is important because schooling for the children must be considered. Teens going to the field for the first time face the challenges of language, culture, and social integration at a time they are transitioning into adulthood.

Other factors will come into play regarding placement, and ability to raise support. One key principle must not be overlooked or pushed aside: the best predictor of future performance is past performance. What is the candidate's history?

The Work of the Missionary

1   What is the first role of a missionary in a cross-cultural setting?

The variety of roles and tasks missionaries fill are numerous. Especially with the opportunities and tools available for the spreading of the gospel, the edification of the saints, and the means of practical and material service, the list is almost endless. Nonetheless, if one thinks of the changing roles of the missionary or missionary team in the progression of the emerging Church, a certain pattern follows.

A missionary must take on the role of learner and must learn the language and culture of the host people. The missionary must also understand his or her own culture—its strengths and weaknesses—and must relate to the host people in ways that provide a credible witness to the truth of the gospel. The importance of language and culture cannot be overemphasized as the melding of these two elements makes for effective cross-cultural ministry.

The basis for all missionary activity is found in the Great Commission as stated in Matthew 28:18–20 and Mark 16:15:

Then Jesus came to them and said, "All authority in heaven and on earth has been given to me. Therefore go and make disciples of all nations, baptizing them in the name of the Father and of the Son and of the Holy Spirit, and teaching them to obey everything I have commanded you. And surely I am with you always, to the very end of the age." (Matthew 28:18–20)

Note that the primary imperative is to make disciples, i.e., learners, followers, propagators, and imitators of Jesus. They are to do this by baptism—having the new converts make a public confession of their conversion from the old life to the new. Then they are to teach them all that Christ taught the apostles. This is to be done among all people, even to the end of the age. Mark echoes the same theme: "Go into all the world and preach the good news to all creation. Whoever believes and is baptized will be saved, but whoever does not believe will be condemned" (Mark 16:15–16). Here the emphasis is on the public proclamation of the gospel throughout the world. Upon the response to this message lies the fate of those hearing the good news. Those who accept, do so both in mind and by public demonstration of their commitment to Christ.

To begin a new work, the missionary must proclaim the gospel with the intent to make disciples. Those committing to Christ are to be taught to know and obey His ways, to live a godly life in obedience to His Word. As the work progresses, the missionary task shifts increasingly to training leaders to follow the pattern set before them. Then, as these believers assume full leadership of the church, the missionary role becomes that of partner and mentor, moving away from control while being available to guide and assist as needed.

Thus we can safely say the three primary functions of a missionary outreach are evangelism leading to church planting, discipling new Christians to maturity, and training leaders to follow the same pattern. This is the clear mandate of the New Testament by precept and example.

Some may want to add the need for holistic ministry, ministering to the whole person and even seeking to change the culture. A full discussion of this position is beyond the scope of this study. Nevertheless, it must be emphasized that whatever is done to meet the physical and material needs of persons—and those are legitimate aspects of missionary activity—they must point to the need of a personal commitment to Jesus Christ as Lord and Savior. Without Christ there will be no life in the eternity of heaven.

Many auxiliary roles can be taken by missionaries. These may include ministries in education, communication using various media, technological support, aviation, medical missions, relief and development, construction, administration, publishing, age group specialties, and many more. The response is based on the need.

In all, the missionary team must ever seek to train church members to assume the role exercised by the missionary, not attempting to carve out for him or her a permanent place of ministry. The new believers must not be looked upon as incapable. A picture comes to mind of an Aborigine from the outback of Australia, garbed in traditional loin cloth and little else, operating a sophisticated video camera. So much for missionary superiority!

Missionary Support

6.1.3
OBJECTIVE

Justify the deputation approach for missionary support.

2 What is the primary method by which missionaries raise support for going to the mission field?

In many evangelical churches, including the Assemblies of God USA, missionaries gain prayer and financial support through the process of deputation. They seek opportunity to present their ministry to the local churches with the hope of gaining what is needed to get to the foreign field.

Having spent one or more terms of service at their post, they return to report to their supporting churches and others they may address to renew that support to meet the increased cost of ministry and fund new projects. At their assigned post, they regularly report to their constituency to seek prayer for special needs, to assure of their worthiness of support, and to stimulate the supporting churches to maintain the vision for missions.

Some feel this is an inefficient method of gaining and maintaining support. Yet there are many reasons to continue this approach. First, people generally give to people, not to central funds or projects disconnected from the missionaries. Secondly, prayer support is at least equally important to financial help. People are most likely to fervently pray for someone with whom they have had personal contact. Third, one of two primary factors behind someone's sensing a call to missionary service was by hearing the message of a missionary. The other was personal prayer. Without missionary participation in the churches, the missionary outreach of the church may well dwindle and even die.

Another reason for missionary itineration is the need for accountability. This is a constant reminder to the missionary that he or she must give account to those who support the work. History has shown that mission boards that have moved from the itineration approach for the gaining of missionary support to a central fund have experienced a severe loss in donations. Difficult as it may seem, the method still seems to be the best.

Long-Term Versus Short-Term Missions

Most missionaries are appointed for three- to four-year terms. This is followed by a one-year period of deputation. Then they return to their field assignment and repeat the cycle, usually staying at least three or more four-year terms. While the World Missions program has long provided for short-term service, increasingly people are signing up for one- to four-year terms, mostly as adjunct to the career missionaries. This is a growing trend and will be dealt with in a later chapter.

Incarnational Missions

3   What is an incarnational missionary?

In popular missions terminology, incarnational missions is intended to mean identification with the host culture. The missionary approaches the people with whom he or she desires to minister as a learner, taking the posture of one among equals. The missionary learns to live like the hosts—eating what they eat, sleeping in their homes, and understanding their problems and aspirations (Van Rheenen 1996, 59). The role model is that of Christ himself, who fully identified with the human race (72–73). Still, there is a clear distinction between Christ as the unique Incarnate God and representing Him through a form of witness that is built upon an intimate relationship with the people.

There are other, more radical, perspectives beyond the scope of this study. They focus on actions by the church to reform society as an extension of Christ's ministry on earth. For a more complete discussion, see Hesselgrave 2006, 142–150.

The Power of the Holy Spirit

Missionary Enablement

While serving in Ivory Coast, West Africa, one Assemblies of God (AG) missionary was invited to the home of another missionary from a non-Pentecostal group to discuss missionary strategy. The work of the Assemblies of God in the country was growing at a phenomenal rate while that of the other organization was progressing much slower. The non-Pentecostal missionary wanted to know what methods AG was using that had resulted in such rapid church growth. The question was asked as to whether the missionary personnel and national pastors of this church were less qualified academically than those serving with the Assemblies. The answer was obviously no. In fact, the missionary personnel possessed considerably more academic training than their Assemblies of God colleagues. A second question was asked about the amount of preaching and training programs being organized and used by the missionaries and national pastors of the non-Pentecostal church. Again, the response was that they were extremely active. The AG missionary's response was that obviously, the primary difference between the two churches had to be the emphasis on and work of the Holy Spirit. The difference was not in human ability but in the Spirit's anointing.

6.2.1
OBJECTIVE
Explain the primary purpose of the baptism in the Holy Spirit.

In the book of Acts, Jesus instructed His followers to "wait for the gift my Father promised, which you have heard me speak about. For John baptized with water, but in a few days you will be baptized with the Holy Spirit" (Acts 1:4–5). In Acts 1:8, He continued by saying, "You will receive power when the Holy Spirit comes on you; and you will be my witnesses in Jerusalem, and in all Judea and Samaria, and to the ends of the earth." The primary purpose of the baptism in the Holy Spirit was to empower the disciples to be witnesses to the ends of the earth. The same experience came to the apostle Paul (Acts 9:17), to the house of Cornelius (Acts 10:45, 46), and to the Ephesians (Acts 19:6).

On the Day of Pentecost, Peter declared that the outpouring of the Spirit was for all people. The people in attendance at the Feast of Pentecost had come from sixteen parts of the world and each heard Jesus' followers speaking in his or her language. They were utterly amazed. Peter announced to them the gospel of the salvation of Christ. He was a totally different person from the one who had earlier denied the Lord!

All of the disciples and apostles in the first century were Spirit-filled. The book of Acts gives Luke's account of the preaching, teaching, and miracles seen under the ministry of the early disciples. After the Day of Pentecost, the first miracle recorded is spectacular as a man who is lame is healed at the gate of the temple in Jerusalem (Acts 3).

In Acts 5, the gift of knowledge was manifested as Peter challenged Ananias and Sapphira about their lying to the Holy Spirit (5:1–11). Acts 5:12 states that "the apostles performed many miraculous signs and wonders among the people." Philip was instructed by an angel to meet the Ethiopian eunuch who was an officer of the queen. After baptizing the eunuch, Philip was suddenly taken away (Acts 8:39). Another incident of empowerment is seen when Peter was delivered from Herod's prison by an angel (Acts 12:10). Paul and Silas were delivered from prison in Philippi when the doors of the prison opened as the result of a mighty earthquake (Acts 16:26). Yet another miracle occurred in Troas when a young man asleep fell from the third floor and was picked up dead while Paul was preaching. By the power of the Spirit, Paul raised the young man from the dead (Acts 20:10–12).

Another aspect of empowering believers for service is the Holy Spirit's giving spiritual gifts to equip them for ministry. Paul gives a list of several spiritual gifts and says, "All these are the work of one and the same Spirit, and he gives them each one, just as he determines" (1 Corinthians 12:11). When the gifts of the Spirit are active, it is another indication of the presence of God thrusting the Church out to powerful ministry in the world.

It is obvious that today, in a time of unprecedented unbelief and resistance to the gospel, there is a great need for the empowering of the Holy Spirit upon our lives and ministries.

Prayer

6.2.2
OBJECTIVE
Discuss three reasons for prayer, and analyze the Spirit's work in our lives.

Prayer is our communion with God, whether it be a petition made to Him, worship, repentance, praise, or thanksgiving. James wrote that "the prayer of a righteous man is powerful and effective" (5:16). The New Testament talks about the idea of being devoted to prayer. In Acts 2:42, Luke recorded the following report about the fellowship of believers of that time: "They devoted themselves to the apostles' teaching and to the fellowship, to the breaking of bread and to prayer." Paul exhorted the church in Rome "to be joyful in hope, patient in affliction, faithful in prayer" (Romans 12:12). He also exhorted the Colossian church by saying, "Devote yourselves to prayer, being watchful and thankful" (Colossians 4:2).

These exhortations indicate that prayer must always be part of everything we do. We must persevere in prayer at all times, in all situations. Paul spoke to Timothy about prayer being "first of all" in his ministry (1 Timothy 2:1). Jesus set the example. He prayed (Matthew 14:23) and taught His followers to pray (Luke 11:1–4).

No matter how intelligent we may be, if we do not continue to pray for God to give us understanding and a believing and humble heart, and if we do not maintain a personal walk with the Lord Jesus, we will misunderstand the teaching of the Word of God. Doctrinal error and disobedience to the Lord will result.

Prayer is not just meant to reveal to God what we need. Jesus said, "Your Father knows what you need before you ask him" (Matthew 6:8). Why then does God want us to pray? One reason is because our prayer expresses our trust in God and allows our trust to increase. Prayer also means we believe in God's wisdom, love, power, and all other attributes which make up His character. However, God does not only want us to have faith in Him, He also wants us to love Him and fellowship with Him. Thirdly, prayer permits us to be involved in activities of eternal consequences. When we pray, the work of the kingdom of God is advanced. James encourages: "You do not have, because you do not ask" (James 4:2). Jesus also said, "Ask, and it will be given you; seek, and you will find; knock and the door will be opened to you. For every one who asks receives, and he who seeks finds, and to him who knocks, the door will be opened" (Luke 11:9–10).

We see examples of the power of prayer in the Old Testament. Lord God declared to Moses that He would destroy the people of Israel because of their sin (Exodus 32:9–10). "But Moses sought the favor of the Lord his God, 'O Lord,' he said, 'why should your anger burn against your people, whom you brought out of Egypt with great power and a mighty hand? Why should the Egyptians say, "It was with evil intent that he brought them out, to kill them in the mountains and to wipe them off the face of the earth"'? Turn from your fierce anger" (Exodus 32:11–12). After this prayer of Moses, "the Lord relented and did not bring on his people the disaster he had threatened" (Exodus 32:14).

Second Chronicles 7:14 expresses a similar thought: "If my people, who are called by my name, will humble themselves and pray and seek my face and turn from their wicked ways, then will I hear from heaven and will forgive their sin and will heal their land." These Old Testament examples clearly tell us the prayers of God's people affect God's actions. We should then be motivated to pray for the salvation of the nations of the world.

The New Testament contains many examples of answered prayer. One spectacular instance took place when Peter was imprisoned after the death of James. Acts 12:5 records, "Peter was kept in prison, but the church was earnestly praying to God for him." God delivered him miraculously! Again, it was after prayer that "the place where they were meeting was shaken. And they were all filled with the Holy Spirit and spoke the word of God boldly" (Acts 4:31).

As we pray for missions, the Holy Spirit is present to assist us. Paul reminds us:

> The Spirit helps us in our weakness. We do not know what we ought to pray for, but the Spirit himself intercedes for us with groans that words cannot express. And he who searches our hearts knows the mind of the Spirit, because the Spirit intercedes for the saints in accordance with God's will. (Romans 8:26–27)

Numerous are the examples of believers being prompted by the Spirit to pray for a missionary or a country at a strategic moment without knowing the situation. This is a demonstration of the work of the Holy Spirit in prayer.

In Guidance

The Bible provides many examples of the Holy Spirit's guiding people. Consider the case of Philip and the Ethiopian eunuch traveling by chariot back to his homeland. The Holy Spirit instructed Philip: "Go to that chariot and stay near it" (Acts 8:29). Later, the Holy Spirit told Peter to go with three men to

Cornelius' household (Acts 10:19–20). The Holy Spirit also instructed the church in Antioch to set apart Barnabas and Saul for the work of ministry (Acts 13:2).

In most cases, the Spirit's guidance is less dramatic than the cases mentioned above. Rather, there is a day-to-day guidance wherein one is led by the Spirit (Romans 8:14, Galatians 5:18), or where one walks according to the Spirit (Romans 8:4). Paul further advises: "I say, live by the Spirit" (Galatians 5:16). The direction and influence of the Holy Spirit is also seen in the decision of the Jerusalem Council in Acts 15:28: "It seemed good to the Holy Spirit and to us not to burden you with anything beyond the following requirements."

Evident in Paul's missionary activity was the guidance of the Spirit. Luke writes that they were "kept by the Holy Spirit from preaching the word in the province of Asia" (Acts 16:6). They also attempted to enter Bithynia, "but the Spirit of Jesus would not allow them" (Acts 16:7). It is comforting to know we can have the guidance of the Holy Spirit in the decisions of the church. When we walk in the Spirit, He guides our ministries and missionary activities.

In Supernatural Gifts

4   What is the main purpose of the gifts of the Spirit?

The pouring out of the Holy Spirit in fullness and power for all believers occurred at Pentecost. During his explanation of the Spirit's arrival on this day, Peter declared that "God has raised this Jesus to life, and we are all witnesses of the fact. Exalted to the right hand of God, he has received from the Father the promised Holy Spirit and has poured out what you now see and hear" (Acts 2:32–33). The spiritual gifts that would accompany this baptism in the Spirit would characterize the new covenant age that began at Pentecost. There would be a distribution of the gifts of the Spirit to all people—sons and daughters, young men and old men, menservants and maidservants.

Consequently, the Church is meant to be a miracle-working agency. The spiritual gifts equip the Church to carry out its ministry until Christ returns. This is evident in Paul's words to the church in Corinth: "You do not lack any spiritual gift as you eagerly wait for our Lord Jesus Christ to be revealed" (1 Corinthians 1:7). The gifts are meant to equip the Church to preach the gospel (Acts 1:8).

The empowering of the Church comes through many gifts. God has given an amazing variety of supernatural gifts to His people for the work of the ministry. The following chart lists these gifts and where they are found in Scripture.

1 CORINTHIANS 12:28	1 CORINTHIANS 12:8–10
• Apostle	• Word of wisdom
• Prophet	• Word of knowledge
• Teacher	• Faith
• Miracles	• Gifts of healing
• Kinds of healings	• Miracles
• Helps	• Prophecy
• Administration	• Distinguishing between spirits
• Tongues	• Tongues
	• Interpretation of tongues
EPHESIANS 4:11	**ROMANS 12:6–8**
• Apostles	• Prophecy
• Prophets	• Serving
• Evangelists	• Teaching
• Pastor-teacher	• Encouraging
	• Contributing
	• Leadership
	• Mercy

In Spiritual Warfare

What is *spiritual warfare*? The term itself is not found in Scripture, but the concept is taught in the Bible. Two of the most commonly associated passages were written by the Apostle Paul.

> Though we live in the world, we do not wage war as the world does. The weapons we fight with are not the weapons of the world. On the contrary, they have divine power to demolish strongholds. We demolish arguments and every pretension that sets itself up against the knowledge of God, and we take captive every thought to make it obedient to Christ. (2 Corinthians 10:3–5)

> Finally, be strong in the Lord and in his mighty power. Put on the full armor of God so that you can take your stand against the devil's schemes. For our struggle is not against flesh and blood, but against the rulers, against the authorities, against the powers of this dark world and against the spiritual forces of evil in heavenly realms. (Ephesians 6:10–12)

Every area of Christian ministry, particularly any form of missions work, is a battleground, but often spiritual resistance is not discerned. Often, we attribute a natural or human explanation to most problems without realizing spiritual warfare is the real explanation. Continued awareness of spiritual warfare is effective in evangelism. We must learn to recognize barriers and strongholds in advance and prepare through prayer, spiritual authority, and ministry.

Another aspect of the work of the Holy Spirit in empowering believers for service is in giving them victory over spiritual opposition to the preaching of the gospel and to God's work in people's lives. This empowerment in spiritual warfare was first seen in the life of Christ who said, "If I drive out demons by the Spirit of God, then the kingdom of God has come upon you" (Matthew 12:28). When Paul was opposed by Elymas, the magician in Cyprus, Paul responded in the power of the Spirit:

> Saul, who was also called Paul, filled with the Holy Spirit, looked straight at Elymas and said, "You are a child of the devil and an enemy of everything that is right! You are full of all kinds of deceit and trickery. Will you never stop perverting the right ways of the Lord? Now the hand of the Lord is against you. You are going to be blind, and for a time you will be unable to see the light of the sun." (Acts 13:9–11)

Luke's account continues by stating that "immediately mist and darkness came over him, and he groped about, seeking someone to lead him by the hand." As a result of the demonstration of the power of the Spirit against Elymas, the Roman proconsul believed the gospel.

The Bible teaches that the gift of "distinguishing between spirits" (1 Corinthians 12:10) is a weapon against the forces of evil. The same is true of the Word of God, "the sword of the Spirit" (Ephesians 6:17).

Test Yourself

Circle the letter of the *best* answer.

1. The conviction of God's call to mission work is important because
a) calls should come through dreams or visions.
b) a growing burden is not sufficient.
c) the Bible reveals God initiates the call, calling those He desires.
d) human talents are unnecessary.

2. The basic principle for predicting successful missionary service is one's
a) level of education.
b) knowledge of cultural factors.
c) evidence of spiritual gifts.
d) past performance.

3. The principle scriptural basis for all missionary work is found in
a) Ephesians 4:11–12.
b) Mark 16:15.
c) Romans 19:9.
d) Philippians 4:19.

4. The three primary functions of a missionary are
a) training leaders, medical missions, and administrative functions.
b) church planting, training leaders, and relief/development.
c) church planting, discipling new Christians, and training leaders.
d) traveling, planting new churches, and training leaders.

5. A primary factor behind someone's sensing a call to missions is
a) reading about missions in a journal.
b) hearing a message by a missionary.
c) through family discussion.
d) through the influence of a friend.

6. Incarnational missions refers to
a) identifying with the host culture.
b) teaching in another culture.
c) a host culture imitating a missionary.
d) speaking a foreign language.

7. The primary purpose of the baptism in the Holy Spirit is
a) distributing the gifts of the Spirit.
b) developing the fruit of the Spirit.
c) exercising more effective pastoral ministry.
d) empowering disciples to be witnesses.

8. One reason for prayer is that it
a) reminds us of our selfishness.
b) allows us to have a significant role in missions.
c) provides God with insights into our character.
d) permits God to know us.

9. Gifts of the Spirit characterized
a) the crucifixion.
b) the end of the apostolic age.
c) the new covenant age.
d) the end of the book of Acts.

10. The term *spiritual warfare* is
a) found in 2 Corinthians 10:3–5.
b) found in Ephesians 6:10–12.
c) found in Matthew 12:28.
d) not found in the Bible.

Responses to Interactive Questions
Chapter 6

Some of these responses may include information that is supplemental to the IST. These questions are intended to produce reflective thinking beyond the course content and your responses may vary from these examples.

1 What is the first role of a missionary in a cross-cultural setting?

Answer: To be a learner

2 What is the primary method by which missionaries raise support for going to the mission field?

Answer: Missionaries gain prayer and financial support through the process of deputation.

3 What is an incarnational missionary?

Answer: A missionary who identifies with the host culture by living, eating, thinking, etc. like them

4 What is the main purpose of the gifts of the Spirit?

Answer: The spiritual gifts are given to equip the Church to carry out its ministry until Christ returns.

Contemporary Strategies in Missions

The Assemblies of God World Missions (AGWM) has four basic goals in its philosophy of missions: reaching, planting, teaching, and touching. To achieve these goals, various methods of outreach—including worldwide church plantings—are engaged. Foundational to this process of church establishment is the idea of teaching others to obey Jesus' commands (Matthew 28:20). Teaching is a primary philosophy of the Assemblies of God World Missions, as is evident in the many institutes and extension centers globally.

To enhance understanding of contemporary approaches in missions, the student of this course must not only join in this education of self and others, but also consider ways in which a church is indigenous. A primary focus on the indigenous principles involves the maturing and advancement of the various churches around the world.

Lesson 7.1   The Four Basic Goals of AGWM

Objectives

7.1.1   Summarize the relationship between evangelism and missions expansion.
7.1.2   Identify motivations for establishing house churches.
7.1.3   Describe the use of tabernacle evangelism in church planting.

Lesson 7.2   The Indigenous Church

Objectives

*7.2.1   Describe the relationship between colonialism and missions in the
         nineteenth century.*
*7.2.2   Relate the importance of self-governance, self-propagation, and self-
         support to the indigenous church.*
7.2.3   Discuss contextualization as it relates to self-theologizing.
7.2.4   Describe the self-missionizing movement around the world.

7.1.1
OBJECTIVE
Summarize the relationship between evangelism and missions expansion.

1   What institution is considered to be the primary source of proclamation and witness?

The Four Basic Goals of AGWM

Reaching and Planting

In recent years, the Assemblies of God World Missions division has characterized its strategy in four succinct words: reaching, planting, teaching, and touching. Each of these refers to a specific focus of the strategy. From its inception, the foreign missions program has focused on proclaiming the gospel message of Jesus Christ by every available means. The early Pentecostal leaders, though small in numbers at the outset, believed in Jesus' command to reach the entire world. Evangelism has ever been the hallmark of the mission as converts share their testimonies; messages from the pulpit proclaim Bible truths; street meetings, literature distribution, radio and television programs are employed; and evangelistic crusades similar to the Billy Graham crusades are held in key locations. However, while methods of evangelism are as varied as imagination allows, the local church is still considered the primary source of proclamation and witness.

Efforts to meet physical, emotional, and spiritual needs through special programs, such as disaster relief, health care, aid for the hungry and homeless, drug and alcohol treatment, and the like are combined with a witness to the saving and delivering power of the gospel through Jesus Christ. The electronic media, such as the Internet, also plays an ever-increasing role in featuring programs to attract the lost and witness for Christ.

The goal of it all is to give every person, young or old, the opportunity to know of the freedom, peace, and joy that comes through a personal relationship with God through Jesus Christ. The intent is that people may commit their lives to Him and be destined for eternity with the Triune God and fellow believers.

Following the New Testament pattern, a second principal facet of the missions outreach is the planting of indigenous churches. Fulfilling the Great Commission requires more than seeking the lost. It requires the discipling of the converted and the gathering of believers into congregations for corporate worship, mutual edification, and witness. To reap a harvest is not enough; it must be conserved. Missionaries have sought from the beginning to establish congregations that could support and govern themselves. This was the pattern of the apostle Paul and has proved its value through the years.

Church planting might be better termed "congregation planting" lest we think of buildings rather than people. Congregations may be established in almost any location, from the shade of a banyan tree to the basement of a public building. From caves to store front buildings, all kinds of locations have been used as gathering places for people to share worship, fellowship, mutual edification, and evangelistic outreach.

The House Church Movement

7.1.2
OBJECTIVE
Identify motivations for establishing house churches.

2   Why has the house church movement been so effective through the centuries?

The establishment of congregations in private homes is as old as the early church. At the beginning of the Church, these homes became the nexus for believers in the area, the place of nurture and fellowship (Acts 2:46–47; 5:42; 20:20; Romans 16:3–5; 1 Corinthians 16:19; Colossians 4:15; Philemon 1:2).

The same method has been used through the centuries for at least three reasons: (1) as a natural family-oriented and community-related place conducive to start a church; (2) for a more intimate environment for fellowship and edification for small groups of believers within larger fellowships; and (3) as an unobtrusive gathering place in lands resistant and hostile to the cause of Christ.

The second of these groups might be better termed *cell groups*, but in reality they can function as congregations within the larger framework of the local church. Pastor David Yonggi Cho of the Yoido Full Gospel Church in Seoul, Korea, established hundreds of cell groups as a means of ministering to the more than 700,000 members. The pattern in Korea was suggested much earlier by Presbyterian missionary John L. Nevius, who urged that converts remain in the context in which they were saved (Nevius 2003, 19).

An even more spectacular example is that of modern day China. The non-registered churches have grown rapidly to number in the millions. While no means the only place on earth where this is happening, it is probably the best example of a house church movement. Originated by the Chinese believers themselves, the pastors of these congregations are most often lay persons—both men and women—who have dedicated themselves to the study of the Word and the preaching of the gospel (Pocock 2005, 140).

Tabernacle Evangelism

7.1.3
OBJECTIVE
Describe the use of tabernacle evangelism in church planting.

Tabernacle evangelism was launched in 1991 to encourage and develop strong, indigenous churches throughout Africa. As of 2005, 588 tabernacle units had been placed in thirty-four African countries (Africa Harvest Ministries 2005). In a meeting of various missionary leaders in April 19, 1993, it was declared that Africa faced the possibility of losing the harvest because of a lack of buildings. In Burkina Faso alone three hundred churches were without buildings (Tabernacle 1993). Due to the poverty of many nations of Africa, it was believed that providing a basic structure for church planting would greatly benefit efforts in evangelism. Otherwise, many evangelistic campaigns were conducted in the open air with no permanent structure to facilitate the meeting together of the new congregations. As a result, many of those initially won during the campaign were lost. It seemed obvious that if outside donations could provide the pillars and roof, the local people would be able to complete the building over time as funds became available to them. While completing the tabernacle, they would be able to conduct services under the roof.

Thus, one method of evangelism used extensively in Sub-Saharan Africa has been the building of tabernacles. These are made of steel trusses and a roof system that can easily be shipped to Africa and set up within a few hours. Tabernacle construction facilitates a partnership between the local churches in the United States, Assemblies of God World Missions, and the national church in another country. This is a practical approach to church growth for many national churches (Africa Harvest Ministries). In one extremely poor country in West Africa, it took years for a local congregation to find the funds to build a permanent building for worship. However, today, with a roof over their heads provided by tabernacle evangelism, believers are able to begin meeting immediately after the first converts are won.

A local church in the United States of America usually provides the funding for the steel structure and/or manpower for setting up the tabernacle. Each unit is purchased at a set price of $5,000.00. This cost includes an amount to assist with shipping to the closest port. The national church provides the manpower and finishes the structure according to their desire.

Donald Tucker of the office of Africa Harvest Ministries commented:

The tabernacle provides an immediate place of worship for a needy congregation. Most places begin having services as soon as the trusses and roof are complete. Many times they begin with a dedication service and continue on with a crusade where many give their hearts to the Lord. We have found that a small congregation will see immediate growth in numbers of attendance. Often, the congregation will double in numbers the first week after the tabernacles is complete. (Tucker 2005)

The Indigenous Church

Training of National Ministers

A major reason behind the growth of AGWM-related Pentecostal churches is the emphasis from the beginning on the training of national ministers. The undergirding belief is that training national ministers offers the greatest prospect for the evangelization of the world. Since the most effective witnessing is done by people reaching others in their own culture, the training of national ministers is critical.

Everywhere Assemblies of God missionaries have gone they have sought to establish Bible schools. The type and level of training depends upon the educational and spiritual level of the believers. Programs have ranged from basic discipleship to graduate courses in both residential and non-residential settings. By the end of 2003, with over 40,250,000 members and adherents around the world, AGWM was reporting 831 Bible schools with over 47,000 students, and another 1,060 extension programs with 43,500 students. That does not include more basic levels of training where nearly 600,000 were being trained through programs related to Global University in cooperation with field missionaries and national churches. The emphasis on producing indigenous churches makes the early training of national pastors and leaders imperative.

History of Indigeneity

From its earliest days, the Church focused on planting churches. Such was the practice of the apostle Paul as recorded in the book of Acts and the Epistles. So it has been ever since, regardless of the particular theological bent of the various streams of Christianity down through the centuries.

Whatever mission agency is involved, whether an individual or an organized missionary society, the church planting effort is necessarily that of an external entity seeking to penetrate a people group other than their own. Several issues then arise. What should the new entity look like? How should it be organized? What should be its relationship to the surrounding culture? How should it be governed? How should it be supported financially? Who should lead it? What should be its relationship with the founding mission, and over what time period? Who should decide?

These questions are not easily answered. How they are answered depends in part on how the foundations are laid in the beginning. Much will be determined by personal relationship with those being won to Christ. Much depends on the missionaries' understanding of the host culture.

That this has not always been the case can be shown throughout history. Even with advanced understanding of anthropology, cross-cultural communications, and the best missiological training, mistakes are made. But lest we lose heart over difficulties and past errors, let us remind ourselves that even within the churches in our own culture and denomination people struggle with similar issues. Witness the problems over the form of worship and style of music!

From the 1500s onward, the western nations used naval and military dominance to explore and conquer other territories in Asia, Africa, North and South America, and many islands. The rule of the day was colonialism—the imposition of the conquering nation's language, lifestyle, governance, and economics of its culture. At times conquerors may felt a kind of benevolence toward less-developed people, though exploitation was their main motive.

Unfortunately, the Cross accompanied the flag; missionaries followed or even accompanied conquering armies. Not only were the colonialists resented by those they dominated, but so too were the missionaries and the churches they represented. Kane describes the reaction in the nineteenth century:

> In Latin America the Spanish colonial system broke up between 1810 and 1824; but in other parts of the world—Asia, Africa, Oceania, and the Middle East— the missionary advance coincided with the rapid expansion of European power. Three major groups were involved in the invasion—the diplomat, the merchant, and the missionary. In the eyes of the nationals, they came to represent three forms of imperialism—political, economic, and cultural. (Kane 1986, 93)

However, as the missionary enterprise grew, missionaries and mission leaders began to recognize the problems caused by the apparent marriage between colonialism and missionary activity. Among them was the father of modern missions, William Carey, who began his missionary career in 1792. He was followed by Henry Venn, Secretary of the Anglican Church Missionary Society (1841–1871), who said that "the 'euthanasia' of a mission takes place when the missionary is able to resign all pastoral work into the hands of the indigenous ministry and congregation." Rufus Anderson, the mission board secretary of the American Congregational Church, had already declared in 1830 the policy of the American Board of Commissioners to create an indigenous ministry. In constant communication with each other, by 1856 they had come to believe that an indigenous church was to be self-governed, self-supported, and self-propagating (Terry, et al. 1998, 306,307).

In the last half of the nineteenth century, John Nevius, a Presbyterian missionary to China, developed a method of church planting that built on the ideas of Venn and Anderson. Rejected in China, he took his plan to Korea and convinced the missionaries pioneering the work to use his method. Nevius felt strongly that the nationals should be in charge almost from the beginning of the work. He also felt that believers should stay within their social and economic positions to be able to retain their bridges of communication to the rest of the population. The result was rapid growth of the Presbyterian churches in Korea, as attested by their great numbers today (Terry 1998, 307–308).

A similar point of view was expressed by Roland Allen, missionary to North China under the auspices of the Anglican Society for the Propagation of the Gospel. His book *Missionary Methods: St. Paul's or Ours?* examined the need to establish indigenous churches following the pattern set by the apostle Paul. His work influenced the missionary philosophy and practice of early Assemblies of God missionaries Alice C. Luce and Henry C. Ball (McGee 1986, 97).

Definition of Indigenous

Indigeneity, or the adjective *indigenous*, comes from the Latin meaning "in-born," or "native." The idea is of something native to a given environment and growing naturally within that environment. The analogy of plant life is often used to illustrate the principle. An indigenous plant is one that grows naturally in its habitat, but is not likely to survive in a very different one. For example, a palm tree will grow naturally in Florida, but not in Alaska.

When we speak of an indigenous church, we mean a local church that will grow naturally where it is located. It is suitably designed to flourish without artificial stimuli. The Madras Conference of the International Missionary Council meeting in 1938 offered the following definition:

> An indigenous church, young or old, in the East or in the West, is a church which, rooted in obedience to Christ, spontaneously uses forms of thought and modes of action natural and familiar in its own environment. Such a church arises in response to Christ's own call. The younger churches will not be unmindful of the experiences and teachings which the older churches have recorded in their confessions and liturgy. But every younger church will seek to bear witness to the same Gospel with new tongues. (Terry et al. 1998, 311)

Note that no geographical boundaries were given and no compromise with the gospel of Christ was suggested. Yet such a church would be characterized by words and actions that have a familiar feel to the native population. This is made even clearer by Beyerhaus:

> To be indigenous means that a church, in obedience to the apostolic message that has been entrusted to it and to the living guidance of the Holy Spirit, is able in its own particular historical situation, to make the gospel intelligent and relevant in word and deed to the eyes and ears of men. (Quoted in Terry et al. 1998, 304)

Drawing from earlier writings and from his mentor, Ralph D. Williams, Melvin L. Hodges articulated the indigenous principles in his popular book *The Indigenous Church*. This book soon became a standard reference among evangelical and Pentecostal missionaries. Hodges (1976) discusses the three primary ingredients of a truly indigenous church: self-governing, self-propagating, and self-supporting. Thus, the indigenous church became characterized as a "three-self church." This philosophy has become the standard for church planting by Assemblies of God missionaries, though not always with stellar success.

In recent years, two additional characteristics have been added to the traditional three-self formula. They are self-theologizing and self-missionizing. In brief, self-theologizing refers to the need of the church to address the particular issues of its cultural context in light of biblical principles. Self-missionizing refers to the need of a truly indigenous church to participate in the mandate of Christ to make disciples of all peoples throughout the earth. These will be dealt with later.

7.2.2
OBJECTIVE
Relate the importance of self-governance, self-propagation, and self-support to the indigenous church.

Self-Governance

Self-governance was considered by Hodges (1976, 22) to be perhaps the most difficult and time-consuming characteristic of indigeneity to achieve. However, no church can be truly indigenous if it is not self-governing. The apostle Paul obviously saw this as vital. The book of Acts records his practice of establishing leaders for each new congregation before moving to another place (Acts 14:23). Interestingly, he seems to have done so very early in their development, almost from the beginning.

To be self-governing requires leaders who are respected as leaders in their congregation and sufficiently equipped by their gifts and training to carry out their tasks. From this arises a number of key questions: Who selects the new leaders? Who evaluates their abilities? Who trains them, and to do what? How does that relate to their context of ministry? If a missionary pioneered the church, when should the reins be turned over to the national leaders? The answers to these questions are not simple.

In our study of missions, the church is assumed to have been started by a missionary team. Ideally, as people are led to the Lord and progress to become members of the church, they will be discipled in the ways of Christ. Some will begin to stand out as leaders and should be afforded advanced training as lay leaders. If they evidence the call of God on their lives, they should be further taught the roles associated with the pastorate. Increasingly, they should be given the responsibility to lead the congregation.

One key issue is when to turn over the leadership of the church to the members themselves. That is followed by the question of whether governance has truly been left in the hands of the national brethren or only in appearance. In one example of a mission where the local church was led by a national, the missionaries proudly attributed this move to indigeneity. Unfortunately, they held all the other leadership positions in the church and were members of the decision-making body. This scenario is a far cry from a truly self-governing church. While self-governance does not suggest that a church should reject advice and counsel from others outside itself, it does mean that, in the end, the church makes its own decisions and plots its own course.

Self-Propagation

A truly indigenous church is one that grows from within, reaching out to the surrounding community through the witness of its own people. Without self-propagation, the church will soon cease to exist. The local church is God's plan to reach the lost in a community. As part of the cultural context in which the church is planted, these believers have natural bridges of understanding and relationship with those around them. Nevius wanted to capitalize on these bridges of natural relationships. Referring to 1 Corinthians 7:20, he observed, "It teaches most emphatically that Christianity should not disturb the social relations of its adherents, but requires them to be content with their lot, and to illustrate the Gospel in the spheres of life in which they are called" (Nevius 2003, 19).

New converts are natural witnesses. Their testimonies may be unstructured or even crude, but they are genuine. They are eager to tell their friends of what this great God has done for them in Christ. It is too tempting to feel we must teach them how to witness, how to get it right, how to make sure the theology is correct. To insist on such at this stage of their experience in Christ is to kill their natural enthusiasm. Those things should come later in the discipleship process.

The church may well receive the added incentive of itinerating evangelists and cooperative evangelistic mass crusades. But, in the end, the principal growth will come from the proclamation of the gospel from the pulpit and from the personal witness of its members. This must be encouraged from the beginning.

Self-Support

While Hodges may be right in stating that the most difficult thing to achieve is self-governance, self-support is an almost equal challenge. Here is where missionaries and their supporting churches raise financial support. Woe to the parent who provides all the material needs of his children without teaching them stewardship principles and self-discipline in financial matters. Woe to the church that has learned to depend on support from the missionaries and well-meaning churches from abroad. Like dealing with one's children in such matters, helping the local church or fellowship of churches requires wisdom and discretion.

New converts, no matter how poor, must be taught from the beginning to tithe. God himself mandates it (Numbers 18:21–26; Deuteronomy 14:22–29;

Malachi 3:8–12; Luke 11:42). Note that Malachi records God's promise of blessing to those who do. Without such instruction, the local church will struggle to maintain itself financially.

4 What is the great temptation of missionaries from more affluent societies?

The great temptation to those of us who come from affluent societies is to want to reproduce our lifestyle in the converts. So often—but not always—the people are truly poor by our standards. Surely, they need financial assistance for everything from personal support to education, church building, and support for the pastor. But if our financial support were to suddenly cease, could the church carry on? Too often when we have gone too far in support, the local church cannot maintain what we created for them. The church building, Bible school, and the pastor cannot continue at the level we instituted.

This is not to say that immediately from the beginning we must avoid financial assistance. The so-called start-up costs must be met. But nothing is wrong in a congregation's beginning under a tree or brush arbor or store-front and learning to pay as they go, establishing programs and buildings as they are able. The buildings, for example, may not look like what we would prefer or think they need, but it is better for them to make those decisions.

Further, learning and practicing self-support brings with it a sense of self-worth and confidence. To be ever dependent upon outside support is demeaning. Those willing to live in that state are not those who will advance the kingdom of God. The focus will remain on themselves. Like children growing up in the home, there is a period where the parents must support them. Yet once they have achieved adulthood, relying on the parents is considered shameful.

The Bible instructs us to care for the truly poor and needy, but it also chastises those who are lazy and unwilling to fend for themselves (Proverbs 12:24; 15:19; 21:25–26; 24:30–34; 26:13–15). To discern real needs and respond to them appropriately requires much prayer and wisdom. Consider the situation in which fourteen of sixteen prospective students in an overseas training program claimed they needed financial assistance, not being able to pay anything. The national pastor agreed to pay their way. Within two weeks, the only students left were those who paid their own way, having taken responsibility for themselves.

In the end, the church that will grow and have an impact on its community is the one that accepts responsibility for its own financial needs based on good stewardship principles.

Indigeneity and Cultural Factors

All this may sound rather straightforward, but is more complex than it seems. For example, it is easy for the missionary to follow the patterns of his or her own culture in establishing the organization. In North America, we are used to a congregational form based on independent local churches with hierarchical levels of governance, where the pastor is often positioned as CEO of the church.

Other cultures may follow a council of elders format or that of the village chief. Another might follow the pattern of a mother church with many daughter churches forming an entire family of churches in a network led by the senior pastor of the mother church. The employ of constitutions and bylaws and practices following Robert's Rules of Order may seem strange. So the imposition of a style of governance based upon our preferences or experience may well stifle, rather than enhance, growth.

Programs that work well in the churches of our home country may or may not serve well in another. Standards of dress and deportment must fit the cultural context of the national church. For example, missionary styles of dress as worn in their home countries have been copied by the nationals in some countries, believing them to be a special sign of spirituality. Unfortunately, suits and ties in a hot, humid climate do not serve well! A gothic-styled church, common in North America, may appear totally out of the norm of building styles in another culture. Music and worship styles must be carefully crafted to fit in another culture as well. We must be careful about what we establish as standards lest we fail to establish a church that is truly indigenous.

Self-Theologizing

5   Why is self-theologizing beneficial to a local culture?

The teaching about indigenous principles has gone beyond the three popular principles dealt with earlier with a call for self-theologizing. The idea of people in different cultures finding ways to express Christian belief and apply them to their own cultures was expressed by the word contextualization in the early 1970s. The greatest example of one's identifying with the culture of a particular people is in the life and ministry of Christ himself. Jesus, the incarnate Word, lived and died a Jew. He commissioned His disciples to go into all the world and share the good news of salvation (Matthew 28:18–20). This was obviously not just in geographical terms, but to be demonstrated in words and illustrations the people of the earth could understand. The gospel was to be applied to their daily lives and their particular situations. It must penetrate the culture of the people and judge the culture at the same time.

As Pentecostal and evangelical students of the Word, we are careful to understand the Bible in its original languages and cultural contexts as God revealed himself to the original authors. However, our work is not complete even when we arrive at such an understanding. The biblical message must be interpreted in such a way that it is properly understood by contemporary people in contemporary times and places (Kraft 1978, 32). There is only one biblical message, but there are many ways to express that message with sensitivity to the symbols of a given culture. Churches should have the right to interpret and read the Scriptures for themselves. This is not a new approach; it is as ancient as the Church itself. Recall how the early church struggled to break loose from its Jewish cultural trappings and enter the Greco-Roman world of the Gentiles.

OBJECTIVE

Discuss contextualization as it relates to self-theologizing.

Contextualization refers to the "process of communicating the gospel in such a way as to make it meaningful to the people of any given cultural context" (Hesselgrave 1995, 139). This gospel must, however, faithfully reflect the meaning of the biblical text. Therefore, the first task of the contextualizer is one of interpretation, which means that one must determine not only what the text says but also the meaning of what has been said. After this has been determined, the truth can be applied to the culture in words and symbols that are meaningful to the people. This is the self-theologizing element. If one is not faithful to the meaning of Scripture, then the result is syncretism—an incompatible mixture of biblical truth and local beliefs and practices. Bong Rin Ro (1985) says that the best protection against syncretism is a mission-centered theology that aims at communicating the gospel to the lost.

Many of the leaders in the churches that were formerly mission fields have been trained in Bible and theology. They face questions unique to their situation, such as ancestors and polygamy in Africa and other areas of the world. In India, the leaders face the question of transmigration and the caste system, as well as meditation (Hiebert 1985, 196). A church that cannot self-theologize is only able to state its beliefs as they were given to them by foreign missionaries and teachers. Such a church does not think or speak for itself. This makes it ill-equipped to respond to local issues that arise within its culture. Local leaders must search the Scriptures to find God's response to issues. In this way, they will be mature and able to voice their opinion in clear, intelligible, biblical terms.

Missionary Warren Newberry (2005) wrote that "until recently national church leaders were not encouraged to develop their own theologies. Any theology that deviated from the standard theological texts from the West was considered suspect, perhaps syncretistic, and even heresy" (111). In East Africa, there is a particular call for a contextualized Pentecostal theology without the dualism and Greco-Roman influence in western theology (Chakwera 1999).

As leaders, teachers, and pastors define theology in their own contexts, the teaching of the Word is better understood and applied. One such example comes from Burkina Faso in the late 1960s. Many of the new converts came from a polygamous society, and the missionaries had refused to baptize them or allow them to become members of the churches. Finally, the national church leaders took up this problem in one of their national meetings. They asked the missionaries to leave the meeting hall while the Africans themselves made a decision about this issue. The national brethren decided the Scripture did not forbid baptism or church membership to polygamists. It did, however, forbid them from being leaders in the church (see 1 Timothy 3:2; Titus 1:6).

Self-Missionizing

7.2.4
OBJECTIVE
Describe the self-missionizing movement around the world.

Self-missionizing refers to a church planted by missionaries that recognizes its responsibility to send missionaries as well. In a special time of study in Malawi, Dr. Lazarus Chakwera, the General Superintendent of the Assemblies of God of Malawi, appealed to a number of leaders from many countries of Africa to become missionary-sending churches (Chakwera 1999).

Earlier, in 1996, Bryant L. Meyers of MARC and World Vision, reported that over half the Christians who live in the Majority World (also referred to as Third World or Two-Thirds World) and nearly seventy percent of all evangelicals live in the non-western world (Meyers 1996). It was also estimated that the number of Protestant missionaries from Africa, Asia, and Latin America, in the year 2000, was approximately 170,000. In 1996, the South Korean churches had sent 4,402 missionaries to Asia, Eastern Europe, Western Europe, the United States, Latin America, Africa, the Middle East and Oceania. The churches of the Philippines are sending missionaries to many countries. The nation of Brazil is also sending missionaries to unreached people groups in a number of continents. This makes the former mission fields full partners in world missions. The technology and finances of the western churches are being matched by the faith, resilience, and numerical strength of the former mission fields (Ezemadu 2000).

Test Yourself

Circle the letter of the *best* answer.

1. The primary source of proclamation and witness is the
a) missionary.
b) pastor.
c) church.
d) evangelist.

2. One principal facet of Assemblies of God missions outreach is
a) Bible schools.
b) education.
c) missionary recruiting.
d) the planting of indigenous churches.

3. One of the reasons stated for the house church method was
a) freedom from an organized church.
b) a family-oriented and community-related place.
c) convenience for lay leadership.
d) that it is superior to the larger fellowship.

4. Tabernacle evangelism
a) provides an entire building for a local congregation in Africa.
b) encourages the local people to provide the pillars for a building.
c) provides pillars and a roof of a building, and the local people complete the building.
d) encourages missions giving in the United States.

5. A reason for AGWM-related, Pentecostal church growth is emphasis on
a) training national ministers.
b) missionaries who serve as evangelists.
c) holistic ministries.
d) church construction.

6. Henry Venn stated that euthanasia of a mission takes place when
a) the missionary leaves the field.
b) the missionary shifts all pastoral work to the indigenous ministry.
c) involvement of outside missions ceases.
d) the mission field is isolated.

7. Self-theologizing refers to
a) teaching another gospel.
b) a church's ability to answer questions raised by its own cultural context.
c) a new approach to scriptural interpretation.
d) the tendency to syncretistic teaching.

8. The key motivation behind self-theologizing is
a) helping churches face questions that are unique to their situation.
b) independence from missionaries and mission societies.
c) embracing a syncretistic gospel.
d) a matter of nationalistic pride.

9. Self-missionizing refers to
a) a church planted by missionaries.
b) self-governance of the national church.
c) a church planted by missionaries sending its own missionaries.
d) a church's ability to be self-supporting.

10. A church's practice of self-support
a) imposes unnecessary strain on its members.
b) demeans the pastor and congregation.
c) brings self-worth and confidence to that local body.
d) does not advance the kingdom of God.

Responses to Interactive Questions
Chapter 7

Some of these responses may include information that is supplemental to the IST. These questions are intended to produce reflective thinking beyond the course content and your responses may vary from these examples.

1 What institution is considered to be the primary source of proclamation and witness?

Answer: The local church

2 Why has the house church movement been so effective through the centuries?

Answer: 1) It is a natural family-oriented and community-related environment; 2) it provides a more intimate environment for fellowship and edification for small groups of believers within larger fellowships; and 3) it is an unobtrusive gathering place in lands where there is open resistance and hostility to the cause of Christ.

3 List the characteristics of an indigenous church.

Answer: An indigenous church grows naturally in the context where it is located. It is suitably designed to flourish without artificial stimuli.

4 What is the great temptation of missionaries from more affluent societies?

Answer: To reproduce their lifestyle in the native people

5 Why is self-theologizing beneficial to a local culture?

Answer: The biblical message must be interpreted in such a way that it is properly understood by contemporary people in contemporary times and places.

Partnership in Missions

Missions involves partnerships of the local, national, and international missionaries with church bodies. In the past two decades, there has been a remarkable awakening in the Majority World as these national churches have launched into world missions. A majority of Christians now live in the southern hemisphere as churches in the western, industrialized nations decline. Since 1974, numerous evangelical conferences have been called to examine how the churches and missions can work better together to bring in the harvest. Non-governmental and religious non-governmental agencies have also increased at a rapid rate to meet the challenge of the need for development in the poor nations of the world.

Lesson 8.1   The Local Level

Objectives
8.1.1   Define the church and its mission.
8.1.2   Explain the role of missions in the local church.
8.1.3   Cite examples of missionary ministry from the New Testament.
8.1.4   Discuss opportunities for involvement in missions giving in the local church.

Lesson 8.2   The National Level

Objective
8.2.1   Explain the need for a national organization of churches.

Lesson 8.3   The International Level

Objectives
8.3.1   Describe the international partnership models of Argentina and Niger.
8.3.2   Outline the origin of non-governmental organizations.
8.3.3   Explain the purpose of the Lausanne conference of 1974.
8.3.4   Describe the composition of the Manila conference.
8.3.5   Discuss the stated function and purpose of the Pentecostal World Fellowship.

8.1.1
OBJECTIVE

Define the church and its mission.

1   How is the triumph of the Church assured?

The Local Level

The Church Defined

In Ephesians 5:22–32, Paul referred to the local church as "a profound mystery" (5:32). The word "church" often refers to a building or a Christian denomination adhering to a particular creed. The word in English comes from the Greek word *ekklesia*, which referred to an assembly of citizens summoned to discuss something of particular interest to the community. In this sense, the term did not have a religious connotation but simply indicated a meeting. It is logical to assume that the assembly came together upon the summons of a responsible authority. The church, then, refers to people called out by God to a special service for Him. These people have a special relationship to God.

The word *church* is found only two times in the Gospels, and both times are in the gospel of Matthew. The first reference is about Peter's confession of who Jesus Christ was, and the second reference concerns church discipline (Matthew 18:17). After Peter confessed that Jesus was the Son of God, Jesus said to him and the other disciples, "You are Peter, and on this rock I will build my church, and the gates of Hades will not overcome it" (Matthew 16:18). Jesus' declaration speaks of the final victory of the "assembled ones" in that the gates of Hades will not overcome them. It is interesting to note that it was at the gate of the village or city in the Middle East where the village or city counsel met. This was where business, politics, and marriages were transacted or decided upon. The "gates of Hades" must refer to Satan and his counsel devising tactics and strategies against the Church. But the Lord of Glory made one thing clear—the evil scheming of Satan will not prevail!

In a broad sense, the word *church* includes all those who, through faith in Christ, have become part of God's family. This would include believers of all periods of history. We call this the "universal church." However, in the book of Acts, Paul mentions churches as smaller units in particular geographical areas (cf. Acts 14:23 and Romans 16:5). Although the term *ekklesia* is used only twice in the Gospels, it is seen 115 times in the New Testament. Eighty-five of these usages refer to the local congregation, while thirty of them designate the universal church.

The following provides a partial list of churches identified by their geographical location:

1.   The church in Jerusalem (Acts 8:1)
2.   The church in Antioch (Acts 13:1)
3.   The church in Philippi (Philippians 1:1–2)
4.   The church of Ephesus (Acts 20:17)
5.   The churches of Galatia (Galatians 1:2)
6.   The churches in Asia (Revelation 1:4).

No church buildings were erected specifically for the assembling of the believers. Rather, they met in homes in specific geographical locations (Acts 12:12; 16:15; Romans 16:23; 1 Corinthians 16:19).

The Church's Mission

2   Who is responsible for the Church's mission?

In Ephesians 2:14 and 15, Paul describes the Church as a new man called out to fulfill the mission not accomplished by Israel. Israel's mission was to be a light to the nations (Isaiah 51:4). However, after Israel failed its mission, the prophet Ezekiel declared the following:

Therefore say to the house of Israel, "This is what the Sovereign Lord says: It is not for your sake, O house of Israel, that I am going to do these things, but for the sake of my holy name, which you have profaned among the nations where you have gone. I will show the holiness of my great name, which has been profaned among the nations, the name you have profaned among them. Then the nations will know that I am the Lord," declares the Sovereign Lord, "when I show myself holy through you before their eyes." (Ezekiel 36:22–23)

Before Christ ascended, His words were clear about the mission of the Church (see Matthew 28:18–20; Mark 16:15; Luke 24:47). Every believer must have this vision of world evangelization. Harold Lindsell (1970) recognized this responsibility of the individual believer: "To know that men are lost and to do nothing about it is irrational. To know that we must give an account of our stewardship and then do nothing to press our stewardship is to act foolishly" (155).

Paul committed himself to a specific mission given to him by Christ on the Damascus road, and this commission applies to every believer. In Acts 26:18, Paul related his mission to King Agrippa: "To open their eyes and turn them from darkness to light, and from the power of Satan to God, so that they may receive forgiveness of sins and a place among those who are sanctified by faith."

Consequently, the Church exists as a result of the will and activity of God. She has been set apart for the purpose of reaching the nations with the gospel. Ephesians 3:10 states, "His intent was that now, through the church, the manifold wisdom of God should be made known to the rulers and authorities in the heavenly realms." It is therefore the Church that serves as God's agent to reconcile the world to himself (2 Corinthians 5:18–20). The very names of the epistles—Romans, Corinthians, Galatians, Ephesians, Philippians, Colossians, Thessalonians—indicate that taking the gospel to the world was an ongoing enterprise. Thus, the contemporary Church must continue the ongoing task of world evangelization.

8.1.2
OBJECTIVE
Explain the role of missions in the local church.

The local church's successful execution of missions involves participation of everyone, from the local church to the national and international church. Missions is the reason for the existence of the local church. It does not simply involve the passive role of providing candidates, funds, and prayer for the mission field. Missions is the guiding principle in all the church's programs. This includes the local setting as well as other areas of the city, state, and world. The pastor and leadership of the local church should have a burning vision and personal conviction about the role of the church in world missions. By their leadership example and preaching of the Word, they can teach and inspire the congregation toward a genuine burden and passion for world missions.

As a supplement to this printed text, a manual titled "The Missions Awareness Team: Checklist for Building Missions in the Local Church" is available as a free PDF download at: http://worldagfellowship.org/wp-content/uploads/2011/08/MANUAL-THE-CHECKLIST1.pdf. This manual was written and designed by long-time missionary Paul Brannan of Assemblies of God World Missions. Please study it along with the text that follows to learn how the missions program of the local church can become highly effective through proper promotion.

The pastoral staff and church leadership need to be exposed to mission realities. This can be done through short-term experiences in visiting different mission contexts; ongoing exposure to various missionaries who are invited to speak to the church; and the pastor's frequent speaking on the subject of world missions. In this way, the members of the local church, particularly the youth, are encouraged to enter the ministry and missionary service.

The church's leadership should organize and encourage intercessory prayer for the lost. Specific facts can be regularly communicated to the congregation about particular countries' religious beliefs and cultural issues. There should also be an exchange of letters with missionaries, updating the congregation on the needs and activities on the field. These things help focus the church on the realities of the missionary enterprise, and the congregation can become personally involved with missionaries they support.

One of the best ways to stay informed and focused on missions is to conduct "missions conventions." The convention speaker should be a missionary who reports on his or her work and leads the church in prayer. There should be an emphasis on praying for missions, giving to missions, and accepting the call to missions. The spiritual benefits are great when a church is involved in worldwide missions.

8.1.3
OBJECTIVE
Cite examples of missionary ministry from the New Testament.

The New Testament provides examples of missionary ministry of local churches. Jerusalem was the starting point of the spread of the gospel. Some of the characteristics of this church are given in the second chapter of the book of Acts (vv. 42–47). This passage states that the members gave themselves to the apostles' teaching and to prayer. They loved one another and shared their resources. They held on to the teaching of the apostles in the face of great persecution. This persecution would be one of the reasons for the scattering of many of the believers in Judea to other parts of the world.

In addition to the many miraculous signs manifested in the Church, we see Philip carrying the gospel with great spiritual fervor to Samaria and beyond (Acts 8:5). Although material resources were scarce among the members of the Jerusalem church, they had an intimate knowledge of God and accomplished great things in His name. Yet this church was the recipient of an offering carried by Paul from churches outside of Judea who responded to the economic hardship and poverty of this area. This is an example of the compassion and care of the members of the churches in the first century.

Another New Testament example of a local church is the one in Antioch, which became a great missionary-sending church. Williams (1990) wrote that the church in Antioch "became the springboard of that great missionary thrust into the Roman Empire" (202). Romans 10:14–15 presents Paul's questions about the focus of missions for the believer and for the church. "How, then, can they call on the one they have not believed in? And how can they believe in the one of whom they have not heard? And how can they hear without someone preaching to them? And how can they preach unless they are sent?" A powerful demonstration of this commission is the sending of Paul and Barnabas by the church in Antioch (Acts 13:3). This brings the role of the local church into clear focus. The church must send the missionaries!

In yet another example of missionary ministry in the New Testament, Paul writes about the generous giving of the church at Philippi (2 Corinthians 8:1–6). This church served as a model of financial support of missionaries. They were the only church that supported Paul in the beginning of his missionary efforts in Macedonia (Philippians 4:15). Yet they gave out of extreme poverty (2 Corinthians 8:2) and were faithful in continued giving (Philippians 4:16). Paul expressed his appreciation for the partnership of the Philippian church, "In all my prayers for all of you, I always pray with joy because of your partnership in the gospel" (Philippians 1:4–5). The Philippian church's example illustrates that missions support is not limited and does not depend on the material wealth of a local church. Such support comes from a heart of generosity motivated by the need to reach the lost with the gospel of salvation.

8.1.4
OBJECTIVE
Discuss opportunities for involvement in missions giving in the local church.

One example of giving to missions comes from a young boy in the state of Virginia in the United States. He was a Royal Ranger in his church. Royal Rangers is a boys' program of the General Council of the Assemblies of God, USA. This boy wanted to carry out an assignment to receive a badge in world missions, so he placed a note at the door of all the neighbors in his area of the city. His request was that they place any pairs of used shoes they wanted to give away outside their door for him to pick up on the following day. The shoes would be sent to an underdeveloped West African country. To his amazement, he collected 1500 pairs of shoes, most of which were in good shape. The shoes were sent to a Muslim country in Africa where the churches were in the beginning stage of development. The pastors sold the shoes at a very low price, but they had enough money from the sale of the shoes to sponsor the entire cost of four hundred children to a youth camp. This boy's creativity and love are a powerful demonstration of how the local church can impact missions locally and abroad.

8.2.1
OBJECTIVE
Explain the need for a national organization of churches.

The National Level

The National Church

With the growth and extension of local churches, the need arises to have a national organization of local bodies to maintain doctrinal purity, to train and appoint ministers and leaders, and to administer national programs including missions. In most countries where missionaries have established Assemblies of God churches, these churches have been organized into general councils of churches. The national churches are indigenous, but maintain a fraternal relationship with the other Assemblies of God churches in the region and around the world. This fraternal relationship is maintained through conference and international organizations, such as the Africa Assemblies of God Alliance, which brings together the superintendents from the different countries of Africa. A primary purpose of this alliance is the coordination and promotion of missions throughout Sub-Saharan Africa.

The leaders chosen for a national church must commit themselves to the task of the Great Commission. They should be men and women of strong spiritual character and vision, who understand this is the reason for the existence of their organization. Missions cannot be a minor concern or be in the margin of the planning and thrust of the national church. It is essential that it be at the center of the church organization, providing a passion and enthusiasm for winning and training the lost.

3   What can a national church do to provide finances for missionaries?

A national office should also be established for both home and foreign missions in the beginning of the national church organization. Leaders must not wait for the membership to become large or until finances are sufficient. The office should provide current information about missions to the local churches and pastors on a continual basis. This includes new churches being planted in the nation, as well as persons sent and sponsored by the national church.

The burden and vision for missions should be instilled in every phase of the national church life—children, youth, and adults. It is advisable that a missions program be developed to include lay persons in mission activities, such as short-term mission assignments. In order to assure the success of the missionary enterprise, the national church must develop a program of intercessory prayer for missionaries and mission fields.

National missions offices need a plan for appointing missionaries, and this should include ways of screening candidates and raising their financial support from local churches in the nation. The North American Assemblies of God uses a faith promise method of raising support through local churches. The various members in the local churches make commitments, by faith, to give a certain amount of money each month for the support of missionaries. The local church then sends this money to the national office to be disbursed to the various missionaries serving both within the nation and in foreign countries. The missionaries maintain contact with the local churches through visits during times they are in the area and by newsletters.

It is also suggested that the national missions office furnish materials and information through the training institutions so leaders can be thoroughly trained in cross-cultural practices and communication. If world missions is to become a part of the ministry of the entire national church, it would be well if the office made every effort to see that missions and cross-cultural studies are a major part of the study program of its Bible colleges and institutes.

Furthermore, the national missions office should establish a means of accounting carefully for all finances designated to missionary work, including reports from missionaries on the use of such funds. It is imperative that all of the funds given for missions be used for the task of fulfilling the purpose of world missions. Proper accounting and reporting of monies will inspire confidence in the members who provide the finances. Administrative fees in the use of these funds should be kept at a minimum.

World missions was the primary motivating factor in the organizing of the Assemblies of God in the United States. When this church was first established in November 1914, one of the stated reasons for such an organization was the coordination of finances and personnel for a more efficient missions effort. One of the resolutions of the meeting brought about the establishment of a missionary-sending agency.

> Whereas, there have sprung up spontaneously . . . Pentecostal centers, . . . and . . . moneys for missionary purposes are being sent to these several centers and distributed upon the missionary field, therefore be it resolved, that the Presbytery be instructed to seek to bring about a more perfect cooperation among these centers, in the matter of distribution of missionary funds and the sending out of missionaries, with a view to greater efficiency (*The New Missionary Manual* 2004, 11).

Morris O. Williams concluded: "No national church can say it is fully obedient to the Great Commission until it makes the 'ends of the earth' part of its outreach. It should care for 'its own,' but it should not neglect the lost of other tribes and nations. Every national church should be a 'sending' church" (Williams 1979, 129).

The International Level

In the beginning of the modern missionary outreach, almost all the missionaries were sent by Europe and North America. Toward the end of the twentieth century, other countries where missionaries had been sent began to engage in foreign missions. Today, more than two-thirds of the world's Christians live in the Majority World. The national churches in the Majority World are becoming increasingly involved in foreign missions. As these churches work on the same mission fields with missionaries from other nationalities, it becomes necessary for them to form partnerships so the work will be more effective. These partnerships usually involve missionaries from several nations working together.

The Model of International Partnership

Argentina

OBJECTIVE

Describe the international partnership models of Argentina and Niger.

4   How are the missionaries from Argentina supported?

National churches are increasingly working together with other nations in planting churches in foreign lands. One example of this is the Argentina Assemblies of God, which has had an active foreign missions program since 1989. This church has about 160 missionaries serving in 37 nations. The missionaries work with existing missionaries from other nations (Walz 2003). To support the missionaries, the Argentina National Church requests mission offerings from each church in the nation, and most of the money is designated to particular missionaries. In Argentina, this is called the "personalization of missions." Money is sent to the missionaries once each month, and 10 percent is retained to cover office expenses. A missions committee comprising eleven members directs the affairs of the mission.

All but seven of the countries served by the missionaries from Argentina are outside Latin America. Of the twenty-one countries in Latin America, eighteen have missions departments. However, of these eighteen countries only four have had a significant number of missionaries sent to other nations—Brazil, El Salvador, Costa Rica, Argentina (Walz 2001).

In a practical example, Pastor Juan Masalykam leads the church in Cordoba, Argentina. He and his church obeyed God's call to become a sending church. The pastor started conducting missions conventions and taught the believers to give "faith promises." He preached about the need for missionaries and taught about this need in cell groups. The local church numbers about four hundred people, and almost everyone is involved in the missions outreach. This church sent out over twenty-five missionaries and gave $50,000 for missionary work during the year 2000.

Niger

The missions efforts in Niger began in 1991, when the Assemblies of God of Burkina Faso was granted official registration by the government of Niger (Johansen 1993, 9). Almost immediately following the first missionary from Burkina Faso, a French missionary couple began ministry in the capital city of Niamey. In November 1992, an American missionary family settled in Maradi, an important interior city of the country. By 1993, there were five churches in Niger (*Convention des Missions* 2002). Adding to these three national missions were three other African nations: Ivory Coast, Nigeria, and Togo.

These six national missions formed a consortium under the leadership of one of the missionaries from Burkina Faso. They also founded a central fund from which monies would be distributed to the various projects in the country. The six missions established a schedule of meeting every three months to report on one another's work and decide on projects, such as the Bible institute, student admission to the institute, ministry assignments, building projects, schools, medical dispensaries, and any other project related to the missions work in the nation. These representatives made decisions by consensus (*Pentecostal Evangel* 2003). The Assemblies of God of Niger has thirty churches, two Bible schools, four elementary schools, and one clinic (B. Teague, pers. comm.). This missionary enterprise is becoming a model of the effectiveness of several nations working together with similar goals, doctrines, philosophies, and methodology. A certain amount of tolerance has been necessary because of some differences in methods, but these differences have been worked out as the missionaries determined to work for the building of the Church in Niger.

Some of the advantages of non-western nations' involvement in missions is their cross-cultural sensitivity and the fact that they can sometimes gain entrance into countries where westerners are not permitted or where entry is difficult. Non-westerners are often able to speak several languages, making it easier for them to learn the language of another country. This allows them to be more proficient in communicating the gospel. Often they also have more experience with spiritual warfare and a stronger belief in miracles. This is particularly true because they do not separate the world into secular and spiritual. Everything is involved in the spiritual realm.

Other Models

The nations of Korea, Malaysia, the Philippines, and Singapore send missionaries to other countries, but have no national coordination of the missions efforts and little, if any, collaboration with other missions on the fields where their missionaries serve. All missionary activities are carried out by the local churches (Snider and Dorsing, personal communication, March 21 and 22, 2003). The same is true for the Assemblies of God churches in Brazil (Walz 2003).

Non-Governmental Organizations

OBJECTIVE
Outline the origin of non-governmental organizations.

5   What is the purpose of NGOs?

A non-governmental organization (NGO) is an organization that is not part of a government and is not founded by states. NGOs are, therefore, typically independent of governments. Although the definition can technically include for-profit corporations, the term is generally restricted to social, cultural, legal, and environmental advocacy groups having primarily noncommercial goals (Willetts 2002). These also include non-governmental organizations set up by missions societies.

The phrase *non-governmental organization* came into use with the establishment of the United Nations in 1945, with provisions in Article 71 of Chapter 10 of the United Nations Charter for a consultative role for organizations that neither are governments nor member states (www.un.org/wiki/Non-governmental_organization). One of the first NGOs to be organized was the International Committee of the Red Cross that began in 1863.

Globalization during the twentieth century was a motivating factor in the rise and importance of NGOs. Many of the problems, particularly in the Majority World, could not be solved by the national governments. While organizations, such as the World Trade Organization, seemed centered on the interests of capitalist enterprises, NGOs gave attention to humanitarian issues. An example of this is the World Social Forum that held its fifth meeting in Porto Alegre, Brazil, in January 2005. There were more than one thousand representatives of NGOs in attendance (Agence France Press 2005).

Korten has identified three stages in the development of NGOs. In the first stage, the NGO focuses on relief and welfare–direct deliveries of services, such as food and health assistance. The second stage has to do with small-scale, self-reliant local development wherein a community is aided in developing structures to become self-sufficient. In the third stage, an NGO attempts to make changes in policies and local institutions or on a national level (Korten 1990, 118).

In the past several years, the Religious Non-Governmental Organizations (RNGOs) have been on the rise. Among the largest are the Salvation Army, World Vision, and Catholic Relief Services. In 2001, they alone reported revenues of over 1.6 billion US dollars and claimed an outreach to over 150 million (Berger 2003, 1).

Convoy of Hope

Sponsored by the Assemblies of God, Convoy of Hope (COH) partners with RNGOs and defines its existence in the following manner: "Convoy of Hope, a 501(c) (3) nonprofit organization, serves in the United States and around the world providing disaster relief, building supply lines and sponsoring outreaches to the poor and hurting in communities. During a COH outreach, free groceries are distributed, job and health fairs are organized and activities for children are provided" (www.convoyofhope.org/who.html). While other RNGOs exist globally within national churches, Convoy of Hope is the largest RNGO operated by the Assemblies of God.

Happy Horizons Children's Ranch

Another RNGO is the Assemblies of God Happy Horizons Children's Ranch in the Philippines. This is a humanitarian ministry and a non-profit organization dedicated to the rehabilitation and defense of street children in the Philippines.

Happy Horizons monitors and cares for hundreds of street children, many of whom have been abandoned or orphaned by civil war, abused or rejected by dysfunctional and poverty-stricken families, and further traumatized by the indifference of the societies in which they live. Ubiquitous and growing in numbers, many far too young to comprehend their fate, they beg, steal, and sell themselves for a hot meal, a hot shower, a clean bed. Living on the edge of survival, they are often swept in an undertow of beatings, illegal detentions, torture, sexual abuse, rape, and murder. Happy Horizons is dedicated to helping these children get off the streets and back on the road to meaningful and productive lives. (www.hhcr.org)

Health Care Ministries

Health Care Ministries (HCM) is the medical arm of the Assemblies of God World Missions. HCM ministers to individuals through short-term medical evangelism teams, emergency medical response, missionary health, and health education and training. HCM makes following statement about its activities:

In order for us to continue the work of Christ, we must find creative ways of reaching nations and ministering to the world. At HealthCare Ministries, we believe in using medicine as a tool to reach people for Christ: a way to gain access to areas that would otherwise be closed, and reach people who would otherwise be unresponsive. Our goal is not merely to care for physical ailments, but we strive to go beyond the stethoscope, to minister to spiritual and emotional needs as well. Not only are we able to instill hope that heals in the people that we minister to, but through our compassionate touch God has opened doors and provided opportunities that may have been impossible otherwise. Our medical teams have been invited to countries that have been closed to traditional missionaries for decades, and through our willingness to listen to our patients we earn the right to be heard. (www.healthcareministries .org/about.htm)

Interdenominational Consultations

OBJECTIVE

Explain the purpose of the Lausanne conference of 1974.

The Lausanne Covenant

The first major interdenominational and evangelical world conference was held in Lausanne, Switzerland, in the summer of 1974. The conference was organized and planned by a committee chaired by evangelist Billy Graham and was a follow-up to the World Congress on Evangelism held in Berlin, Germany, in 1966. Over 2,300 evangelical Christian leaders gathered from 150 nations were present in the Palais de Beaulieu to discuss world evangelization. The theme of the conference was "Let the earth hear His voice." The conference produced the Lausanne Covenant, and the drafting committee for the covenant was headed by John Stott of England. The Lausanne Covenant is one of the most important documents in modern evangelical Christianity as it proclaimed a basic united doctrine, purpose, and mission for all evangelical churches and missions.

The Lausanne Covenant reaffirmed the primary doctrines of the evangelical community, including the uniqueness of Christ in salvation. On the nature of evangelism, the covenant stated the following:

> Evangelism itself is the proclamation of the historical, biblical Christ as Saviour and Lord, with a view to persuading people to come to him personally and so be reconciled to God. In issuing the gospel invitation we have no liberty to conceal the cost of discipleship. Jesus still calls all who would follow him to deny themselves, take up their cross, and identify themselves with his new community. The results of evangelism include obedience to Christ, incorporation into his Church and responsible service in the world. (Lausanne Covenant)

Article 5 opened a dialogue among the evangelical missions leaders as to the responsibility and calling of evangelism in the social and political areas of life.

> We affirm that God is both the Creator and the Judge of all men. We therefore should share his concern for justice and reconciliation throughout human society and for the liberation of men and women from every kind of oppression. Because men and women are made in the image of God, every person, regardless of race, religion, color, culture, class, sex or age, has an intrinsic dignity because of which he or she should be respected and served, not exploited. Here too we express penitence both for our neglect and for having sometimes regarded evangelism and social concern as mutually exclusive. Although reconciliation with other people is not reconciliation with God, nor is social action evangelism, nor is political liberation salvation, nevertheless we affirm that evangelism and socio-political involvement are both part of our Christian duty. For both are necessary expressions of our doctrines of God and man, our love for our neighbor and our obedience to Jesus Christ. The message of salvation implies also a message of judgment upon every form of alienation, oppression and discrimination, and we should not be afraid to denounce evil and injustice wherever they exist. When people receive Christ they are born again into his kingdom and must seek not only to exhibit but also to spread its righteousness in the midst of an unrighteous world. The salvation we claim should be transforming us in the totality of our personal and social responsibilities. Faith without works is dead. (Lausanne Covenant)

The covenant concluded with a call for united work in achieving the goals laid out in Lausanne.

> Therefore, in the light of this our faith and our resolve, we enter into a solemn covenant with God and with each other, to pray, to plan and to work together for

the evangelization of the whole world. We call upon others to join us. May God help us by his grace and for his glory to be faithful to this our covenant! Amen, Alleluia! (Lausanne Covenant)

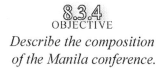

8.3.4
OBJECTIVE

Describe the composition of the Manila conference.

The Manila Conference

Numerous other conferences were held between 1974 and 1989. However, the conference in July 1989, in Manila, Philippines, was an important event. This gathering of 4,300 leaders was to examine how successful their networking had been over the previous years and to strategize taking the whole gospel to the whole world. The Manila conference was significant in that it would lead the evangelical world into the last decade of the twentieth century. It was called "Lausanne II." Those in attendance included the Soviet Union, Eastern Europe, and a larger number of women, lay persons, and younger leaders than at previous conferences. The conclusions of the conference were published in twenty-one affirmations in the Manila Manifesto.

At this conference, Bill O'Brien called for more concerted effort among evangelicals. He decried the division as he spoke on "Ecclesial Superiority":

The names of the actors have changed, but the first-century drama is still playing. Sadducees versus Pharisees are present in interchurch, intrachurch, and parachurch rivalries. From [the] bases of tradition, doctrine, or praxis, the competition has escalated until today [there] are more than twenty-two thousand denominations and twenty thousand parachurch entities in the world. . . . Modern Zadoks are exclaiming, "My church, my tradition, my movement." (Manila Conference 1989, 206)

Australian Robyn Claydon concluded his remarks to the conference with the following statement:

The task of taking the whole gospel to the whole world will only be effective if the whole church catches the vision of working with God and with each other, acknowledging each other and each other's ministries, encouraging each other, praying for each other, strengthening, and supporting each other, so that there will be an ever-growing, dynamic network of God's believing, praying, called, and commissioned witnesses covering the whole world. (Manila Conference 1989, 215)

These conferences have created an increasing awareness of the need for cooperative efforts in reaching the world for Christ. Over two-thirds of the leaders are now representing the Majority World—as Latin America, Africa, and Asia are experiencing phenomenal growth and rapidly increasing their presence in worldwide missions.

The Pentecostal World Fellowship

8.3.5
OBJECTIVE

Discuss the stated function and purpose of the Pentecostal World Fellowship.

6   What is the basic function of the Pentecostal World Fellowship?

To encourage cooperation among Pentecostals, the Pentecostal World Fellowship organized the Pentecostal World Conference, beginning with the conference held in Switzerland in 1947 and the last conference in Indonesia in 2007. Eighteen other conferences were held in intervening years.

This organization articulates its existence and function as follows:

The Pentecostal World Fellowship is a cooperative body of Pentecostal churches and groups worldwide of approved standing. It is not a legislative body to any national entity, but it is rather a coalition of commitment for the furtherance of the Gospel to the ends of the world and thus shall function as a service agent to:

- uphold one another in prayer.
- support and encourage one another in the task of missions and evangelism.
- promote Christian fellowship and cooperation among Pentecostal people throughout the world , primarily through the triennial Pentecostal World Conference.
- provide means of consultation and cooperation among the members and related agencies.
- share mutual concerns and insights relating to any crucial spiritual and temporal issues of the Church.
- administer relief in times of crises.
- promote exchange of personnel in special areas of ministry.
- disseminate helpful information and up-to-date statistics for the benefit of the Church.
- voice to the world and governments in defense of the faith, social justice, and persecuted believers, as the PWF. (Pentecostal World Fellowship 2009)

The PCCNA

Another organization of Pentecostal denominations is the Pentecostal/Charismatic Churches of North America (PCCNA). This is the successor of the Pentecostal Fellowship of North America (PFNA) that was formed in 1948 in Des Moines, Iowa. The charter members of this organization were the Assemblies of God, Church of God (Cleveland, Tennessee), Foursquare Gospel Church, Pentecostal Holiness Church, and the Open Bible Standard Churches.

The Pentecostal/Charismatic Churches of North America (PCCNA) was formed as part of a unification of charismatic and Pentecostal bodies and a movement toward racial reconciliation. Whereas the PFNA was formed to help bridge doctrinal divisions, the PCCNA set a broader goal of also reconciling the racial and cultural gaps. At a meeting in 1994 in Memphis, Tennessee, the Pentecostal Fellowship of North America was dissolved, and the Pentecostal/Charismatic Churches of North America was formed. PCCNA headquarters are in Los Angeles, California. Thirty-seven different churches joined this new body. (Pentecostal/Charismatic Churches of North American website).

On the website of the PCCNA the following statement is made about its purpose: The purpose of the Pentecostal/Charismatic Churches of North America is to provide a framework for fellowship, dialogue, and cooperation between the various Pentecostal and charismatic denominations, churches, and ministries in North America that agree with the purposes and goals of the organization. Since these churches and fellowships share a common history of Holy Spirit renewal and an overriding goal of evangelizing the world, they wish to join in a common witness to the outpouring of the Holy Spirit upon all flesh in the last days (www.pctii.org/pccna/mission.html).

Test Yourself

Circle the letter of the *best* answer.

1. The word *church* is used only twice in the Gospels, both times in
a) Mark.
b) Luke.
c) John.
d) Matthew.

2. The guiding principle in all church programs is
a) good administration.
b) pastoral delegation.
c) missions.
d) financial accountability.

3. The church serving as springboard for evangelizing the Roman Empire was
a) Jerusalem.
b) Antioch.
c) Philippi.
d) Corinth.

4. A model for supporting missionaries was the church in
a) Philippi.
b) Antioch.
c) Jerusalem.
d) Corinth.

5. In Argentina, the "personalization of missions" means
a) the missionaries travel to churches to raise their support.
b) the national church finances personal missionaries from its general budget.
c) the national church requests an offering for missions from each church, and this money is designated to particular missionaries.
d) it is the personal responsibility of the missionaries to raise their support.

6. One of the first NGOs to be organized was
a) CARE International.
b) the International Committee of the Red Cross.
c) World Vision.
d) the World Trade Organization.

7. The first major interdenominational world conference on evangelism was held in
a) Rome in 1972.
b) Lausanne in 1974.
c) Manila in 1989.
d) Amsterdam in 1982.

8. In the Lausanne Covenant, social concern and evangelism were
a) seen as mutually exclusive.
b) not both considered necessary expressions of doctrines.
c) both seen as our Christian duty.
d) not seen as equal Christian responsibility.

9. The conference called Lausanne II was held in
a) Amsterdam 1985.
b) Manila 1989.
c) Berlin 1982.
d) South Africa 2004.

10. The Pentecostal/Charismatic Churches of North America (PCCNA) set a broader goal of
a) bringing doctrinal unity among Pentecostal and Charismatic bodies.
b) bringing worship styles into conformity.
c) reconciling racial and cultural gaps.
d) bringing administrative unity to member bodies.

Responses to Interactive Questions
Chapter 8

Some of these responses may include information that is supplemental to the IST. These questions are intended to produce reflective thinking beyond the course content and your responses may vary from these examples.

1 How is the triumph of the Church assured?

Answer: After Peter confessed that Jesus is the "Son of God," Jesus said to him and the other disciples, "'You are Peter, on this rock I will build my church, and the gates of Hades will not overcome it'" (Matthew 16:18). This speaks of the final victory of the "assembled ones" in that the power of Hades will not overcome them.

2 Who is responsible for the Church's mission?

Answer: Every believer must have the vision of world evangelization.

3 What can a national church do to provide finances for missionaries?

Answer: It is important that the national missions office establish a plan for the appointment of missionaries, and this should include ways of screening candidates and raising their financial support from the different local churches in the nation.

4 How are the missionaries from Argentina supported?

Answer: The Argentina National Church requests an offering for missions from each church in the nation, and most of the money is designated to particular missionaries. In Argentina, they call this the "personalization of missions." This money is sent to the missionaries once each month and only ten percent is retained to cover office expenses.

5 What is the purpose of NGOs?

Answer: NGOs provide social, cultural, legal, and environmental aid to nations for noncommercial purposes.

6 What is the basic function of the Pentecostal World Fellowship?

Answer: To encourage cooperation, including missions partnerships, among participating Pentecostal groups

---

UNIT PROGRESS EVALUATION 3

Now that you have finished Unit 3, review the lessons in preparation for Unit Progress Evaluation 3. You will find it in Essential Course Materials at the back of this IST. Answer all of the questions without referring to your course materials, Bible, or notes. When you have completed the UPE, check your answers with the answer key provided in Essential Course Materials. Review any items you may have answered incorrectly. Then you may proceed with your study of Unit 4. (Although UPE scores do not count as part of your final course grade, they indicate how well you learned the material and how well you may perform on the closed-book final examination.)

Response to the Missions Mandate

The second Lausanne congress, known as Lausanne II, took place in 1989 in Manila, Philippines; the gathering revealed the great shift in missions as most delegates came from the Majority World. The many nations represented indicated the globalization of the missionary enterprise, and as we now move into the twenty-first century, new trends in missions continue to evolve. Among these trends is a renewed interest in compassion ministries by the many churches and mission agencies around the world. In this unit, the reader will examine the biblical foundations and practicality of this approach to missions individually and worldwide.

Current Trends in Missions

The world is constantly changing—everything from the physical features of the planet to the ways of the people living on it. To realize this, one needs only to look at the vast changes in transportation and communication that have accelerated since the industrial revolution. These changes have greatly influenced thought and behavior. In some sense, the world is becoming flatter, for cultures continue to be a mixture of languages, religious beliefs, and ways of life. In another sense, hope exists for equality, for similar opportunity for economic prosperity and mutual understanding. There is, at the same time, a desire to hold onto cultural boundary markers, philosophy, language, and religions.

To this world the Church and its missions outreach must relate. To illustrate the extent that change impacts missions strategy, the reader is directed to the following resources. David J. Bosch (1991) traces paradigm shifts in the theology of missions from the early church to the present, listing at least sixteen key trends. Stan Guthrie (2005) speaks of twenty-one key trends for the twenty-first century, and Pocock et al. (2005) deal with twelve. There is considerable overlap among them, but the point is clear: great change is on the modern scene, and missions strategies must adjust in order to continue to draw people to Christ.

While we will address a few of the current trends, the reader is urged to continue to examine these and other trends as the world marches toward the great event, the return of Christ.

Lesson 9.1   Shift to the Majority World and Globalized Missions

Objectives
9.1.1   Describe the shift of Christendom's center over the past century and its impact on western missions.
9.1.2   Describe the missions efforts of Majority World Protestant churches.

Lesson 9.2   From Long-Term to Short-Term Missions

Objectives
9.2.1   Indicate factors that have contributed to the rapid increase in short-term missions in recent years.
9.2.2   Discuss the potential benefits and pitfalls of short-term mission efforts.

Lesson 9.3   Toward Entrepreneurship in Missions

Objective
9.3.1   Describe the difference between missions by process and missions by project.

Lesson 9.4   Technology in Missions

Objective
9.4.1   Discuss advantages and disadvantages to the missionary task of increased connectivity through technology.

Lesson 9.5   Theological Drift

Objectives
9.5.1   Explain why theological drift exists in today's Church.
9.5.2   Describe the current shift in presenting the gospel to postmodernists.

9.1.1
OBJECTIVE
Describe the shift of Christendom's center over the past century and its impact on western missions.

Shift to the Majority World and Globalized Missions

At the start of the twentieth century, Christendom was largely centered in the West, that is, in Europe and North America. Colonialism was still strong and the cry of churches was for the evangelization of the rest of the world. The two world wars changed the landscape considerably as these wars began and were fought largely among so-called Christian nations. Europeans, especially, were disillusioned. They had had enough of war over the centuries, often due to competing "Christian" factions. Materialism, therefore, became the rule of the day for them.

Yet Jesus declared He would build His Church, and the gates of hell would not overcome it (Matthew 16:18). The evangelical churches reacted to the two world wars in a different manner. If peace were to come to the world, it would only be by the Prince of Peace. The world needed Christ as never before, so a great missionary movement was spawned, especially to the so-called Third World (now referred to as the Majority World) of Africa, South America, and Asia. If missionaries were no longer welcome in the Soviet Union and China, they would deploy to places where they could take the gospel.

The growth of the Church in these areas is astounding. Guthrie reports that in 1960 an estimated fifty-eight percent of the world's Christians were westerners, but in 1990 just thirty-eight percent. Latin American evangelicals had grown from perhaps 300,000 in 1900 to over 55 million in 2004! [The majority are Pentecostals]. Across the world, from 1960 to 1990 the number of evangelicals jumped from 57.7 million to 95.9 million in the West, but from 29 million to over 208 million outside the West (Guthrie 2000, 159, 160). These data indicate that the center of Christendom has shifted from the West and North to the Majority World and the southern hemisphere.

The rate of growth of these churches is striking. While the world's population is growing by approximately 1.6 percent per year, Protestants are growing by 2.9 percent overall. But within those figures is a 5.9 percent growth among evangelicals and an astounding 7.3 percent growth rate among Pentecostals and Charismatics. At that rate, the Pentecostals and Charismatics will double every ten years (US Center for World Missions 2006).

1   What attitudes and practices of western missions hindered the maturing of the Majority World churches?

This being the case, First World Christians of the West are not, so to speak, in the driver's seat. Leaders of evangelical churches of the Majority World have proven themselves fully capable of leadership. No matter of what language, culture, or physical appearance, they are often more aggressively evangelistic, more enthusiastic, and more willing to put their lives on the line for Christ than their First World counterparts. Perhaps the most important role for western missionaries is to help them avoid the mistakes of past generations and to provide theological education as needed. Nevertheless, the key word today is *partnership*, not *oversight*. Above all, we must not squelch their enthusiasm and growth by insisting on inappropriate western trappings.

The natural outgrowth of a healthy, emerging church should be the impetus to take the gospel to the rest of the world. However, this is not always so if congregations focus inward and become receivers rather than givers. Unfortunately, many missions took a paternalistic attitude toward the churches they helped establish, maintaining the new church's dependency on the mission instead of encouraging them to become self-sufficient and reach out in their own missions efforts. Theological education often fell short of teaching world missions. After all, world missions was the responsibility of the western missionaries, those specifically trained for the task, wasn't it? Surely these emerging churches were not ready.

Fortunately, that mentality began to break. The Majority World Protestant churches—mostly evangelical and primarily Pentecostal—were growing and maturing. Missions conferences such the 1974 International Conference on World Evangelization in Lausanne, Switzerland, drew representatives from around the world. A major impact was the impassioned plea of Ralph Winter to concentrate efforts on evangelizing the more than sixteen thousand unreached people groups of the world (Johnstone 1998, 103). That and many subsequent missions conferences hammered home the need for all of evangelical Christianity—West and non-West alike—to spread the gospel everywhere, not just in their backyards.

9.1.2
OBJECTIVE
Describe the missions efforts of Majority World Protestant churches.

2   What are some examples of Majority World churches that are sending missionaries?

To the surprise and, at first, somewhat dubious acceptance of western missions, the Majority World churches began to spread the gospel. Whether outside their country or to other ethnic groups within, the churches began, in earnest, to send missionaries to spread the Good News. Today, that movement has spawned mission partnerships, whereby missionaries from various countries, who hold to similar theological positions, band together to reach the lost. Several examples follow.

The Korean Pentecostal churches have many missionaries among Korean populations in other parts of the world. The Argentine Assemblies have sent out many missionaries, especially to Africa, southern Europe, and the Middle East, often working in conjunction with missionaries of the Assemblies of God World Missions, USA. In French West Africa, American, French, Burkina Faso, and Brazilian missionaries can be found working together. And the Brazilian Assemblies of God has engaged in aggressive missionary efforts in many other countries.

A growing phenomenon is the sending of missionaries from other countries to the United States to evangelize and nurture believers of the missionaries' language and culture in America. This is missions in reverse.

Reuben Ezemadu of Nigeria, at the Celebrate Messiah 2000 conference, spoke of the role of the African Church in world missions. He shared the following statistics:

In the year 2000, Protestant missionaries from Africa, Asia, and Latin America numbered about 170,000, accounting for over seventy percent of the total world Protestant missionaries.

India had over 100 mission agencies with about 12,000 missionaries.

The Philippines had an estimated 2,000 missionaries abroad.

Some 700 missionaries had been sent by Chinese churches outside Mainland China, most from Singapore and Hong Kong.

In 1996, South Korea had sent 4,402 missionaries to Asia, Eastern Europe, Western Europe, Latin America, Africa, Middle East, and Oceania.

Many missionaries were sent from Brazilian Protestant churches to unreached people groups, particularly Africa, the Middle East, and southern Europe.

The Nigeria Evangelical Missions Association had over 50 mission agencies with a total of more than 3,000 missionaries.

Ezemadu (2000) noted that many western mission agencies are recruiting workers from churches that once were the object of their own outreaches. These agencies are attracted by the church's spirituality and shift of wealth from the West to the East. "The numerical strength, the cross-cultural experience gained from its pluralistic contexts, the resilience developed from its sufferings and limited resources, and the resultant trust in God, the preponderance of unreached people groups, all made the Majority Church a vehicle that has advanced greatly the cause of the kingdom of Christ" (www.ad2000.org/celebrate/ezemandu.htm).

3 Explain some of the problems faced by Majority World missionaries.

With all the greatness of this phenomenon—and it is to be welcomed and applauded—it is not without its problems. Justin Long reported:

> Stories [were told] of missionaries returning home, unable to raise their support or to be able to accomplish anything, problems with financial accountability; difficulties in leadership training; barriers in cross-cultural sensitivity; and the overwhelming shadow of persecution, which is much harder on Third-World missionaries than on westerners.

> The problems boil down to these three issues: (1) How can the global body of Christ best help Third-World missions sustain what they have already started? (2) How can we help them to become more effective in what they are presently doing? (3) How can we help them to expand to do new things? (www.gordonconwell.edu/ockenga/gobalchristianity/mmrc/mmrc9642.htm)

Nonetheless, this is a welcome and growing feature of missions today. The key to success is partnership, the joining of evangelical Christians of all nations to take the gospel to all peoples. Where a white face and western passport is a problem, missionaries from Majority churches may find entrance. To be effective, they need help to avoid the same mistakes western missions have made. Effective training of missionaries is part of the answer. Continue on this venture we must. As an earlier vision statement of this university declared, the gospel should to out "from all nations to all nations." May it be so.

9.2.1
OBJECTIVE

Indicate factors that have contributed to the rapid increase in short-term missions in recent years.

From Long-Term to Short-Term Missions

The western mission world has seen an explosion of short-term missions [STM] over the past forty years or so. Scenes from *National Geographic* magazines, stories and pictures from returning missionaries, and the striking vistas on television of exotic lands drew the attention of evangelical Christians. Seeing the plight of the many poor and deprived abroad stirred within them the desire to do something about it themselves, not just put money in the offering plate. The relative ease, speed, and low cost of travel made it plausible, and an American passport with a tourist visa made it possible.

In America, part of the impetus behind this movement has stemmed from the generations born after World War II and the resulting changes in culture. Now, people are less likely to support any venture, whether financially or personally, without firsthand experience of it. Many were most interested in projects with tangible results at the end (Guthrie 2005, 106). Undoubtedly shaped by a culture focusing on instant results, they could avoid the painstaking efforts to learn a language, a culture, and religious bent of the people.

Mission agencies themselves saw this as a good opportunity. If more people visited the fields and saw the need firsthand, surely they would be inspired to give financial and prayer support. Some would determine to become missionaries themselves. Practical help, from bookkeeping to building, would be most welcome. In the contemporary world of missions, specialists in many fields could provide much-needed help. National churches appreciated the assistance, if done properly, and especially the financial aid it brought.

Everything from two weeks to two-year assignments became generally welcomed and encouraged. In a fascinating series in *Christianity Today*, Abram Huyser Honig (2005) observes, "Short-term missions trips to foreign countries are the biggest trend to hit the evangelical Christian outreach scene since vacation Bible school. Between

1 million to 4 million North American Christians reportedly participated in STMs in 2003, and the number keeps rising."

The series captured an interchange between Kurt Ver Beek of Calvin College and Robert Priest of Trinity Evangelical Divinity School on the value of these STMs. Their discussion focused on STMs lasting only two weeks or so, with the results being somewhat predictable. In spite of proper orientation and debriefing, most of these STMs had little effect on the participants. STMs are supposed to result in participants who are changed forever—give more to missions, pray more for missions, and the like. In fact, for those studied over the long term, this did not happen. Good intentions got swallowed up in the face of daily routines back at home.

Are we then to abandon the practice? Not likely; the movement is here to stay for at least awhile. The issue, rather, is how to make it more effective. Priest observes:

> STM provides a fertile setting for Christians to reflect on such things as witness, service, community, sacrifice, spirituality, poverty, materialism, suffering, hedonism, self-denial, justice, racism, ethnocentrism, inter-ethnic relations, globalization, stewardship, and vocation. The context is valuable, even if STM leaders do not foster these reflections among participants. (Honig 2005)

Those are factors that should impact the individuals involved. But what about the groups? Ver Beek and Priest speak of the factors of bonding and bridging. Bonding builds relationships among members of the group, whereas bridging builds relationships across cultural divides, for example, between STM participants and their hosts. There can be no doubt that such trips create bonding among the participants. Just as important is the question of whether the trip created bonding among the host nationals, resulting in their wanting to maintain close relationships among themselves.

Whether bridging occurs depends on the extent of the contact between the groups—such as working side by side over a lengthy period—and the ability to create meaningful dialogue. Most likely, bridging will be short-term. The STM team will leave with great expectations of maintaining contact, but their initial enthusiasm will be swallowed up by life.

Many STMs do have positive results. Some short-term participants do become more dedicated to prayer, giving, personal involvement in the cause of missions, or even become missionaries themselves. Congregations come alive to the missions potential of their church and the need to support the missions enterprise. Unfortunately, the belief that increased STMs will result in more career missionaries has not been verified by the data. While STMs have increased dramatically, the number of career missionaries has stayed about the same (Guthrie 2005, 110).

STM is to be applauded. However, if it detracts from the support of long-term missions efforts and career missionaries, it is to be questioned. There is no substitute for living within a culture over time, learning the language and the culture itself, and building lasting relationships that will serve to build the indigenous church. Neither should the frequency of such trips to given fields change the role of established missionaries into tour guides and STM team "go-fers."

Certain questions need to be raised when considering short-term efforts, whether by a group or by individuals. Who pays the bill? Is this the best stewardship of resources in time and money, considering all factors? Will there be adequate pre-trip orientation and post-trip debriefing in a way that leads to real growth in understanding and commitment? Do field missionaries and/or host churches really want such a visit, or are they simply accommodating the visit with an eye on the financial fall-out? Is there adequate pre-trip coordination with the field personnel so as to maximize effectiveness and efficiency? Is this trip really about missions or an excuse for exotic travel at the expense of others?

In 2003, the Fellowship of Short-Term Mission Leaders issued their "US Standards of Excellence in Short-Term Missions." These include: (1) God-centered Kingdom growth; (2) partnership; (3) mutual design; (4) reliable set-up and administration; (5) qualified leadership; (6) training and equipping; and (7) debriefing and follow-up (Guthrie 2005, 113).

4 Discuss key factors in lasting results for short-term missionaries.

Short term mission ventures are here to stay as far as North American evangelical churches are concerned. The likelihood of long-term benefit will be directly linked to the length of stay in the host context. Building relationships is key, and that cannot be done in a day or a month.

The issue is one of balance. Positive results can and do happen from STMs done right. But if STMs are seen as the wave of the missions future, a substitute for long-term involvement, the real work of missions will be shortchanged. Ralph Winter (1996) probes this issue:

> Where are we? One mission leader told me, "There is a great tide of missionary interest and giving, but it is geared to a wide variety of vested interests without a unifying focus. 'Missions,' it seems, has become any Christian volunteering to be sent anywhere in the world at any expense to do anything for any time period." Is this the re-amateurization [of mission]?

Missions pastor, Tom Steller, takes a different view:

> This is thrilling to me. I think it is a stimulation to missions. I don't think it is robbing mission dollars from long-term missionaries but rather widening the pool of informed mission supporters, both the returning short-termers as well as the support networks they have tapped into. (Guthrie 2005, 111)

9.3.1
OBJECTIVE
Describe the difference between missions by process and missions by project.

5 Why is missions by project attractive to some?

Toward Entrepreneurship in Missions

Partly an offshoot of the STM experience, churches are increasingly "sending out their own people, bypassing the traditional agencies in the name of better efficiency and stewardship. . . . These churches and groups are sending more and more short-termers, while the long-term force continues to decline" (Guthrie 2005, 107).

Citing what they see as the high cost and ossified thinking of traditional mission agencies, a sizable block of churches, sometimes called "megachurches" for their size and clout, have decided to go it alone. . . .Of course they risk making the same mistakes and relearning the same lessons the agencies have done over the decades—worst of all, needlessly. (Guthrie 2005, 4)

What has happened is an increasing divide between mission mobilizers and strategists. Guthrie (2005) observes two major streams of action: missions as process and missions by project. Missions as process is the perspective of traditional missions efforts for long-term strategies to fulfill the Great Commission everywhere in the world. Missions by project focuses on the unreached people groups (Guthrie 2005, 107). Missions by project may also be focused on other specific targets for short-term high-impact involvement. Here, participants have a sense of immediate gratification for a job well done.

North Americans, today, live in a "high tech/high touch" world of instant gratification. This is infused with confidence that as Americans, with American money and know-how, they can solve the world's problems. They desire personal involvement and efficiency; they like to get things done and showcase the results. After all, this stimulates more enthusiasm, greater involvement, and dedication to do even more.

This is not altogether bad, for legitimate projects can be completed and the participants can be gratified by their efforts. However, there can also be a certain naïveté and assumption that appearances equal reality. For example, the assumption that if people wear American-style clothes and play contemporary American music, they think like Americans. Perhaps even worse is the assumption that the folks over there just cannot do it without us, and they really desire our help.

Missions by project can lose sight of the long-term benefits of missions as process. When that happens, the church begins to refocus its mission funds on self-directed efforts on the mission field, bypassing the mission agency, and removing support from long-term missionaries. Such mind-sets fail to see that long-term effectiveness is achieved through those missionaries who learn the language and culture and build positive relationships with their hosts.

Proverbs 15:22 advises, "Without consultation, plans are frustrated, but with many counselors they succeed" (NASV). Hence, missions by project are most effective when done in close collaboration with the long-term missionaries and leadership of the national churches. Key questions include whether the project will help draw people to Christ, establish local congregations, and/or contribute to the cause of the Kingdom in ways that make economic and strategic sense. Will it build dependency on the sending church or foster indigenous church principles? Projects have been undertaken by well-meaning entrepreneurial churches that inadvertently helped dissident elements of a national church bent on personal ambition. Others started projects the national church could neither complete nor maintain without continued outside help.

To minimize these occurrences, missions must be embraced as both process and project; it is not an either/or issue. Both are to be desired when done in concert and partnership with the national church where one exists.

OBJECTIVE

Discuss advantages and disadvantages to the missionary task of increased connectivity through technology.

Technology in Missions

The Neo-Electronic Age

The world of the twenty-first century indeed is amazing. It is a world of continual technological change as the speed and frequency with which new technology appears on the scene is almost breathtaking. By the time this lesson is published, the technology currently in vogue may be out of date or out of use.

Nevertheless, the advent of electronic media has brought with it new opportunities for education and training. The Internet is especially attractive, for it allows ready access to research and study at whatever time is available to the student. While most prevalent in the First World countries, the Internet is sweeping the globe. Even some of the most remote places in underdeveloped countries boast Internet cafés.

The purpose of this lesson is not to discuss any particular products with a view for developing a strategy around them. Rather, the intent is to urge creativity in exploring how such technologies may be employed in the cause of missions. Further, we must consider the impact of technology on daily living and ministry in this century.

Pocock, Van Rheenen, and McConnell (2005) list seven issues that arise from the technological trend:

1. Enhanced connectivity
2. Escalation of the pace of life
3. High tech/high touch
4. E-learning
5. Digital divide
6. Digital deflation
7. Security issues

Pocock and others (2005) point out that technology is not just a neutral tool for improving methodology, but one that can be used to solve or minimize problems (301–318).

Enhanced Connectivity

6   What does increased connectivity mean to the missionary?

The last fifty years have seen the development of the Internet, cell phones, e-mail, instant messaging, satellite television, low-cost telephone rates, low-cost radio transceivers, DVDs, hand-held miniature telephone-computer combinations, and many more cutting edge trends in technology. Wireless telephone transmission across the globe is possible via satellite transmission. Global positioning systems can communicate where you are, direct you to where you want to go, and even tell others where you are.

Such connectivity has revolutionized interactions between the home base and the missionary. The ability to receive instant feedback on any issue, to allow real-time strategic decision-making, to provide immediate assistance in times of emergency, and much more profoundly affects how missions business is accomplished. The gospel can be made available almost anywhere electronically. Digital images can be simply and inexpensively employed to reach pre-literate, visually-oriented societies. High-tech societies can receive the gospel in streaming video on their hand-held devices. Missionaries also can readily communicate with their families and home churches while yet on the field. The ability to transmit funds electronically via automated teller machines (ATMs) is an added benefit. This is not only a quick means of accessing funds, but does away with the need to carry large amounts of cash or traveler's checks.

But what is an advantage can become a drawback. The convenience of connectivity with home can lead to avoidance of connecting with the local culture and its people. Missionaries can become fascinated with the latest in technology and forget the purpose of the mission itself.

Another concern is the sharing of personal information. Not only is there potential for revealing embarrassing personal data, but also what is transmitted can be used as incriminating evidence in restrictive countries. Nonetheless, the advantages of connectivity far outweigh the disadvantages. After all, connectivity is part of the promise of the gospel.

Escalation of the Pace of Life

A price must sometimes be paid for the advantages of technology. One price is the focus on speed—the need to get every task, every decision, and every response completed quickly. Quality is now measured by both content and speed. Not only in North America, but increasingly in the entire world, the importance of prayer, meditation, and rest is being lost in the name of productivity and efficiency. The question must be asked whether, in the interest of high-speed information acquisition and exchange, interpersonal relationships are minimized. This leads us to the next issue to be addressed.

High Tech/High Touch

The phrase *high tech/high touch* highlights the problem attending the focus on technological solutions. These so-called solutions do not exist in isolation. They create a greater need for face-to-face interaction or at least real-time voice-to-voice. One illustration of this is the frustration felt when instead of getting a person on the phone, one gets an answering machine. Part of the reaction to this need for personal relationship is the increase of chat rooms and virtual "pen pals" on the Internet, a somewhat superficial attempt to bridge the gap.

On the other hand, this same technology allows immediate and more frequent interaction for those with whom an interpersonal relationship is already established. For example, missionaries can be in contact with families, friends, supporters, and mission leadership with relative ease and frequency.

E-Learning

One of the great advantages of electronic technology is the ability to deliver education without space-time requirements. Two key words summarize the demands of much of the world today: *access* and *asynchronous*. Increasingly, people want their desire for something met wherever they are and whenever they want it. Thus the plethora of automatic teller machines (ATMs) and 24-hour stores of all kinds. Such convenience is also true of the delivery of education. As access to the Internet continues to expand around the globe—even among the most impoverished—the distribution of high quality education worldwide is becoming a possibility.

Modifications to accommodate cultural and language differences are relatively easy. Moreover, digital images, video clips, and even gaming can be incorporated to enhance the learning experience. Virtual cohort groups can be established even if the participants are thousands of miles apart. If not delivered in real time, the same lesson can be reviewed as often as needed to master the subject. Video conferencing can be incorporated if real-time virtual face-to-face interaction is preferred. Access to extensive information resources via the Internet is an extremely valuable aspect to e-learning, and such virtual libraries are growing by leaps and bounds.

Another advantage to e-learning is the ability to deliver education and training at a relatively low cost on a per-student basis. No campuses are required, nor are lecture halls or lecturing professors needed once the course is developed. The initial cost of development is expensive, but can be distributed over thousands of students. Nonetheless, e-learning at present is as much an art as a science, and there is much to be learned about using it effectively.

Digital Divide

Like the distribution of wealth, haves and have-nots exist in the world of technology. While direct cost to the user is a factor, of greater concern is the ability and cost to government and industry to provide the infrastructure necessary for speed and quality of transmission. A key issue is the need for broadband width sufficient to distribute video and other digital images.

Because of the relative ease of transmission at low cost—only a tower is required, no land lines—cell phones are appearing everywhere on the globe. Text-messaging already is a reality. Similar economies may eventually be achieved through direct broadcast via satellite and the appearance of interactive television where speed and bandwidth already exist.

Still, dependence upon global electronic communication of high quality must be categorized as a hope that awaits future fulfillment. A multi-pronged strategy must still hold sway.

Digital Deflation

Digital deflation refers to the continued development of technology—in reality, not just digital—that allows products of greater value to cost less. One example is the development of micro-miniaturization that allows devices of great capacity to be built cheaply into many applications. Think of telephone answering devices that use only a crystal with no moving parts, or of wireless technologies that eliminate the use of expensive landline support infrastructures. Computers of high speed and high capacity are a fraction of the price of a few years ago. Such developments, at relatively low cost, bode well for missions use around the world.

Security Issues

One drawback of increased use of advanced communication devices, such as the Internet and wireless transmission, is the loss of personal anonymity. What is "out there" can be seen, read, or heard by others. Today, most societies police electronic communications. This may be done to protect the citizenry from problems, such as identity theft or those who prey on the unwary. But for missionaries in countries with restricted access, real danger exists. Any material that can be found on the Web or captured from cell phone conversations can be used against them.

The result is the on-going development of security measures, such as encryption software and compression techniques. Still it is an ongoing race between those seeking to protect the user and those seeking ways to hack into the system. Perhaps the best attitude in high-risk situations is to assume what is communicated is most likely to be found out.

The Benefits of New Technologies

Apart from the issues just reviewed, these new technologies are revolutionizing the way mission ventures are accomplished. Look at the impact on the military, not only in military hardware, but also in strategy and battle management. The United States military strategy during the Gulf War was directed from the command center in Tampa, Florida, thousands of miles away from the military action. Today, church planting strategies can be guided by experienced missionaries far away. Databases of various kinds can be used as resources.

The Internet offers great possibilities for delivering evangelism and training materials. Online digital libraries serve as virtual libraries, saving considerable cost and effort to build library facilities for hard-copy texts and periodicals. Done properly, without anti-government rhetoric, the Internet provides great promise for sharing the Word, even in countries with restricted access.

Highly interactive training materials that include both text and video segments can be distributed inexpensively through DVD and other technologies. Today, the promise that all the world will hear the gospel (Matthew 24:14) is more possible than ever.

9.5.1
OBJECTIVE

*Explain why theological
drift exists
in today's Church.*

Theological Drift

Through the ages, the theological stance of the church has been influenced by its cultural and historical contexts. This also is true today. As Christians in the West have experienced an influx of non-Christian populations into their cities and workplaces, they have found it increasingly difficult to maintain the exclusivity of the gospel as being the only road to heaven. Postmodernism has produced a shift away from focus on the escape from hell to a focus on the glory of God. Pentecostals, observing the success stories of other evangelicals, have tended to de-emphasize the need for the baptism in the Holy Spirit. However, in an uncertain world that appears to be in chaos, there is the desperate need for a theology firmly rooted in the unchanging Word of God.

Those Who Do Not Believe

The biblical perspective of a Christ-less hell of real torment and punishment is abhorrent to many who find it difficult to picture their unsaved neighbors in such a state. Our natural tendency is to seek some other way to heaven, some other status before God. Some theologians solve the problem by declaring a wider hope for the lost, that somehow God will accept their good works or good efforts through other religions to open the door to heaven. Others take the view that unbelievers will not suffer the torments of hell, but will be annihilated at death. Guthrie (2005), however, muses, "Perhaps we find it difficult to believe in hell because we find it difficult to believe in our own sin" (47).

If we hold fast to the Word and its record of Christ's teaching, then we must carefully examine what it has to say. We cannot base our actions on personal preferences. Even a cursory review of the Scriptures leads us to conclude that no matter what we may wish, the Word makes it clear there is no other way to be made right with God (John 3:16–18; 14:6; Acts 4:12; Romans 10:12–15).

For Christian missions, an important question must be answered. If those who have never heard the gospel will be saved because they did not hear, why share the gospel with them? To do so would open the possibility of their rejecting the gospel and thereby losing their "free ticket" to heaven! But the Bible makes it clear no one is excused from judgment apart from faith in Jesus (Romans 1:18–32). The reality of hell is addressed throughout Scripture (see Matthew 3:7–12; 8:12–18; 10:28; 18:8–9; 25:41–46, Mark 9:40–48; Luke 16:19–31; Romans 2:5–12; 2 Thessalonians 1:6–9; Jude 5–12; Revelation 14:9–11; 20:10, 15).

Therefore, to seek Christ and urge others to seek Him to avoid the realities of hell is critical. We must never cease taking the gospel to all peoples that they might turn from the hell they face to the God of grace and mercy.

The Glory of God

9.5.2
OBJECTIVE

*Describe the current shift
in presenting the gospel to
postmodernists.*

At the beginning of this course, we emphasized the importance of the worship of God as a primary motivation for missions. This emphasis is at least partly due to the cultural shift in the West from modernism to postmodernism. Modernism saw scientific advances as leading to a future utopia, basing their confidence on scientific "facts." That has given way to postmodernism with its distrust of science as a final answer and an increasing focus on self as the determiner of truth. "Your truth is yours, and mine is mine, and they may well not be the same."

7   How do postmodernists
view truth?

Postmodernists believe Christian teaching is but one of many options. If the Church is to demonstrate the validity of its message, it must speak to this generation in ways that demonstrate the benefits to be derived from following in this way as opposed to others. This leads to focusing not on what is to be avoided (i.e., hell) but what is to be gained. The idea of being "lost" is redefined, not to mean destined for a Christless eternity, but rather as lacking a relationship with a loving and gracious Father, who desires that all experience the glory of His presence in heaven forever (Pocock et al. 2005, 161–181).

At first glance, this approach seems a weakening of the clear teaching of Scripture. However, it must be remembered that a major emphasis of the early church was upon the glory of God and His gracious blessings awaiting those who believe and place trust in Him (see 2 Corinthians 3:1–4:18; 1 John 1:1–4).

However one defines *lost*, the reality is that apart from a true commitment to Christ, there awaits eternal separation from Him and His blessings. There is no other way except the way of the Cross and the One who paid for the sins of all humankind. We are once again reminded of our obligation to tell the unbelieving world of this glorious gospel:

> "Anyone who trusts in him will never be put to shame." For there is no difference between Jew and Gentile—the same Lord is Lord of all and richly blesses all who call on him, for, "Everyone who calls on the name of the Lord will be saved." How, then, can they call on the one they have not believed in? And how can they believe in the one of whom they have not heard? And how can they hear without someone preaching to them? And how can they preach unless they are sent? (Romans 10:11–15)

Baptism in the Holy Spirit

8 Explain the importance to missions of the baptism in the Holy Spirit.

In some Pentecostal circles there seems to be a muting of the Pentecostal message and practice. What once was an unwavering belief in the need for the baptism in the Holy Spirit is no longer thought necessary or even important. There are several reasons for this. The Charismatic movement introduced alternative interpretations of Holy Spirit baptism. Many pastors and evangelists seem to have powerful and influential ministries without claiming such an enduement; some speak forcefully against it. This brings a measure of confusion and perplexity to those in the Pentecostal camp.

The answer must be a renewal of clear teaching from Scripture on the importance of Holy Spirit baptism. Space does not permit that here. Yet it must be remembered that Jesus emphasized the importance of the Holy Spirit in His followers' lives (see John 14–16). After His resurrection, He told His followers, on at least two occasions, to wait to receive power that would make them witnesses of Him (Luke 24:49; Acts 1:8). Acts records how the 120, filled with the Holy Spirit, became powerful witnesses in both word and deed, and supernatural gifts and miracles were common among them.

In most of the Majority World, Pentecostal churches are growing rapidly. Miraculous signs and wonders still accompany the gospel, to the glory of God. Jesus' instruction still rings true. We are to seek the empowering of the Holy Spirit, and when that happens, we will witness.

Test Yourself

Circle the letter of the *best* answer.

1. When the twentieth century began, Christians were primarily in
a) Latin America.
b) Asia.
c) Africa.
d) the West.

2. In the early part of the twentieth century, many evangelical and Protestant missions
a) were known for establishing indigenous churches on the foreign field.
b) held a paternalistic attitude toward the churches they established.
c) emphasized the teaching of world missions in the churches they established.
d) encouraged independence of the churches on the mission field.

3. The greatest problem Majority World missionaries have is
a) resilience.
b) language skills.
c) cross-cultural experience.
d) difficulty in leadership training.

4. Short-term missionaries who spent about two weeks on the mission field
a) showed that they were not greatly affected by their experience.
b) generally gave more to missions upon their return home.
c) generally prayed more for missions upon their return home.
d) were changed forever in their attitude toward missions.

5. Missions by project
a) has the perspective of traditional missions efforts for long-term strategies.
b) tends to have participants with a sense of immediate gratification for a job well done.
c) is often rather impersonal.
d) is usually not focused on a particular project.

6. Missions by project is most effective when
a) the funds are adequate to complete the project.
b) a skilled team is recruited for the project.
c) done in close collaboration with career missionaries and national leaders.
d) a church is able to be self-directed.

7. A disadvantage of modern technology is
a) missionaries may avoid connecting with local culture.
b) producing an electronic gospel.
c) that digital images are expensive.
d) that it is not globally accessible.

8. One drawback of increased use of advanced communication devices is
a) an increase in personal anonymity.
b) more personal freedom.
c) it is virtually impossible for one's conversations to be policed.
d) the compromising of one's personal data.

9. Pentecostals observing the success of other evangelicals tend to de-emphasize the need for
a) salvation.
b) church membership.
c) evangelism.
d) the baptism in the Holy Spirit.

10. Postmodernism
a) trusts science.
b) saw scientific advances as leading to a future utopia.
c) provides a firm foundation of belief based upon scientific "facts."
d) has an increasing focus on self as the determiner of truth.

Responses to Interactive Questions
Chapter 9

Some of these responses may include information that is supplemental to the IST. These questions are intended to produce reflective thinking beyond the course content and your responses may vary from these examples.

1 What attitudes and practices of western missions hindered the maturing of the Majority World churches?

Answer: 1) many missions took a paternalistic attitude toward the churches they helped establish, maintaining the new church's dependency on the mission instead of encouraging them to become self-sufficient and reach out in their own missions efforts. 2) Theological education often fell short of teaching world missions.

2 What are some examples of Majority World churches that are sending missionaries?

Answer: The Korean Pentecostal churches have many missionaries among Korean populations in other parts of the world. The Argentine Assemblies have sent out many missionaries, especially to Africa, southern Europe, and the Middle East, often working in conjunction with missionaries of the Assemblies of God World Missions, USA. In French West Africa, American, French, Burkina Faso, and Brazilian missionaries can be found working together. The Brazilian Assemblies of God has engaged in aggressive efforts in many other countries.

3 Explain some of the problems faced by Majority World missionaries.

Answer: Return of missionaries who are unable to raise their support; problems with financial accountability; difficulties in leadership training; barriers in cross-cultural sensitivity; and the overwhelming shadow of persecution

4 Discuss key factors in lasting results for short-term missionaries.

Answer: Short term mission ventures are here to stay, but the likelihood of long-term benefit is directly linked to the length of stay in the host context. Building relationships is critical, and that cannot be done in a day or a month.

5 Why is missions by project attractive to some?

Answer: Participants have a sense of immediate gratification for a job well done. After all, this stimulates more enthusiasm, greater involvement, and dedication to do even more.

6 What does increased connectivity mean to the missionary?

Answer: Such connectivity has revolutionized interactions between the home base and the missionary. The ability to get almost instant feedback on any issue, to allow real-time strategic decision-making, to provide immediate assistance in times of emergency, and much more has a profound effect on how missions business is accomplished.

7 How do postmodernists view truth?

Answer: Postmodernists see truth as relative; self is the determiner of truth.

8 Explain the importance to missions of the baptism in the Holy Spirit.

Answer: After the believers were filled with the Holy Spirit, they became powerful witnesses in word and deed, and supernatural gifts and miracles were common among them.

Holistic Missions in the Socio-Political Context

For years, the Assemblies of God hesitated to emphasize any type of social action as a major part of its strategy. Like most evangelical agencies it was an overreaction to a growing tendency of mainline churches to move away from evangelism and focus on meeting physical and social needs. In part, their reaction was a fear that donor support would diminish. Even so, a good bit of ministry to the suffering was quietly carried on. In recent years, however, the church as a whole has recognized that ministry to the hurting not only meets real needs but is a demonstration of God's love that can open the door for effective witness.

At no time in history has the Church received more pressure to respond to both physical and spiritual needs. War and social upheaval have increased, leaving millions of people poverty-stricken or in refugee camps. Millions of people in the Third World are affected by HIV/AIDS and are dying, and millions of children are orphans. Thus, the church must reexamine its role in these crises. One of the hindrances to meeting these needs has been a modern dualism that separates body from spirit, science from religion, and natural from supernatural. This division means some see evangelism through preaching alone while leaving ministries to earthly human needs to secular agencies.

Lesson 10.1   A Balanced Perspective

Objective
10.1.1 Articulate the need for both proclamation and social service.

Lesson 10.2   The Biblical Basis

Objectives
10.2.1 Explain the implications of the cultural mandate at creation.
10.2.2 Examine how the doctrine of salvation is presented in the Old and New Testaments.
10.2.3 Discuss the effectiveness of a holistic approach to the gospel ministry.
10.2.4 Identify four works of compassion within the Assemblies of God.

Articulate the need for both proclamation and social service.

A Balanced Perspective

This part of our study of missions discusses touching, the fourth cardinal facet of the philosophy and outreach of Assemblies of God World Missions. The social and political context of world missions is an important study in view of the socio-political challenges facing the church on an international scale. The mission of God is the unifying theme for the revelation of God in Holy Scripture. However, how do the people of God carry out their responsibilities in response to His mission? Is it possible to divide these responsibilities between secular and spiritual aspects? To what extent has western culture influenced our way of doing evangelism? The answers must come from the Bible. If our message is one of salvation of the whole person, this must necessarily include ministry to both the physical and spiritual needs of humanity. Such ministry presents a theological Christ who does not ignore the socio-political and historical realities of people's lives.

Unfortunately, some missionaries have focused on ministry to human needs—providing food and medical assistance, education and other development projects—without proper emphasis on the salvation of souls. The student needs to be aware of the urgency of a balanced approach to world missions.

One of the basic questions we may ask about evangelism is whether the gospel is best shared by using both words and actions. If it is, this would include acts of mercy and justice. Ronald Sider (1999) stated that "many, while believing that evangelism is primary, insist that evangelism and social responsibility are both important. Mission includes both" (3). Social responsibility refers to "activities related to relieving human need, philanthropy, seeking to minister to individuals and families, and works of mercy" (Nicholls 1985, 9). Evangelism is "the proclamation of the good news that God sent his only begotten son to redeem man from his sin in order to restore him to fellowship with God and to serve God in his Church" (Ro 1985, 13). No missions endeavor would be maximized without the melding of these two elements.

1 What is Christ's Kingdom message meant to bring to humanity?

A majority of the poor of this world live within the 10/40 window, and despite advances in technology, the number of poor in the world is rapidly expanding. "Fifty percent of Bombay's [known as Mumbai] ten million people live in slums. By 2020 the percentage will be 75%. More than 50% of the Indian population... live below the poverty line. Among this 50%, at least in the cities, there are very few churches (World Evangelical Fellowship 1993, 7). Jesus' message of "good news for the poor" (Luke 4:18; 7:22) is meant to bring wholeness to all humanity. This will be fully accomplished at His return, but in the meantime we are to do our best to alleviate human suffering through ministries of compassion and development.

Explain the implications of the cultural mandate at creation.

The Biblical Basis

The cultural mandate originated with God at creation. Before the fall, when God announced the creation of the first human beings, He said, "Let us make man in our image, in our likeness, and let them rule over the fish of the sea and the birds of the air, over the livestock, over all the earth, and over all the creatures that move along the ground" (Genesis 1:26). In this way, Adam and Eve received their first responsibility, and this was followed by the first commandment: "Be fruitful and increase in number; fill the earth and subdue it" (Genesis 1:28). Hence, humans received a delegated sovereignty over creation, and they would act in the place of God over His creation. This was a cultural mandate.

Jesus refers to this mandate in His response to the Pharisees about the greatest commandment. Jesus said, "Love the Lord your God with all your heart and with all your soul and with all your mind. This is the first and greatest commandment. And the second is like it: Love your neighbor as yourself" (Matthew 22:37–39). True Christian love is deeply concerned about the well-being of one's neighbor. Jesus' Sermon on the Mount adds many other expectations of the believer. John the Baptist expressed this through his preaching: "The man with two tunics should share with him who has none, and the one who has food should do the same" (Luke 3:11). The cultural mandate has never been cancelled and will be in effect until Jesus returns.

Salvation in the Old Testament

The meaning of the biblical word *salvation* is central to our understanding of how the gospel works in human beings and human society. In the Old Testament, God is always portrayed as the author of salvation. God alone can rescue His people or save them (Ezekiel 34:22; Hosea 1:7). In the Psalms, He is called "God our Savior" (Psalm 68:19). All areas of life are included in the teaching of salvation in the Old Testament. This certainly applies to God's divine justice for the poor and the oppressed. At the exodus, it was God who delivered His people by miracles and signs (Exodus 7–14). However, the salvation or deliverance of God's people in the Old Testament is always related to His covenant with them (Psalm 3:8; 62:1–2; 68:20; 85:9).

Salvation in the New Testament

In the New Testament, salvation is closely related to the kingdom of God. This is illustrated in the story of the rich young ruler (see Mark 10:17–26). After the rich young ruler had left Jesus in sorrow because he could not accept the admonition to sell his goods and give the proceeds to the poor, Jesus told the disciples that it is difficult for the rich to "enter the kingdom of God." To experience salvation meant a radical transformation of all the thinking and relationships of the person. This is also illustrated in Jesus' Sermon on the Mount (Matthew 5:3–16).

To Zacchaeus, who repented of his dishonest and corrupt gain of money, Jesus affirmed, "Today, salvation has come to this house" (Luke 19:9). This story shows us that salvation has to do with a person's social and personal life, as well as his or her relationship with God. Salvation involves the whole person—physical, spiritual, and social. The Gospel of Luke presents salvation in five dimensions: economic, social, physical, psychological, and spiritual (Musasiwa 1996, 198).

The New Testament presents the redeemed as members of a new society. Jesus redefined one's neighbor in His parable of the Good Samaritan (Luke 10:29–36). The Jews understood their "neighbor" to mean friends or relatives (Leviticus 19:18). In fact, after Jesus gave the meaning of the Great Commandment to a certain lawyer, He followed this teaching by demonstrating and defining who one's neighbor is. Through the parable, Jesus illustrated that attempting to do one's religious duty while failing to assist a wounded person is disobedience to the God's Law.

Clearly, our ministry must involve proclamation and service–word and deed–to both the spiritual and physical or social human being. A proverb in Burkina Faso says, "An empty sack cannot stand." In Sierra Leone, the same idea continues: "An empty belly has no ears." In Nigeria, a Yoruba saying states,

10.2.2
OBJECTIVE
Examine how the doctrine of salvation is presented in the Old and New Testaments.

2   To what extent does transformation take place at salvation?

10.2.3
OBJECTIVE
Discuss the effectiveness of a holistic approach to the gospel ministry.

"A hungry man has no ears for words." These sayings simply mean a hungry person cannot listen to sermons (Adeyemo 1985, 51). Therefore, the mission of preaching the gospel must include everything, even the socio-responsibility of the church and its members.

The local church is the most effective distribution center for ministering to human need. Church leaders can best judge the reality of needs in the community and determine the most effective way of meeting them. Those helped through a demonstration of Christ's compassion can then identify with a group of believers from within their own culture and community.

A great example of the effectiveness of this holistic approach is seen in one of the Muslim countries of Africa. The church and mission in one nation are actively involved in both preaching and social service. A recent medical mission that combined the service of medical personnel with evangelism brought positive response from the government. The director of the national hospital proposed to an American missionary that there be a Christian chapel designated in the hospital and that a chaplain be named to visit the sick. He also proposed a chapel at the national mortuary for Christian ministry.

This bears out the truth that social service and evangelism are equally important in the witness of the believers to the world. Both of these activities appear to be included in Jesus' declaration in Luke 4:18: "The Spirit of the Lord is upon me, because he anointed me to preach the gospel to the poor. He has sent me to proclaim freedom for the prisoners, and recovery of sight for the blind, to release the oppressed." Jesus' mission and that of His followers is to preach the gospel, heal the sick, and feed the hungry. It does not appear these activities are given primary or secondary roles. They are done together.

3   Why do dispensationalists view proclamation as the only valid ministry?

Dr. Tokunboh Adeyemo (1985) summarized the different options for social service and evangelism among evangelicals. His summary began with social action seen by those who hold an extreme view of **dispensationalism** to be a distraction. They believe the only legitimate activity is the proclamation of the gospel or evangelism. They are waiting for the return of Christ at any moment, and any social activity would simply distract them from the task of the Church. This perspective fails to engage the believer in the marketplaces of the world and interaction with the human's whole being.

The second option among evangelicals is that social action is a betrayal of evangelism. The world is hopelessly lost, and any effort toward redemption of society apart from evangelism is a waste of time. The ship is sinking, and one simply needs to man the lifeboats. The "salt and light" function of the Church is lost in this view.

A third view has social action as evangelism. In this way, no distinction is made between the two. However, when Jesus fed the multitude, would He have considered this action the same as proclaiming the gospel (see John 6:15–29)? Certainly, the apostles made a distinction between ministry of the Word and waiting upon tables (Acts 6:1–8).

A fourth view is that social action is a means to evangelism—a bridge or preparation for evangelism. This would be useful in places where the doors are not open for the proclamation of the gospel. This is certainly true of work among the 1.3 billion Muslims, where missionaries are involved in different types of compassion ministry, from education to medical work (Adeyemo 1985, 48–52).

At least three types of social issues involve relief, development, and structural change. When we refer to relief, we mean ministering to victims of disasters, feeding the hungry, and providing clothing and medical services. In the area of development, we refer to helping people obtain skills and knowledge to care for themselves. This may mean improving agricultural methods, supplying wells, or providing education. There is relevance in the saying that when you give a person a fish, you feed that person for a day, but when you teach a person to fish, you feed that person for a lifetime. Therefore, relief provides food for people who are starving today, but development provides self-sufficiency.

The challenges of relief and development should not be left to a denomination or missions society. The responsibility rests on every believer to do whatever he or she has the power to do. James probes:

> What good is it, my brothers, if a man claims to have faith but has no deeds? Can such faith save him? Suppose a brother or sister is without clothes and daily food. If one of you says to him, "Go, I wish you well; keep warm and well fed," but does nothing about his physical needs, what good is it? In the same way, faith by itself, if it is not accompanied by action, is dead. (2:14–17)

When we refer to structural change, we mean the political and economic areas of life. What role does the Christian play in bringing about changes in freedom, economic justice, and positive changes in the environment in general? Jesus did not join a political party in Palestine*. He did not come to earth as a military leader to drive out the Romans and oppressors of the Jews. He taught a gospel of repentance, love, and righteousness that would bring about a new society of the redeemed and change society from the inside. The believers were to be salt and light in the world. They were to model justice and love. This penetrates and transforms society in general. The redeemed community influences the total social order. Ephesians 2:11–22 shows how the gospel of Christ can overcome ethnic hatred and create a new community in Christ. Ephesians 3:6–7 reveals that Gentiles and Jews become one people in a new, redeemed community of all races. They are heirs together of the blessings and promises of Christ.

Social Service in the Assemblies of God

Orphanage in Egypt

One great work of compassion was established in the early years of the Assemblies of God by Lillian Trasher. She was called the "Mother of the Nile" for her work in the orphanage she established in Assiout, Egypt in 1911. "Hundreds of Egyptian youngsters found food, shelter, and instruction over the years" (McGee 1986, 99).

Lillian was born in Jacksonville, Florida, on September 27, 1887. As a young adult, she served in a faith-operated orphanage in North Carolina. After hearing a missionary speak, Trasher abandoned her plans to marry. After slowly raising funds, she went to Egypt in 1910 and settled in Assiout to begin a traditional missionary career. Lillian was asked to visit a dying Egyptian woman. When she arrived at the woman's home, she found an emaciated, severely malnourished three-month-old baby. When the mother died, the baby was given to Lillian. This was the beginning of the orphanage.

Since she had no funds for her work, Trasher begged the Egyptians for money. By 1916 she had fifty orphans. Then, she was able to collect enough money to purchase half an acre of land on which she constructed the first new building for her orphans. The construction was completed on March 23, 1916. Gradually, she was able to purchase more land until she had nine acres. In 1919 the orphanage became a part of the overseas ministry of the Assemblies of God, and Lillian Trasher was appointed a foreign missionary. By 1961, Lillian had 1,400 children.

Please Note:
*The term *Palestine* is used throughout this course to identify the geographic region generally located between the Sea of Galilee and the Negev desert and west of the Jordan River. Although this term is not an official political label for this area either now or during the first century AD, it is a convenient way to reference a geographic area that is very difficult to name due to its tumultuous political, ethnic, and religious history. This descriptive term has been used since the fifth century BC, even though it was not officially applied as a political designation until the second century AD. It is used for convenience because of its general recognition and does not intend any historical, political, or ethnic implications.

OBJECTIVE

Identify four works of compassion within the Assemblies of God.

4   What can we learn about compassion ministry and motivation from Lillian Trasher?

In September, 1941, at the beginning of World War II, Trasher and the orphanage were cut off from funds, mail, and supplies. Their clothes were tattered, and the food was gone. Lillian called a prayer meeting with all her staff and presented their desperate situation to the Lord. Shortly after the prayer, the Ambassador of the United States in Egypt informed her of a shipment of supplies meant for Greek refugees that could not reach its destination. The ship had docked in Alexandria. Its cargo included thousands of dresses for women and girls, shirts and pants for men and boys, clothes for babies, hundreds of kegs of powdered milk, huge sacks of rice, flour, and beans. All the supplies were given to the orphanage! Many leaders and workers in the Assemblies of God Fellowship in Egypt came from the orphanage (Assemblies of God Fellowship Archives 2001).

Twenty-five years after Lillian Trasher's death, there was a celebration at the orphanage in memory of her, at which was present J. Philip Hogan, the then Executive Director of the Division of Foreign Missions. Thirteen thousand people attended this 75th anniversary of the orphanage. Zaki Badr, the governor of Assiout, and his staff were present. He awarded a special brass tray to Rev. Hogan in honor of Trasher and her work. On the front of the tray was the Lord's Prayer in Arabic, and, on the back, the governor's seal. There was also a citation written on papyrus from the Egyptian government (Hogan 1986, 22–23).

Latin America ChildCare

5   What should be the primary purpose of a Christian school?

Latin America ChildCare was established by John and Lois Bueno in El Salvador. After John and Lois arrived there in 1961, they became pastors of a local church of about one hundred people. This congregation eventually grew to over twenty-two thousand in Sunday attendance and planted more than 120 other churches in the area.

John was burdened with the plight of the children of El Salvador and sought to demonstrate to them that God loved them. Consequently, he started a school in the church, and an entire Christian school system developed that was called Liceo Cristiano (Christian Schools). This first school presently has 2,400 students, a medical clinic, laboratory, pharmacy, and a dental clinic. The entire school system of 38 campuses has 22,000 children enrolled. One of the primary focuses of the school system is to bring the children to a saving knowledge of Jesus Christ (Hurst 2005, 24–27). Joaquin Garcia, director and general administrator of the school system, mentioned, "Our main focus and responsibility at Liceo Cristiano is that our students become Christians so they will have eternal life" (Hurst 1998, 11).

Amidst this progress, the Buenos realized there were too few trained Christian teachers. They founded the Christian University of the Assemblies of God that is fully accredited by the government (Hurst 1998, 11). These schools, spread throughout twenty countries, have served over 457,000 children and currently serve 80,000 needy children.

The children in the Latin America ChildCare are often sponsored by people in the United States. One touching story is about Jaime Francisco Moreno Mejia. Over thirty years ago, he was a student in this program in El Salvador. His sponsors sent him letters, Christmas cards, and gifts on special occasions. Eventually, Jaime continued his studies and completed an MBA in Business Counseling. He always remembered the love and care of his sponsors in the United States and wanted to meet them. During a business trip to the Washington D.C. area, he recalled his sponsors were from that part of the United States. He found their contact information on the internet and went to their home. They were in their nineties by then! Jaime had lunch with them and thanked them for sponsoring him and giving him a foundation for his education. During his visit, his sponsors showed him a special treasure—a chest full of his letters, birthday cards, and thank you notes. Moved to tears, he said, "They treated me like a son" (Life Stories 2003, 84–85).

Mission of Mercy

Another well-known ministry of compassion—Mission of Mercy—was founded in 1954 by Mark and Huldah Buntain in Calcutta, India. The Buntains were sent to India as temporary missionaries, but they continued as full-time missionaries and established the Mission of Mercy as they were feeding and educating more than two hundred children. In 1968, they established an outpatient clinic that later became a full hospital. They quickly saw the need to both evangelize and care for the poor of Calcutta.

Today, more than twenty-five thousand people are being fed in Calcutta, and Mission of Mercy outreaches involve support of child sponsorships, daily feeding programs, total care orphanages, schools (elementary, secondary, and vocational), leadership training centers, clinics, hospitals, and mobile medical units. Leaders of this ministry are aware that people do not live by bread alone. Their vision is to see children's lives transformed by introducing them to Jesus Christ (www.ministrywatch.com).

In January 1990, the Mission of Mercy merged with Bethesda Ministries of Colorado Springs, Colorado.

New Hope Town Leper Colony

Florence Steidel founded a leper colony in Liberia. At first, she worked as a missionary nurse in a girls' school at Newaka. However, she contracted tuberculosis and returned to the United States for treatment in Missouri. After she was cured, she took a course in elementary building construction at Central Bible Institute (later Central Bible College) and returned to Liberia, where she established a home for lepers. Hundreds of lepers were treated in the colony named "New Hope," and more than one hundred buildings were constructed. It was estimated that more than five hundred patients were treated each day at the colony, and ninety percent of them found a new life in Christ.

One of the nurses reported the arrival of a woman who came crawling up the pathway to the clinic on her hands and knees. She was wearing only a small loincloth, and she had traveled for two months to get help at New Hope, crawling almost the entire distance. When the nurse bathed her and gave her a clean dress, tears streamed down lady's face. She repeated, "A-wee'a" (thank you). She accepted Christ, and two weeks after her arrival went to be with the Lord (Legacy of Compassion 2000, 21).

Florence Steidel was recognized at Liberia's Centennial Celebration in April 1957. The decoration of Knight Official of the Humane Order of African Redemption was conferred on her by President William Tubman. She was the first woman missionary in Liberia to be so honored (Assemblies of God Fellowship Archives 2001, 5).

Test Yourself

Circle the letter of the *best* answer.

1. One hindrance to meeting socials needs has been a dualism that separates
a) society from the church.
b) government from the church.
c) human mind and the human spirit.
d) body from spirit.

2. Social responsibility is
a) limited in definition to disaster relief.
b) limited to education.
c) meant to refer to activities related to human need.
d) limited to acts of justice.

3. A majority of the poor of this world live in
a) Africa.
b) the 10/40 window.
c) Latin America.
d) Asia.

4. Humans' delegated sovereignty over the creation is called the
a) evangelistic mandate.
b) cultural mandate.
c) salvation mandate.
d) gospel mandate.

5. In the Gospel of Luke, salvation has these dimensions:
a) economic, social, physical, psychological, and spiritual.
b) social, physical, and spiritual.
c) economic, physical, and spiritual.
d) social, psychological, and spiritual.

6. Those believing missionaries should only proclaim the gospel are
a) the evangelicals in general.
b) those holding an extreme view of dispensationalism.
c) those who see social action as preparation for evangelism.
d) those who see social actions as evangelism.

7. Those who hold that social action is evangelism also believe that
a) any effort toward redemption of society is a waste of time.
b) there is no distinction at all between the two.
c) social action is a bridge for evangelism.
d) proclamation betrays evangelism.

8. Relief differs from development in that relief indicates
a) helping people obtain skills and knowledge to care for themselves.
b) providing self-sufficiency.
c) ministering to victims of disaster.
d) improving agricultural methods or education.

9. In the context of missions, structural change
a) is limited to changes in the environment.
b) means the political and economic areas of life.
c) is restricted to political changes.
d) refers to changes needed within the church.

10. Lillian Trasher's ministry shows that
a) virtue and tenacity can reshape history.
b) women are more effective in foreign missions than in home missions.
c) marriage is a hindrance to every ministry.
d) money is the most important asset in any mission.

Responses to Interactive Questions
Chapter 10

Some of these responses may include information that is supplemental to the IST. These questions are intended to produce reflective thinking beyond the course content and your responses may vary from these examples.

1 What is Christ's Kingdom message meant to bring to humanity?

Answer: Christ's Kingdom message brings wholeness to all humanity and creation. This will be fully fulfilled at His return, but in the meantime we are to do our best to alleviate human suffering through ministries of compassion and development.

2 To what extent does transformation take place at salvation?

Answer: To experience salvation means a radical transformation of all the thinking and relationships of a person. Zacchaeus' relational transformation is a good example of this.

3 Why do dispensationalists view proclamation as the only valid ministry?

Answer: They are expecting the return of Christ at any moment, and view any social activity as distracting from the task of the Church.

4 What can we learn about compassion ministry and motivation from Lillian Trasher?

Answer: Lillian Trasher had a great heart of Christian compassion and gave herself to this ministry without any apparent hope of receiving the financial assistance necessary.

5 What should be the primary purpose of a Christian school?

Answer: The main focus and responsibility must be that the students become Christians—or remain in Christ—so they will reap eternal life.

CHAPTER

The Believer and Missions

Knowledge of the nature of missions, its purpose, strategies, and mandate to the Church is not enough. Ultimately, responsibility for reaching the lost is on the individual Christian. After all, people make up the Church. People are who respond to Christ's call. Jesus came as the first Apostle and missionary, and one of His first acts in ministry was the calling of people to follow Him. Among those who responded were the Twelve.

Jesus has not stopped calling people to become His ambassadors to the world. Whether at home or abroad, we are to be His witnesses. While some people are called to full-time service, we are all called to involvement in the mission task of taking the whole gospel to the whole world.

Lesson 11.1   Individual Responsibility toward Missions

Objectives

11.1.1   Relate the lordship of Jesus to our personal involvement in missions.

11.1.2   Discuss the importance of prayer to the cause of missions.

11.1.3   From 2 Corinthians 8, identify the seven principles of financial support.

11.1.4   Discuss the biblical view of the laity as the people of God.

11.1.1
OBJECTIVE

Relate the lordship of Jesus to our personal involvement in missions.

1 What does it mean that Jesus is Lord over our lives?

Individual Responsibility toward Missions

The Lordship of Christ

The lordship of Christ is a fact, not a wish or a hope. It is not an option. Either He is Lord of our lives or we are not Christians. The apostle Peter made this clear on the Day of Pentecost when he declared, "Let all Israel be assured of this: God has made this Jesus, whom you crucified, both Lord and Christ" (Acts 2:36). The level of one's obedience is another matter, but it does not change the fact that He is Lord. No one can accept Jesus as Savior without committing to Him as Lord (cf. Kane 1976, 108–114).

Lord over Our Lives

All people belong to God by creation, but Christians belong to Him by right of redemption (Ephesians 1:7; Colossians 1:14; Titus 2:14). The apostle Paul speaks to the lordship of Jesus in his first letter to the Corinthians: "Do you not know that your body is a temple of the Holy Spirit, who is in you, whom you have received from God? You are not your own; you were bought at a price. Therefore honor God with your body" (1 Corinthians 6:19–20).

Among the many articulations of Jesus' lordship, however, the strongest assertion comes from Christ himself:

Anyone who loves his father or mother more than me is not worthy of me; anyone who loves his son or daughter more than me is not worthy of me; and anyone who does not take his cross and follow me is not worthy of me. Whoever finds his life will lose it, and whoever loses his life for my sake will find it. (Matthew 10:37–39)

For true followers of Christ, the direction of our lives is in the hands of the Lord himself. Our duty is to follow and obey Him. We are to walk as directed by the Spirit of God, to keep in step with Him (Galatians 5:25). That being so, we must focus on the Lord's purposes in this world–the redemption of humankind.

All of the Old Testament pointed to redemption, and the incarnation and Calvary accomplished it. The New Testament demonstrates God's plan and purpose for the Church. 2 Samuel states: "Like water spilled on the ground, which cannot be recovered, so we must die. But God does not take away life; instead, he devises ways so that a banished person may not remain estranged from him" (2 Samuel 14:14). The Cross was—and is—the only means of salvation. But believers are responsible to follow the Spirit's leading in presenting the gospel to all people (Mark 16:15–16, Matthew 28:18–20).

Lord over Our Possessions

The psalmist reminds us that "the earth is the Lord's and everything in it, the world, and all who live in it" (Psalm 24:1). God gives us the ability to acquire wealth (Deuteronomy 8:16–18) and to enjoy it (Ecclesiastes 5:19). But we are to be wise stewards of its use (Luke 16:1–13) and of all God's blessings (1 Peter 4:10). How a person uses finances will indicate his or her priorities in life (Luke 12:15–21). All believers are to contribute of their means to help reach the lost with the gospel.

Lord over Our Talents and Occupation

The call of the Twelve and the call of the apostle Paul are clear examples of the Lord's sovereignty over one's vocation. For Paul, it was a complete turnaround of his plans. Today, many Christians are surprised by God's sovereign direction in their lives. This does not necessarily mean assignment as a minister or missionary; it does mean being open to whatever and whenever God calls. God has the right position at the right time for every believer. Paul makes it clear that all gifts [special enabling] come from God and are to be used for the building up of the whole body of Christ until all attain the maturity and unity God desires (Ephesians 4:8–16).

If Jesus is Lord of all, it is our duty to obediently carry out His plans for us. Whatever they may be, they will always be within the framework of His desire to see all people brought into fellowship with the Father. The true follower of Christ will joyfully join that purpose in whatever way the Lord chooses.

The World Christian

2   What are the characteristics of a world Christian?

What is a world Christian? This does not mean "worldly," enamored and enticed by the things of this world. It means, rather, one who has caught a vision of God's purpose, the mission of God for the people of this planet. It speaks of one who has seen the plight of the billions who do not know Christ—sheep without a shepherd. The world Christian is willing to take the risks, to make the sacrifices, to do what can be done within his or her capacity to take the gospel to the unreached everywhere. He or she is willing to go or stay as led by the Spirit. Such a Christian—regardless of role or status in life—sees as the highest priority the need to know Christ and to make Him known.

Through Prayer

3   Why is prayer so important to the cause of missions?

11.1.2
OBJECTIVE
Discuss the importance of prayer to the cause of missions.

A motto of the foreign missions enterprise was "Pray, give, go." The motto still has meaning true today. A primary responsibility of the believer is to pray. When Jesus saw the multitudes wandering as lost sheep, He told the disciples to pray (Matthew 9:35–38). Throughout His ministry, Jesus resorted to prayer as a communication link with the Father, leaving His followers a paramount example. If Jesus had to pray, being the Son of God in the limitations of a human body, how much more His disciples! The Twelve saw Him praying and asked to be taught how they too should pray, and He taught them (Luke 11:1–13).

Prayer demonstrates humans' dependence on God for everything. To stand in awe of God leads to praise; to stand in need of Him leads to prayer. Any attempt to do God's will without seeking His direction through prayer is likely to come up short. The cause of missions begins with and depends upon prayer, not only by those sent but by those who send them.

There are various forms of prayer: repentance, petition, and intercession. The prayer of repentance asks God's forgiveness for wrongdoing or for what we have failed to do. Psalm 51 is a good example of a prayer of repentance. Failure to support God's purpose to draw all people to himself is also a reason to repent.

Another kind of prayer is that of petition or a call for help. This is the kind of prayer Jesus instructed His disciples to pray in Matthew 9:35–38. A third form of prayer is intercession, praying on behalf of someone in need. Such an example is praying for sinners who need a savior or missionaries who have a special need. To intercede is to serve as a go-between, for example like a petitioner before a judge seeking mercy for a client.

All of these forms of prayer are vital to the cause of missions. Whether one is sent or stays behind, prayer is no option. The one going calls upon God for direction, for the supply of what is needed for success in the mission, and intercedes for those to be reached. The one who stays is called upon to pray for direction as to how best to help in the missions cause, for God to supply what is needed to support the missionaries and the mission, and intercedes for both the missionaries and the target peoples. Missions depends upon the prayers of the believers.

Through Material Support

The motto "Pray, give, go" is not a list of options but of the essential responsibilities of every believer. If we are serious about prayer, inevitably we will be moved to give, to be part of the solution. It is not that we take over God's responsibility to provide. Rather He pours into our lives what He wants us to use for His purposes; we become His channels of supply. The more we are open to let God's provisions flow through us, the more He will pour in.

This is no guarantee that God will make the giver rich. He knows how much a person can handle without becoming selfish and focused on personal wealth. That is why Jesus taught us to pray, "Give us each day our daily bread" (Luke 11:3). This attitude is seen earlier in Proverbs 30, where the petitioner prays, "Give me neither poverty nor riches, but give me only my daily bread. Otherwise, I may have too much and disown you and say, 'Who is the Lord?' Or I may become poor and steal, and so dishonor the name of my God" (Proverbs 30:8–9).

11.1.3
OBJECTIVE
From 2 Corinthians 8, identify the seven principles of financial support.

We must remember Jesus' example of whom the apostle Paul said, "You know the grace of our Lord Jesus Christ, that though he was rich, yet for your sakes he became poor, so that you through his poverty might become rich" (2 Corinthians 8:9). In 2 Corinthians 8, the apostle Paul gives several principles regarding the financial support of missions efforts:

4   What are the principles of financial support to missions as given in 2 Corinthians 8?

1. Giving is to be seen as a privilege (v. 4).
2. Giving is preceded by a full commitment to Christ (v. 5).
3. Giving is to be considered integral to the believer's life (v. 7).
4. Giving is to be voluntary, not coerced (v. 8).
5. Giving is to be proportional to the financial means of the giver (v. 12).
6. The basis of giving is to meet real need, not make someone else rich (vv. 13–15).
7. There must be proper accountability for the funds (vv. 18–22).

Financial giving is not only for the ones who stay at home and support the missionary cause. The missionaries themselves must also support the missions cause, not just their own work, but that of others. One of the great temptations of the deputation process is to turn those who have determined to follow Christ's call to missions into those who focus upon what they can get for themselves. Placed on a pedestal by admiring supporters, the missionary is tempted to use that platform for personal gain. The example of Gehazi in the Old Testament should serve as a warning (2 Kings 5:20–27). Covetousness comes with a price.

One of the great missionaries of the past, C.T. Studd once said, "If Jesus Christ is God and died for me, nothing that I can ever do for Him should be called a sacrifice" (Kane 1976, 112). Many a missionary has echoed the same.

Through Service

Service is the "go" element of individual responsibility. Though often thought of as representing a response to the call to missionary service, it applies to all believers. Not all are called to become missionaries, but all are called to contribute their time and talents to the cause of world missions.

11.1.4
OBJECTIVE
Discuss the biblical view of the laity as the people of God.

Unfortunately, a distinction is too often made between clergy and laity, between those considered especially called to service and those who provide support, encouragement, and applause. The Bible makes no such distinction among the people of God, the Church. Van Engen says it well:

The term *laity*, if used, must be given its biblical sense of the "people (Gk. *laos*) of God," with distinction of gift, function, and ministration—but not distinction in holiness, prestige, power, commitment, or activity. Today we often use the term *layperson* in contra-distinction from the word *professional*, and we mean that the layperson in a certain discipline is one who dabbles, muddles, tries hard, but certainly does not have expertise. The "professional" is "in the know," the expert, the person dedicated to competence in the discipline. There is no biblical basis for such a distinction in the Church, and the unbiblical practice has only served to place the "professional" clergy on a pedestal as being "close to God," removing the vast majority further from holiness and the activity of the Spirit in their lives. (Van Engen 1991, 151)

If this is true regarding the "professional clergy," it is even more so with "professional missionaries." There are differences in callings, gifts, and abilities. But this only reveals the diversity of people in God's great family. All believers have their part to play in fulfilling God's mandates to the Church, including the missionary task.

Military leaders say it takes about ten to eleven personnel behind the lines to support one on the front lines. Those who stand behind the missionary effort with their own form of commitment are extremely valuable to the cause. Serving on a missions committee, helping create and coordinate a missions convention, and hosting missionaries and mission speakers are some examples of getting involved in the process. Helping with newsletters, writing to missionaries, and securing and shipping needed supplies are others.

5   How can all believers be directly involved in the cause of missions?

There are more direct ways of involvement, short of full-time missionary service. Short-term assignments may be from a couple of weeks to a couple of years, providing help in areas of personal expertise. These may include teaching, preaching, assisting in evangelistic meetings, medical and disaster relief, library work, accounting, printing, construction, child care, training in development efforts, and a host of other possibilities. Church-sponsored building teams have done much to assist in field projects while at the same time inspiring team members to support the missions cause and encourage others to do so. Retired persons can use their expertise as self-supported short-term workers. The list is almost limitless.

The Bible is replete with examples of God-given responsibilities. Think of Adam, Noah, Abraham, Moses, Joshua, Gideon, Samuel, David, Elijah, Isaiah, Ezekiel, John the Baptist, the Twelve, Paul, and many more. Most were simply "laypersons" God called to perform tasks He wanted done. These people were not capable or great in their own strength, but God called and equipped them and walked with them on the journey. God is not necessarily looking for those with expertise, but rather for those willing to use their abilities for missions.

To conclude, King David demonstrated an important principle of the kingdom of God: "The share of the man who stayed with the supplies is to be the same as that of him who went down to the battle. All will share alike" (1 Samuel 30:24). No matter how small or insignificant the task, whether at home or on a mission field, God rewards those who contribute their efforts to the cause.

Test Yourself

Circle the letter of the *best* answer.

1. That Jesus is Lord of our lives primarily implies
a) we are Christians.
b) Jesus is to be worshipped.
c) we are responsible to Him in all we do.
d) He knows everything about us.

2. The principle Old Testament passage stating God owns everything is
a) Psalm 24:1.
b) Psalm 100.
c) Deuteronomy 8:16–18.
d) Ecclesiastes 5:19.

3. Prayer for the cause of missions is vital because
a) sacrifice demands it.
b) praise moves the hand of God.
c) it gets our heart in tune with God.
d) we are totally dependent on God.

4. Intercession is for the purpose of seeking God's
a) forgiveness for yourself.
b) help for others.
c) help for yourself.
d) help in defeating the devil.

5. Praying, "Give us this day our daily bread" is
a) asking for all of our various needs to be met.
b) asking for miraculous provision by God.
c) asking for provisions appropriate for the need of the day.
d) asking the Lord to help us understand the intended meaning of Bible passages.

6. One principle of giving listed in 2 Corinthians 8 is that
a) certain persons are especially called to support missions.
b) pastors should determine the giving amounts for both the rich and the poor.
c) giving is to be proportional to the means of the individual.
d) giving to missions follows the principles of sowing and reaping.

7. The distinction between clergy and laity is
a) foreign to the Bible.
b) a good way of distinguishing between the experts and novices.
c) distinguishing between the Twelve Apostles and the other disciples.
d) helpful to show who qualifies to become a missionary.

8. The responsibility for missions outreach is given to
a) missionaries called by God.
b) all members of the Church.
c) the missions committee of the church
d) the pastor, board, and missions committee.

9. In fulfilling responsibilities for missions, recognize that
a) certain persons are called to serve on behalf of all members.
b) a missionary "call" is required to participate.
c) if you do not have a burden for missions you are excused.
d) every believer has God-given gifts and talents to help the missions cause.

10. When King David said (in Samuel 30:24) that the soldiers fighting on the battlefield and the people supporting the cause in other ways will "share alike," it implies that
a) individuals in both groups will experience the same sorrow.
b) the level of individual commitment in both groups does not matter.
c) no matter the role of the individual serving the Lord's cause, each will share in the rewards.
d) God will reward both groups with material wealth.

Responses to Interactive Questions
Chapter 11

Some of these responses may include information that is supplemental to the IST. These questions are intended to produce reflective thinking beyond the course content and your responses may vary from these examples.

1 What does it mean that Jesus is Lord over our lives?

Answer: For true followers of Christ, the direction of our lives is in the hands of the Lord himself. Our duty is to follow and obey Him. We are to walk as directed by the Spirit of God, to keep in step with Him (Galatians 5:25). We must focus on the Lord's purposes in this world—the redemption of humankind.

2 What are the characteristics of a world Christian?

Answer: Willingness to take risks, to sacrifice, and to do everything possible to take the gospel to the unreached. The world Christian is willing to go or stay as led by the Spirit. Such a Christian—regardless of role or status in life—sees as the highest priority the need to know Christ and to make Him known.

3 Why is prayer so important to the cause of missions?

Answer: Prayer demonstrates our dependence on God for everything. Any attempt to do God's will without seeking His direction through prayer is likely to come up short.

4 What are the principles of financial support to missions as given in 2 Corinthians 8?

Answer: Giving is to be seen as a privilege; it is preceded by a full commitment to Christ; it is integral to the life of a believer; it is to be done voluntarily, not by coercion; it is to be proportional to the financial means of the giver; it is to meet real need, not make someone else rich; and there must be proper accountability for the funds.

5 How can all believers be directly involved in the cause of missions?

Answer: By doing short-term missions assignments including teaching, preaching, assisting in evangelistic meetings, medical and disaster relief, library work, accounting, printing, construction, child care, training in development efforts, and a host of other possibilities

UNIT PROGRESS EVALUATION 4 AND FINAL EXAMINATION

You have now concluded all of the work in this independent-study textbook. Review the lessons in this unit carefully, and then answer the questions in the last unit progress evaluation (UPE). When you have completed the UPE, check your answers with the answer key provided in Essential Course Materials at the back of this IST. Review any items you may have answered incorrectly. Review for the final examination by studying the course objectives, lesson objectives, self-tests, and UPEs. Review any lesson content necessary to refresh your memory. If you review carefully and are able to fulfill the objectives, you should have no difficulty passing the closed-book final examination.

Taking the Final Examination

1. **All final exams must be taken closed book.** You are not allowed to use any materials or outside help while taking a final exam. You will take the final examination online at www.globaluniversity.edu. If the online option is not available to you, you may request a printed final exam. If you did not request a printed final exam when you ordered your course, you must submit this request a few weeks before you are ready to take the exam. The Request for a Printed Final Examination is in the Forms section of Essential Course Materials at the back of this IST.

2. Review for the final examination in the same manner in which you prepared for the UPEs. Refer to the form Checklist of Study Methods in the front part of the IST for further helpful review hints.

3. After you complete and submit the online final examination, the results will be immediately available to you. Your final course grade report will be e-mailed to your Global University student e-mail account after your Service Learning Requirement (SLR) report has been processed.

4. If you complete the exam in printed form, you will send your final examination, your answer sheets, and your SLR report to Berean School of the Bible for grading. Your final course grade report will be sent to your GU student e-mail account. If you do not have access to the Internet, your grade will be sent to your mailing address.

 # Glossary

Reference List

Achtemeier, Elizabeth. 1986. *Nahum-Malachi.* Atlanta: John Knox Press.

Adeyemo, Tokunboh. 1985. A Critical Evaluation of Contemporary Perspectives. In *In Word and Deed:Evangelism and Social Responsibility,* ed. Bruce J. Nichols. Grand Rapids: Eerdmans.

Africa Harvest Ministries. 2005. *Africa Tabernacle Evangelism.* www.africawatch.com/tabernacle.htm (accessed June 10, 2009).

Agence France Press. 2005. More than 1,000 NGOs Launch Anti-Poverty Appeal at Porto Alegre. Global Policy Forum. www.globalpolicy.org/ngos/advocacy/conf/2005/0127ngoslaunch.html (accessed June 10, 2009).

Allen, Roland. 1962. *Missionary Methods: St. Paul's or Ours?* Grand Rapids: Eerdmans.

Arndt, William and F. Wilbur Gingrich. 1957. *A Greek-English Lexicon of the New Testament and Other Early Christian Literature.* Chicago: University of Chicago Press.

Assembly of God Fellowship Archives. 2001. Club Connection. www.ag.org.

Assemblies of God World Missions. 2004. Statistics.

———. 2005. Statistics.

Bavinck, John H. 1969. *An Introduction to the Science of Missions.* Translated by David H. Freeman. Grand Rapids: Baker.

Beaver, R. Pierce. 1968. Missionary Motivation through Three Centuries. In *Reinterpretation in American Church History,* ed. Jerald C. Brauer. Chicago: University of Chicago Press.

Berger, Julie. 2003. *Religious Non-Governmental Organizations: An Exploratory Analysis.* Paper, International Society for Third-Sector Research and the John Hopkins University. Boston: Harvard University.

Blumhofer, Edith L. 1989a. *The Assemblies of God: A Chapter in the Story of American Pentecostalism.* Vol. 1. Springfield, MO: Gospel Publishing House.

———. 1989b. *The Assemblies of God: A Chapter in the Story of American Pentecostalism.* Vol. 2. Springfield, MO: Gospel Publishing House.

Boer, Harry. 1961. *Pentecost and Missions.* Grand Rapids: Eerdmans.

Bosch, David J. 1991. *Transforming Mission: Paradigm Shifts in Theology of Mission.* Maryknoll: NY: Orbis Books.

Broyles, Craig C. 1999. Psalms. Vol. 11 of the *New International Commentary.* Peabody, MA: Hendrickson Publishers, Inc.

Cairns, Earle E. 1996. *Christianity through the Centuries: A History of the Christian Church.* 3rd ed. Grand Rapids: Zondervan.

Chakwera, Lazarus. 1999. *Eleventh Hour Institute Missions Reader,* ed. Murriel McCulley. July 26–August 18. Africa Theological Training Service.

Cohen, Raymond. 1991. *Negotiating across Cultures: Communication Obstacles in International Diplomacy.* Washington, DC: United States Institute of Peace Press.

Convention des Missions. 2001. 13 February.

Convoy of Hope. 2008. Who We Are. www.convoyofhope.org/go/who/ (accessed June 9, 2009).

Covell, Ralph R. 1977. W. A. P. Martin, *Pioneer Progress in China.* Grand Rapids: Eerdmans.

———. 1993. Class notes at Denver Seminary, doctoral course.

Cross Cultural Communications. 2003. www.cultureandlanguage.net/home.html (accessed June 10, 2009).

Cullman, Oscar. 1950. *Christ and Time: The Primitive Christian Conception of Time and History.* Translated by Floyd V. Filson. Philadelphia: Westminster Press.

Elwell, Walter A., and Robert W. Yarbrough. 1998. *Encountering the New Testament: A Historical and Theological Survey.* Grand Rapids: Baker.

Ezemadu, Reuben. 2000. Role of the African Church. http://www.ad2000.org/celebrate/ezemandu.htm (accessed June 10, 2009).

Gibbon, Edward. 1845. *The Decline and Fall of the Roman Empire.* Vol. 1. New York: Hurst & Company.

Glasser, Arthur F. 1989. *Kingdom and Mission.* Pasadena, CA: Fuller Theological Seminary School of World Missions.

Guthrie, Stan. 2005. *Missions in the Third Millennium: 21 Key Trends for the 21st Century.* United Kingdom: Paternoster Press.

Happy Horizons Children's Ranch. 2008. Our Mission. http://www.hhcr.org/from-the-founders/our-mission/ (accessed June 10, 2009).

HealthCare Ministries. 2008. Bringing the Hope that Heals to the Nations of the World. http://www.healthcareministries.org/about/bringing-the-hope-that-heals-to-the-nations-of-the-world.html (accessed June 10, 2009).

Hedlund, Roger E. 1985. *The Mission of the Church in the World.* Grand Rapids: Baker.

Hesselgrave, David J. 1991. *Communicating Christ Cross-Culturally: An Introduction to Missionary Communication.* 2nd ed. Grand Rapids: Zondervan.

———. 1995. Great Commission Contextualization. In *International Journal of Frontier Missions* 12, no. 3:139–144.

———. 2006. *Paradigms in Conflict: 10 Key Questions in Christian Missions Today.* Grand Rapids: Kregel Publications.

Hiebert, Paul G. 1985. *Anthropological Insights for Missionaries.* Grand Rapids: Baker.

Hodges, Melvin. 1976. *The Indigenous Church.* Springfield, MO: Gospel Publishing House.

Hogan, J. Philip. 1986. The "Mamma Lillian" Meeting. *Pentecostal Evangel*, April 13, 22–23.

Honig, Abram H. 2005. Study Questions Whether Short-Term Missions Make a Difference. *Christianity Today* 49 (June, Web-only). http://www.christianitytoday.com/ct/2005/125/12.0.html (accessed June 10, 2009).

Horton, Stanley M. 2000. *Isaiah.* Springfield, MO: Logion Press.

Hurst, Randy. 1998. A Way of Escape. *Pentecostal Evangel*, August 2, 4–12.

———. 2005. Noble Friends of El Salvador. *Pentecostal Evangel*, March 6.

Johansen, David. 1993. A Chance to Hear. *Pentecostal Evangel*, July 25, 9.

Johnstone, Patrick. 1998. *The Church Is Bigger Than You Think: The Unfinished Work of World Evangelisation.* Great Britain: Christian Focus Publications.

Kane, J. Herbert. 1976. *Christian Missions in Biblical Perspective.* Grand Rapids: Baker.

———. 1986. *Understanding Christian Missions.* Grand Rapids: Baker.

Kinsler, F. Ross. 1978. Mission and Contest: The Current Debate about Contextualization. *Evangelical Missions Quarterly* 14:1.

Korten, David C. 1990. *Getting to the 21st Century: Voluntary Action and the Global Agenda.* West Hartford, CT: Kumarian Press.

Kraft, Charles H. 1978. The Contextualization of Theology. *Evangelical Missions Quarterly* 14:1, 32.

———. 1996. *Anthropology for Christian Witness*. Maryknoll, NY: Orbis Books.

Latourette, Kenneth Scott. 1970. *The Great Century, AD 1800–AD 1914*. Vol. 4 of *A History of the Expansion of Christianity*. New York: Harper & Brothers.

———. 1975a. *A History of Christianity*. Rev. ed. Vol. 1. New York: Harper & Row.

———. 1975b. *A History of Christianity*. Rev. ed. Vol. 2. New York: Harper & Row.

Lausanne Covenant. 1974. Articles 4, 5, and conclusion.

Legacy of Compassion. 2000. *Pentecostal Evangel*, December 3.

Life Stories. 2003. Springfield, MO: Latin America Child Care.

Limburg, James. 1988. *Hosea-Micah*. Atlanta: John Knox Press.

Lindsell, Harold. 1970. *An Evangelical Theology of Missions*. Grand Rapids: Zondervan.

Long, Justin D. *Megatrend 11: Thousands of Third-World Mission Agencies*. Gordon Cornwell Theological Seminary. http://www.gordonconwell.edu/ockenga/gobalchristianity/mmrc/mmrc9642.htm.

Lyon, Ruth A. 1992. *A History of Home Missions of the Assemblies of God*. Springfield, MO: Division of Home Missions of the Assemblies of God.

Manila Conference. 1989. Cooperation in Evangelism I and II.

McClung, Grant. 2006. Pentecostals: The Sequel. *Christianity Today* 50, no. 4. http://www.christianitytoday.com/ct/2006/april/7.30.html (accessed June 10, 2009).

McGee, Gary B. 1986. *This Gospel Shall Be Preached: A History and Theology of Assemblies of God Foreign Missions to 1959*. Vol. 1. Springfield, MO: Gospel Publishing House.

———. 1989. *This Gospel Shall Be Preached: A History and Theology of Assemblies of God Foreign Missions since 1959*. Vol. 2. Springfield, MO: Gospel Publishing House.

McNeill, John T. 1974. *The Celtic Churches: A History A.D. 200 to 1200*. Chicago: University of Chicago Press.

Ministry Watch. http://www.ministrywatch.com (accessed June 10, 2009).

Morris, Carol. 2002. *Cultural and Language Barriers in the Workplace*. Charlotte-Mecklenburg Workforce Development Board. http://www.charlotteworks.org/clbpositionpaper.pdf (accessed June 10, 2009).

Musasiwa, Roy. 1996. Missiological Reflections. In *Serving with the Poor in Africa*, ed. Tetsunao Yamamori, Bryant L. Myers, Kwame Bediako, and Larry Reed. Monrovia, CA: MARC.

Myers, Bryant L. 1996. *The New Context of World Mission*. Monrovia, CA: MARC/World Vision.

Neill, Stephen. 1986. *A History of Christian Missions*. New York: Penguin Books.

Nevius, John. 2003. *The Planting and Development of Missionary Churches*. Monadnock, NH: Monadnock Press.

Newberry, Warren B. 2005. Contextualizing Indigenous Church Principles: An African Model. *Asian Journal of Pentecostal Studies* 8, no. 1:1, 111.

Nicholls, Bruce J., ed. 1985. In *In Word and Deed: Evangelism and Social Responsibility*. Grand Rapids: Eerdmans.

Padilla, C. René. 1985. *Mission between the Times: Essays*. Grand Rapids: Eerdmans.

Pentecostal/Charismatic Churches of North America. 2007. Mission of the PCCNA. http://www.pccna.org/mission.php (accessed June 9, 2009).

Pentecostal World Fellowship. 2009. http://www.pentecostalworldfellowship.org (accessed June 10, 2009).

Peters, George W. 1972. *A Biblical Theology of Missions*. Chicago: Moody.

Piper, John. 1993. *Let the Nations Be Glad! The Supremacy of God in Missions*. Grand Rapids: Baker.

Pocock, Michael, Gailyn Van Rheenen, and Douglas McConnell. 2005. *The Changing Face of World Missions: Engaging Contemporary Issues and Trends*. Grand Rapids: Baker.

Ro, Bong Rin. 1985. The Perspectives of Church History from New Testament Times to 1960. In *In Word and Deed: Evangelism and Social Responsibility*, ed. Bruce J. Nicholls. Grand Rapids: Eerdmans.

Severy, Merle. 1977. The Celts. *National Geographic* 151, no. 5:582–632.

Shelley, Bruce. 1982. *Church History in Plain Language*. Waco, TX: Word Publishing.

Sider, Ronald J. 1999. *Good News and Good Works: A Theology for the Whole Gospel*. Grand Rapids: Baker. Orig. pub.: *One-Sided Christianity*, 1993.

Stamps, Donald C., gen. ed. 1992. *The Full Life Study Bible: New International Version*. Grand Rapids: Zondervan.

Steyne, Philip M. 1992. *In Step with the God of the Nations: A Biblical Theology of Missions*. Houston: Touch Publications.

Synan, Vinson. 1987. *The Twentieth-Century Pentecostal Explosion: The Exciting Growth of Pentecostal Churches and Charismatic Renewal Movements*. Altamonte, FL: Creation House.

Tabernacle Evangelism. 1993. Meeting Minutes. April 19.

Terry, John Mark, Ebbie Smith, and Justice Anderson, eds. 1998. *Missiology: An Introduction to the Foundations, History, and Strategies of World Missions*. Nashville: Broadman and Holman.

Tucker, Donald. 2005. Letter. *Africa Harvest Ministries*. November 4.

Van Engen, Charles. 1991. *God's Missionary People: Rethinking the Purpose of the Local Church*. Grand Rapids: Baker.

Van Rheenen, Gailyn. 1996. *Missions: Biblical Foundations and Contemporary Strategies*. Grand Rapids: Zondervan.

Walz, Brad. 2001. Case study. January.

———. 2003. E-mail letter and documents. March 20.

Watts, John D. W. 1987. *Isaiah 34–66*. Vol. 25 of *Word Biblical Commentary*. Waco, TX: Word Books.

Willetts, Peter. 2002. What Is a Non-Governmental Organization? Centre for International Politics, City University, London. http://www.staff.city.ac.uk/p.willetts/CS-NTWKS/NGO-ART .HTM#Summary (accessed June 11, 2009).

Williams, David J. 1990. *Acts*. New International Biblical Commentary. Peabody, MA: Hendrickson Publishers.

Williams, Morris O. 1979. *Partnership in Mission*. Springfield, MO: Department of Foreign Missions.

Winter, Ralph D. 1996. The Re-amateurization of Missions. *Occasional Bulletin*, Evangelical Missiological Society (Spring).

World Evangelical Fellowship Theological Commission. 1993.

Essential Course Materials

CONTENTS

CHECKLIST OF MATERIALS TO BE SUBMITTED TO BEREAN SCHOOL OF THE BIBLE

at Global University; 1211 South Glenstone Avenue; Springfield, Missouri, 65804; USA:

❑ Service Learning Requirement Report (required)
❑ Round-Tripper Forms (as needed)
❑ Request for a Printed Final Examination (if needed)

Service Learning Requirement Assignment

BEREAN SCHOOL OF THE BIBLE

SLR INSTRUCTIONS

This Service Learning Requirement (SLR) assignment requires you to apply something you have learned from this course in a ministry activity. Although this assignment does not receive a grade, it is required. You will not receive credit for this course until you submit the satisfactorily completed SLR Report Form. This form will not be returned to you.

Seriously consider how you can design and complete a meaningful ministry* activity as an investment in preparing to fulfill God's calling on your life. If you are already involved in active ministry, plan how you can incorporate and apply something from this course in your ongoing ministry activity. Whether or not full-time ministry is your goal, this assignment is required and designed to bring personal enrichment to all students. Ask the Holy Spirit to guide your planning and completion of this ministry exercise.

> * Meaningful ministry is defined as an act whereby you give of yourself in such a way as to meet the needs of another or to enhance the well-being of another (or others) in a way that exalts Christ and His kingdom.

You will complete the SLR by following these instructions:

1. Complete a ministry activity of your choice that you develop according to the following criteria:

    a. Your ministry activity must occur during your enrollment in this course. Do not report on activities or experiences in which you were involved prior to enrolling in this course.

    b. Your ministry activity must apply something you learned in this course, or it must incorporate something from this course's content in some way. Provide chapter, lesson, or page number(s) from the independent-study textbook on which the activity is based.

    c. Your ministry activity must include interacting with at least one other person. You may choose to interact with an individual or a group.

    d. The activity you complete must represent meaningful ministry*. You may develop your own ministry activity or choose from the list of suggestions provided in these instructions.

    e. Consider a ministry activity outside your comfort zone such as sharing the message of salvation with unbelievers or offering loving assistance to someone you do not know well.

2. Then fill out the SLR Report Form following these instructions OR online by accessing the online course. Students who will take the final exam online are encouraged to complete the online report form.

3. Sincere reflection is a key ingredient in valid ministry and especially in the growth and development of your ministry knowledge and effectiveness.

4. Global University faculty will evaluate your report. Although the SLR does not receive a grade, it must be completed to the faculty's satisfaction before a final grade for the course is released. The faculty may require you to resubmit an SLR Report Form for several reasons, including an incomplete form, apparent insincerity, failing to interact with others, and failure to incorporate course content.

Do NOT submit your SLR notes, essays, or other documents; only submit your completed SLR Report Form. No prior approval is needed as long as the activity fulfills the criteria from number one above.

Suggested SLR Ministry Activities

You may choose to engage in any valid and meaningful ministry experience that incorporates this specific course's content and interacts with other people. The following list of suggestions is provided to help you understand the possible activities that will fulfill this requirement. Choose an idea that will connect well with your course material. You may also develop a ministry activity that is not on this list or incorporate content from this course in ministry activity in which you are actively involved at this time:

- Teach a class or small group of any size.

- Preach a sermon to any size group.

- Share the gospel with non-believers; be prepared to develop new relationships to open doors to this ministry. We strongly encourage you to engage in ministry that may be outside your comfort zone.

- Lead a prayer group experience or pray with individual(s) in need, perhaps over an extended period.

- Disciple new believers in their walk with Jesus.

- Interview pastors, missionaries, or other leaders on a topic related to something in your course (do not post or publish interview content).

- Intervene to help resolve personal conflicts.

- Personally share encouragement and resources with those in need.

- Organize and/or administer a church program such as youth ministry, feeding homeless people, transporting people, visiting hospitals or shut-ins, nursing home services, etc.

- Assist with starting a new church.

- Publish an online blog or an article in a church newsletter (include a link in your report to the content of your article or blog).

- For MIN327 only: present a summary of risk management to a church board or other leadership group; interview community business people regarding their opinion of church business practices.

To review sample SLR Reports and to access an online report form, go to this Web address: library. globaluniversity.edu. Navigate to the Berean School of the Bible Students link under "Resources for You." Another helpful resource is our GlobalReach website: www.globalreach.org. From that site you can download materials free of charge from Global University's School for Evangelism and Discipleship. These proven evangelism tools are available in many languages.

BSB SERVICE LEARNING REQUIREMENT (SLR) REPORT

Please print or type your responses on this form, and submit the form to Berean School of the Bible. Do not submit other documents. This report will not be returned to you.

MIN261 Introduction to Assemblies of God Missions, Second Edition

Your Name... **Student Number** .... **Date** ....

1. Ministry activity date .... **Description of ministry activity and its content:** Briefly describe your ministry activity in the space provided. (You are encouraged to engage in ministry such as sharing your faith with unbelievers, or other activities that may be outside your comfort zone.)

....

....

....

Identify related course content by chapter, lesson, or page number. ....

....

2. Results: What resulted from your own participation in this activity? Include descriptions of people's reactions, decisions to accept Christ, confirmed miracles, Spirit and water baptisms, life changes, etc. Describe the individuals or group who benefited from or participated in your ministry activity. Use numbers to describe results when appropriate (approximate when unsure).

....

....

....

....

Record numbers here: Unbelievers witnessed to?.................. New decisions for Jesus?.....................

Holy Spirit baptisms?...................... Other?...

3. Reflection: Answer the following questions based on your experience in completing this assignment:

Did this activity satisfy an evident need in others? How so? ....

....

Were you adequately prepared to engage in this activity? Why or why not? ....

....

What positive or negative feelings were you aware of while you were completing this activity? ....

....

In what ways were you aware of the Holy Spirit's help during your ministry activity? ....

....

What would you change if you did this ministry activity again? ....

....

What strengths or weaknesses within yourself did this assignment reveal to you?.......................................

....

Did you receive feedback about this activity? If so, describe: ....

....

Unit Progress Evaluations

The unit progress evaluations (UPEs) are designed to indicate how well you learned the material in each unit. This may indicate how well prepared you are to take the closed-book final examination.

Taking Your Unit Progress Evaluations

1. Review the lessons of each unit before you take its unit progress evaluation (UPE). Refer to the form Checklist of Study Methods in the How to Use Berean Courses section at the front of the IST.

2. Answer the questions in each UPE without referring to your course materials, Bible, or notes.

3. Look over your answers carefully to avoid errors.

4. Check your answers with the answer keys provided in this section. Review lesson sections pertaining to questions you may have missed. Please note that the UPE scores do not count toward your course grade. They may indicate how well you are prepared to take the closed-book final examination.

5. Enter the date you completed each UPE on the Student Planner and Record form, located in the How to Use Berean Courses section in the front of this IST.

6. Request a printed final examination **if** you cannot take the final examination online. You should do this a few weeks before you take the last unit progress evaluation so that you will be able to take the final examination without delay when you complete the course.

UNIT PROGRESS EVALUATION 1
MIN261 Introduction to Assemblies of God Missions, Second Edition
(Unit 1—Chapter 1–3)

MULTIPLE CHOICE QUESTIONS

Select the best answer to each question.

1. *Missions* is defined and restricted to
   a) people in other geographical areas.
   b) unsaved people outside a local church.
   c) representing the gospel across geographical and cultural boundaries.
   d) winning people in gospel-destitute areas.

2. The term missionary is from a Greek word meaning
   a) "to send."
   b) "to shepherd."
   c) "to teach."
   d) "to preach."

3. Missions exists
   a) to provide food and shelter for people living in extreme poverty.
   b) to bring people to worship the true God.
   c) to alleviate all forms of human suffering.
   d) because people are worthy of being saved.

4. The principal motivation for witnessing is
   a) the fact that it is commanded in the Bible.
   b) the lostness of humankind.
   c) an intimate knowledge of the Lord.
   d) to attempt to alleviate suffering.

5. The level of authenticity in our witness will depend upon
   a) our level of biblical knowledge.
   b) our knowledge of culture.
   c) the gifts of the Spirit manifested through us.
   d) our closeness to the Lord.

6. The period between Christ's first coming and second coming is the
   a) age of the church.
   b) apostolic age.
   c) post-apostolic age.
   d) age of the prophets.

7. Both church and missions are creations of
   a) history.
   b) the institutional church.
   c) the Holy Spirit.
   d) the apostles.

8. The first prophecy of the coming of a Savior is found in the story of
   a) Abraham.
   b) Noah.
   c) the offspring of Eve.
   d) the sacrifice of Abel.

9. Most Old Testaments statements about God's mission are in the
   a) book of Proverbs.
   b) Song of Solomon.
   c) Psalms.
   d) book of Nehemiah.

10. The book of Habakkuk is primarily concerned with
    a) the realization of God's will for the world.
    b) suffering in the face of the powers of evil.
    c) the national worship of Israel alone.
    d) Israel being subject to God's will.

11. Joel's prophecy in the third part of his book applies to
    a) Israel.
    b) Babylon.
    c) Assyria.
    d) all people.

12. Old Testament prophecy climaxes in the book of
    a) Psalms.
    b) Ezekiel.
    c) Isaiah.
    d) Jeremiah.

13. In Isaiah, God's "servant," was to be a
    a) witness.
    b) king.
    c) prophet.
    d) judge.

14. The suffering servant in Isaiah portrays
    a) only Israel.
    b) only the Messiah.
    c) Israel and the Messiah.
    d) the Church.

15. The New Testament was written by
    a) apostles.
    b) evangelists.
    c) pastors.
    d) missionaries.

16. Matthew closes his gospel with the
    a) story of the passion.
    b) Great Commission.
    c) story of the resurrection.
    d) story of the ascension.

17. The central theme of the Gospel of Mark is
    a) the parables.
    b) the supernatural nature of Christ.
    c) Christ's conflicts with the Jewish leaders.
    d) the call of the disciples.

18. God called Paul to
    a) take the gospel to the Jews through preaching in the synagogues.
    b) proclaim Christ in the marketplaces.
    c) take the gospel to the Gentiles.
    d) abolish Jewish customs.

19. Worldview refers to assumptions that are
    a) conscious and known.
    b) explicit beliefs of a people.
    c) unconscious and taken for granted.
    d) the manifestation of the behavior of a culture.

20. Contextualization means that the
    a) gospel is relative.
    b) message changes from one culture to another.
    c) gospel is communicated by means of human culture.
    d) culture must change.

21. Western theology is mostly
    a) rationalistic.
    b) emotional in nature.
    c) concerned with faith issues.
    d) oriented toward the miraculous.

22. Languages are
    a) always complex.
    b) often primitive.
    c) only in rare occasions simple.
    d) essentially the same across cultures.

23. Body language is interpreted differently in different cultures. For example, in some places in Africa or Asia, averted eyes are a sign of
    a) shyness.
    b) belligerence.
    c) respect.
    d) indifference.

24. In individualistic cultures, communication is
    a) indirect.
    b) implicit.
    c) direct.
    d) sensitive to relationship building.

25. Tone of the voice communicates
    a) contextualization.
    b) paramessages.
    c) body language.
    d) primary messages.

After answering all of the questions in this UPE, check your answers with the answer key. Review material related to questions you may have missed, and then proceed to the next unit.

UNIT PROGRESS EVALUATION 2
MIN261 Introduction to Assemblies of God Missions, Second Edition
(Unit 2—Chapter 4–5)

MULTIPLE CHOICE QUESTIONS

Select the best answer to each question.

1. The Bible does not record when churches were established in
   a) Troas.
   b) Pontus.
   c) Lystra.
   d) Iconium.

2. Gregory had a ministry of signs and wonders in
   a) Cappadocia.
   b) Armenia.
   c) Derbe.
   d) Lystra.

3. The most dominant force in the spread of Christianity was
   a) apostles.
   b) evangelists.
   c) elders.
   d) ordinary Christians.

4. In AD 410, Rome was conquered by
   a) Attila the Hun.
   b) Alaric and the Goths.
   c) the Burgundians.
   d) the Lombards.

5. The New Testament was translated into the Gothic language by
   a) Clovis.
   b) Boniface.
   c) Giovanni Bernerdone.
   d) Ulfilas.

6. The state of the Franks was first led by
   a) Clovis.
   b) Childeric.
   c) Charlemagne.
   d) Geovanni Bernerdone.

7. When the Saxons accepted Christianity, their faith was one of
   a) profound depth.
   b) spiritual shallowness.
   c) spiritual commitment.
   d) missionary zeal.

8. *Immigrant missionary* meant the missionary
   a) became a part of the people and culture.
   b) was sent and supported by people from his or her culture.
   c) maintained a separate identity.
   d) was always known as a foreigner.

9. A better approach to Islam was stimulated by
   a) Giovanni Bernadone.
   b) Dominic.
   c) Ulfilas.
   d) Ramon Lull.

10. The Christian Order inspired by Matthew 10:7–10 was the
    a) Dominicans.
    b) Franciscans.
    c) Jesuits.
    d) Templar Knights.

11. Devoted to the conversion of heretics were the
    a) Franciscans.
    b) Jesuits.
    c) Dominicans.
    d) Augustinians.

12. The founder of Pietism was
    a) Spener.
    b) Zinzendorf.
    c) Ludwig.
    d) Melancthon.

13. The Moravians were
    a) people who opposed missionaries in northern Europe.
    b) devout Catholics who taught personal holiness.
    c) missionaries who used and taught their vocations while spreading the gospel.
    d) associates of William Carey.

14. Faith missions were so called because they
    a) were the precursors of other missions.
    b) had strong denominational support.
    c) were guaranteed local support.
    d) depended on faith for their support.

15. An affect of Pentecostal revival on the missionary movement was
    a) the prominent role of women.
    b) an emphasis on missions education.
    c) a unique sense of being led by the need on the field.
    d) denominational financial support.

16. J. Roswell Flower
    a) established broad criteria for missionary appointment.
    b) established field leadership.
    c) established a basic budget for individual missionaries.
    d) gave individual initiative to the missionaries in the area of projects.

17. Noel Perkin was troubled that missions work often depended on
    a) untrained men.
    b) women missionaries.
    c) single men.
    d) unspiritual missionaries.

18. One important change after WW II was
    a) a new emphasis on Europe.
    b) that Asia became the primary focus.
    c) that Africa became the primary focus.
    d) strategic planning became a part of missions planning.

19. An important decision made in the 1955 General Council was the
    a) establishment of Field Directors.
    b) establishment of the Foreign Missions Board.
    c) top leader of Foreign Missions became an Assistant General Superintendent.
    d) Foreign Missions Board was expanded to include six pastors.

20. To bring efficiency to AGWM, J. Philip Hogan emphasized
    a) the individual finances of the missionaries.
    b) the naming of new field (or regional) directors.
    c) an annual school of missions.
    d) the individual vision of the missionaries.

21. Hogan believed compassion ministries were
    a) equal to ministries of proclamation.
    b) superior to evangelism.
    c) not to be recognized.
    d) a kind of pre-evangelism.

22. At first, the primary function of Home Missions was
    a) prison ministry.
    b) church planting and overseeing Bible schools.
    c) ministry to college campuses.
    d) establishing urban centers.

23. The recent attention to immigrant ministry
    a) appeals to immigrants around the world.
    b) is as narrow-minded as that of previous years.
    c) targets immigrants in the United States who maintain their culture.
    d) conflicts with the United States sense of nationalism.

24. Structurally, Teen Challenge was placed under the
    a) Prison Department.
    b) Intercultural Ministries Department.
    c) Youth Department.
    d) Urban Centers Department.

25. Chi Alpha is a program designed to reach
    a) international students.
    b) high school students.
    c) Assemblies of God college students.
    d) all college students.

After answering all of the questions in this UPE, check your answers with the answer key. Review material related to questions you may have missed, and then proceed to the next unit.

UNIT PROGRESS EVALUATION 3

MIN261 Introduction to Assemblies of God Missions, Second Edition
(Unit 3—Chapter 6–8)

MULTIPLE CHOICE QUESTIONS

Select the best answer to each question.

1. Jesus began His ministry by
   a) calling and discipling people.
   b) preaching.
   c) performing miracles.
   d) turning water into wine.

2. The best predictor of a missionary candidate's success is
   a) knowing his or her level of education.
   b) knowing his or her past success.
   c) adequate training in cultural studies.
   d) the evidence of spiritual gifts.

3. A missionary must first take on the role of
   a) teacher.
   b) cross-cultural communicator.
   c) learner.
   d) preacher.

4. The preferred approach for raising a missionary budget is through
   a) a denominational central fund.
   b) appeals by letters.
   c) interviews with church boards.
   d) the deputational cycle.

5. An incarnational missionary is a missionary who
   a) lives in another culture.
   b) learns another language.
   c) takes the posture of one among equals.
   d) learns to teach in another culture.

6. The baptism in the Holy Spirit in Acts was to
   a) manifest the fruit of the Spirit.
   b) exercise the gifts of the Spirit.
   c) be a witness.
   d) receive the anointing for the office of an overseer.

7. The power of prayer is demonstrated in the fact that
   a) God depends on our communication to exist.
   b) it moves us to tears.
   c) God may know us personally.
   d) it affects God's actions.

8. Assemblies of God World Missions focus is
   a) evangelism.
   b) social and compassion ministries.
   c) medical work.
   d) education.

9. Tabernacle evangelism was conceived in Africa to
   a) conserve the harvest of souls.
   b) provide an entire building for a congregation.
   c) encourage missions giving in the United States.
   d) provide a temporary structure.

10. Assemblies of God missionaries always seek to establish
    a) schools.
    b) Bible schools.
    c) medical clinics.
    d) agricultural education.

11. The house church movement was successful because of the
    a) global persecution of Christian missionaries.
    b) low cost in maintaining house churches.
    c) lack of pastoral training in the church.
    d) intimacy of the small, virtually inconspicuous gathering.

12. The church planting endeavor is external in that
    a) it does not involve personal relationships with converts.
    b) it is aimed at cultures outside of one's own.
    c) it focuses on the missionary's own life and culture.
    d) the missionary's life is not of any concern to the church.

13. The indigenous church philosophy was taken to Korea by
    a) Venn.
    b) Anderson.
    c) Nevius.
    d) Carey.

14. The principal growth of a local church comes from
    a) itinerating evangelists.
    b) the pulpit and the witness of members.
    c) evangelistic mass crusades.
    d) social service to the community.

15. The most difficult indigenous-church principle to achieve is
    a) self-propagation.
    b) self-support.
    c) self-theologizing.
    d) self-governance.

16. Contextualization refers to
    a) teaching another gospel.
    b) a local approach to interpreting Scripture.
    c) expressing Christian belief in one's own culture.
    d) the tendency to syncretism.

17. Mixing biblical truth with local beliefs and practices is called
    a) syncretism.
    b) contextualization.
    c) self-theologizing.
    d) self-missionizing.

18. *Ekklesia*, the Greek word for church,
    a) had a strong religious connotation.
    b) referred to a meeting.
    c) was a mystery.
    d) is used only twice in the Bible.

19. The Church exists as a result of the
    a) will and activity of God.
    b) development of the institutional church.
    c) ministry of the apostles.
    d) administration of the church fathers.

20. The guiding principle in a local church's program is
    a) the manifestation of godly leadership.
    b) the Spirit-led selection of deacons.
    c) missions.
    d) the pursuit of sound financial accountability.

21. The church modeling financial support of missionaries was in
    a) Ephesus
    b) Antioch
    c) Jerusalem
    d) Philippi

22. A reason for establishing the Africa Assemblies of God Alliance was to
    a) encourage a more centralized church government on the continent.
    b) organize conferences in the different regions of the continent.
    c) arbitrate in disputes in the various churches.
    d) coordination and promotion of missions.

23 A national church's establishing a missions program depends on
    a) a sufficient financial base from which to send missionaries.
    b) obedience to the Lord's command to reach all nations.
    c) providing enough ministers for the local churches.
    d) first establishing of a home missions program.

24. The term *non-governmental organization* came into use
    a) with the establishment of social action within missions agencies.
    b) with the founding of the Red Cross.
    c) as an alternative to the World Trade Organization.
    d) with the establishment of the United Nations.

25. The purpose of the Lausanne Conference in 1974 was
    a) promoting world evangelization.
    b) bringing unity within the Pentecostal churches.
    c) examining globalization.
    d) discussing theological unity.

After answering all of the questions in this UPE, check your answers with the answer key. Review material related to questions you may have missed, and then proceed to the next unit.

UNIT PROGRESS EVALUATION 4

MIN261 Introduction to Assemblies of God Missions, Second Edition
(Unit 4—Chapter 9–11)

MULTIPLE CHOICE QUESTIONS

Select the best answer to each question.

1. Christendom's center has shifted from
   a) the Far East to the western nations.
   b) western nations to the Majority World.
   c) Europe to America.
   d) North America to South America.

2. After WW II western missions affected Majority World churches by
   a) stimulating fervent missionary activity.
   b) demonstrating they no longer needed significant financial support.
   c) slowing their growth through paternalism.
   d) failing to give adequate guidance.

3. For the Majority World, evangelizing unreached people groups
   a) was a major motivating factor for the rapid growth in missions efforts.
   b) was discouraging due to their poor economies.
   c) was frustrating since they had no missionary training programs.
   d) caused them to redirect their already strong missions efforts.

4. An advantage of Majority World missionaries is
   a) their ease of gaining financial support from their own churches.
   b) not having to learn another language.
   c) their cross-cultural experience in a pluralistic setting.
   d) their high level of missionary training before being sent out.

5. Majority World missionaries are not always successful because of their
   a) tendency to want to dominate in leadership.
   b) lack of pre-field training in mission principles and practices.
   c) lack of resiliency in cross-cultural settings.
   d) over dependence on western missionaries.

6. An impetus to project-oriented short-term mission outreaches is the
   a) greater ease for short-termers to adjust to the language and culture.
   b) desire for first-hand experience with immediate measurable results.
   c) closing of former mission fields to career missionaries.
   d) opposition of many national churches to full-time career missionaries.

7. Western missions accept short-term mission outreaches due in part to
   a) their belief that they could stop recruiting career missionaries.
   b) the long-term benefits from the relationships built with the national churches.
   c) the reduced expectations of the national churches to receive funds from short-termers.
   d) the belief it would increase the interest and giving to missions.

8. In short-term missions, bridging is building relationships
   a) between the group and the host people.
   b) between the mission and the national church.
   c) among the members of the short-term group.
   d) among the host people in gratefulness to the team.

9. Benefits of short-term mission outreaches include
   a) reduced need for full-time career missionaries.
   b) reduced need for learning a language and adapting to culture.
   c) increase in the development of national church self-support.
   d) home congregations coming alive to their mission potential.

10. A key to success of short-term missions is
    a) teaching team members the language of the host people.
    b) avoiding the career missionaries in order to introduce new ways.
    c) adequate pre-trip orientation and training.
    d) avoiding the "red tape" of mission agencies to maximize efficiency.

11. Mega churches have a marked increase in
    a) financial giving through the mission agency of their denomination.
    b) entrepreneurship as missions by project.
    c) missions as process.
    d) all-night prayer meetings for missions.

12. A focus on missions by project may result in
    a) acceleration of growth of the national church.
    b) excessive drain on church finances.
    c) depreciation of the need for long-term missionaries.
    d) avoiding the problems associated with mission as process.

13. A key factor for success in a mission project is
    a) making sure the project is controlled by the team itself to avoid mistakes.
    b) close collaboration with the career missionaries and host nationals.
    c) insuring the nationals pay their fair share of the cost.
    d) being prepared to use western methods to insure efficiency within the time.

14. A benefit of technology in missions today is
    a) enhanced connectivity between the home base and the missionary.
    b) the challenge to those in the host culture to use technology in ministry.
    c) the low cost in obtaining the latest technology to be more efficient.
    d) the time economy in relating to people in the host culture.

15. Theological drift is most likely caused by
    a) antagonism from highly visible and vocal non-Christian religions.
    b) failure to use the King James Authorized Version of the Bible.
    c) excessive emphasis on particular theological distinctives.
    d) the effects of local culture and history.

16. Scripture which teaches salvation only through faith in Christ is
    a) Acts 4:12.
    b) Acts 1:8.
    c) Romans 14:1–8.
    d) Galatians 5:1.

17. The trend in Pentecostal circles toward evangelicalism is due to
    a) a preference for contemporary music instead of older songs and hymns.
    b) the more rapid growth among evangelical churches.
    c) misunderstanding the nature and purpose of the baptism in the Holy Spirit.
    d) the prestige of association with evangelicals like Rick Warren.

18. The proper attitude toward preaching the gospel and social service is
    a) proclamation must be preferred, for social service can put off salvation.
    b) proclamation and social service are both involved in sharing the gospel.
    c) social service is to be preferred to show God's love.
    d) proclamation is the duty of missionaries, not social service.

19. Cultural mandate refers to
    a) the command to subdue all cultures.
    b) God's command to Adam to till the earth.
    c) the application of the gospel to all cultures.
    d) the authority given to man to govern creation.

20. Jesus illustrates the cultural mandate by the
    a) parable of the sower and the soils.
    b) parable of the talents.
    c) emphasis on loving and caring for neighbors.
    d) reference to himself as the Good Shepherd.

21. Salvation in the Bible is best defined as
    a) the transformation of one's soul.
    b) a radical change in a person's whole being and relationships.
    c) separation from the world, the flesh, and the devil.
    d) deliverance from bondage.

22. The idea that Jesus is Lord of our lives means
    a) He is behind everything that happens to us, good or bad.
    b) whatever we do is because He is sovereignly directing our steps.
    c) the direction of our lives is ultimately up to Him as we obey.
    d) He rules and reigns over all creation.

23. Our responsibility to be good stewards because all we have is God's
    a) is spelled out in 2 Kings 5:20-25.
    b) was stated in Luke 11:3.
    c) is the theme of Acts 2:36.
    d) summarizes the meaning of Psalm 24:1.

24. Paul gives the most extensive teaching on financial giving in
  a) 2 Corinthians 8:1–24.
  b) Romans 15:22–29.
  c) Philippians 4:13–19.
  d) 1 Corinthians 16:1–4.

25. Missions is the responsibility of
  a) missionaries specially called by God.
  b) pastors with a heart for missions.
  c) missionaries, pastors, and prayer warriors.
  d) all believers.

After answering all of the questions in this UPE, check your answers with the answer key. Review material related to questions you may have missed. Review all materials in preparation for the final exam. Complete and submit your SLR assignment and take the closed-book final examination.

Taking the Final Examination

1. **All final exams must be taken closed book.** You are not allowed to use any materials or outside help while taking a final exam. You will take the final examination online at www.globaluniversity.edu. If the online option is not available to you, you may request a printed final exam. If you did not request a printed final exam when you ordered your course, you must submit this request a few weeks before you are ready to take the exam. The Request for a Printed Final Examination is in the Forms section of Essential Course Materials at the back of this IST.

2. Review for the final examination in the same manner in which you prepared for the UPEs. Refer to the form Checklist of Study Methods in the front part of the IST for further helpful review hints.

3. After you complete and submit the online final examination, the results will be immediately available to you. Your final course grade report will be e-mailed to your Global University student e-mail account after your Service Learning Requirement (SLR) report has been processed.

4. If you complete the exam in printed form, you will send your final examination, your answer sheets, and your SLR report to Berean School of the Bible for grading. Your final course grade report will be sent to your GU student e-mail account. If you do not have access to the Internet, your grade will be sent to your mailing address.

Answer Keys

- Compare your answers to the Test Yourself quizzes against those given in this section.

- Compare your answers to the UPE questions against the answer keys located in this section.

- Review the course content identified by your incorrect answers.

ANSWERS TO TEST YOURSELF

MIN261 Introduction to Assemblies of God Missions, Second Edition

Answers below are followed by the number of the objective being tested. For any questions you answered incorrectly, review the lesson content in preparation for your final exam.

Chapter 1
1. D 1.1.1
2. B 1.1.1
3. A 1.1.2
4. B 1.2.1
5. C 1.2.2
6. B 1.2.3
7. C 1.2.3
8. A 1.3.2
9. C 1.3.3
10. C 1.2.2

Chapter 2
1. B 2.1.1
2. D 2.1.1
3. B 2.1.1
4. A 2.1.2
5. C 2.1.2
6. C 2.1.3
7. C 2.2.1
8. A 2.2.1
9. C 2.2.3
10. B 2.2.4

Chapter 3
1. B 3.1.1
2. C 3.1.1
3. B 3.1.1
4. B 3.1.1
5. C 3.1.1
6. B 3.1.1
7. C 3.1.1
8. A 3.1.2
9. C 3.1.2
10. D 3.1.2

Chapter 4
1. C 4.1.1
2. D 4.1.1
3. B 4.1.1
4. D 4.1.1
5. B 4.1.2
6. C 4.1.2
7. D 4.2.2
8. A 4.3.2
9. C 4.4.1
10. B 4.4.2

Chapter 5
1. C 5.1.1
2. B 5.1.2
3. C 5.2.1
4. A 5.2.1
5. B 5.3.2
6. C 5.4.1
7. C 5.4.1
8. C 5.4.1
9. B 5.4.2
10. C 5.4.2

Chapter 6
1. C 6.1.1
2. D 6.1.2
3. B 6.1.2
4. C 6.1.2
5. B 6.1.3
6. A 6.1.3
7. D 6.2.1
8. B 6.2.2
9. C 6.2.2
10. D 6.2.2

Chapter 7
1. C 7.1.1
2. D 7.1.1
3. B 7.1.2
4. C 7.1.3
5. A 7.1.3
6. B 7.2.1
7. B 7.2.2
8. A 7.2.3
9. C 7.2.4
10. C 7.2.2

Chapter 8
1. D 8.1.1
2. C 8.1.2
3. B 8.1.3
4. A 8.1.3
5. C 8.3.1
6. B 8.3.2
7. B 8.3.3
8. C 8.3.3
9. B 8.3.4
10. C 8.3.5

Chapter 9
1. D 9.1.1
2. B 9.1.1
3. D 9.1.2
4. A 9.2.2
5. B 9.3.1
6. C 9.3.1
7. A 9.4.1
8. D 9.4.1
9. D 9.5.1
10. D 9.5.2

Chapter 10
1. D 10.1.1
2. C 10.1.1
3. B 10.1.1
4. B 10.2.1
5. A 10.2.2
6. B 10.2.3
7. B 10.2.3
8. C 10.2.3
9. B 10.2.3
10. A 10.2.4

Chapter 11
1. A 11.1.1
2. A 11.1.1
3. D 11.1.2
4. B 11.1.2
5. C 11.1.3
6. C 11.1.3
7. A 11.1.4
8. B 11.1.4
9. D 11.1.4
10. C 11.1.4

UNIT PROGRESS EVALUATION ANSWER KEYS

MIN261 Introduction to Assemblies of God Missions, Second Edition

Answers below are followed by the number of the objective being tested. For any questions you answered incorrectly, review the lesson content in preparation for your final exam.

UNIT PROGRESS EVALUATION 1

1.	C	1.1.1	14.	C	2.1.3
2.	A	1.1.1	15.	D	2.2.1
3.	B	1.2.1	16.	B	2.2.1
4.	C	1.2.1	17.	B	2.2.1
5.	D	1.2.2	18.	C	2.2.3
6.	A	1.3.3	19.	C	3.1.1
7.	C	1.3.3	20.	C	3.1.1
8.	C	2.1.1	21.	A	3.1.2
9.	C	2.1.1	22.	A	3.1.1
10.	A	2.1.2	23.	C	3.1.2
11.	D	2.1.2	24.	C	3.1.2
12.	C	2.1.3	25.	B	3.1.2
13.	A	2.1.3			

UNIT PROGRESS EVALUATION 2

1.	B	4.1.1	14.	D	5.1.1
2.	A	4.1.1	15.	A	5.1.2
3.	D	4.1.1	16.	C	5.2.1
4.	B	4.1.1	17.	B	5.3.1
5.	D	4.1.1	18.	D	5.3.3
6.	B	4.1.1	19.	B	5.4.1
7.	B	4.1.2	20.	C	5.4.1
8.	A	4.1.2	21.	D	5.4.1
9.	D	4.2.1	22.	B	5.4.2
10.	B	4.2.2	23.	C	5.4.2
11.	C	4.2.2	24.	A	5.4.2
12.	A	4.3.2	25.	D	5.4.2
13.	C	4.3.2			

UNIT PROGRESS EVALUATION 3

1.	A	6.1.1	14.	B	7.2.2
2.	B	6.1.2	15.	D	7.2.2
3.	C	6.1.2	16.	C	7.2.2
4.	D	6.1.3	17.	A	7.2.3
5.	C	6.1.3	18.	B	8.1.1
6.	C	6.2.1	19.	A	8.1.1
7.	D	6.2.2	20.	C	8.1.2
8.	A	7.1.1	21.	D	8.1.3
9.	A	7.1.3	22.	D	8.2.1
10.	B	7.2.1	23.	B	8.2.1
11.	D	7.1.2	24.	D	8.3.2
12.	B	7.2.1	25.	A	8.3.3
13.	C	7.2.1			

UNIT PROGRESS EVALUATION 4

1.	B	9.1.1	14	A	9.4.1
2.	C	9.1.1	15	D	9.5.1
3.	A	9.1.2	16	A	9.5.1
4.	C	9.1.2	17	C	9.5.2
5.	B	9.1.2	18	B	10.1.1
6.	B	9.2.1	19	D	10.2.1
7.	D	9.2.1	20	C	10.2.1
8.	A	9.2.1	21	B	10.2.2
9.	D	9.2.1	22	C	11.1.1
10.	C	9.2.2	23	D	11.1.1
11.	B	9.3.1	24	A	11.1.3
12.	C	9.3.1	25	D	11.1.4
13.	B	9.3.1			

Forms

The following pages contain two course forms: the Round-Tripper and the Request for a Printed Final Examination.

1. For students who do not have access to e-mail, we are including one **Round-Tripper** for your use if you have a question or comment related to your studies. If you do not have access to the Internet, you will want to make several photocopies of the Round-Tripper before you write on it. Retain the copies for submitting additional questions as needed. Students who have access to e-mail can submit questions at any time to bsbcontent@globaluniversity.edu.

2. Students who do not have access to the Internet-based tests may request a printed final examination. For faster service, please call Enrollment Services at 1-800-443-1083 or fax your **Request for a Printed Final Examination** to 417-862-0863.

ROUND-TRIPPER

MIN261 Introduction to Assemblies of God Missions, Second Edition

Date ....

Your Name .... Your Student Number ....

Send questions and comments by e-mail to bsbcontent@globaluniversity.edu. If you do not have access to e-mail, use this form to write to Berean School of the Bible with questions or comments related to your studies. Write your question in the space provided. Send this form to Berean School of the Bible. The form will make its return, or round-trip, as Berean School of the Bible responds.

YOUR QUESTION:

FOR BEREAN SCHOOL OF THE BIBLE'S RESPONSE:

PN 02.14.01

GLOBAL UNIVERSITY

1211 South Glenstone Springfield, MO 65804
1-800-443-1083 * Fax 1-417-862-0863
www.globaluniversity.edu

BEREAN SCHOOL OF THE BIBLE
REQUEST FOR A PRINTED FINAL
EXAMINATION

NOTE: All final exams are to be taken closed-book.

Final examinations are available online at www.globaluniversity.edu.

Taking the test online gives immediate results and feedback. You will know your test grade and which learning objectives you may have missed.

Students who do not have access to the Internet-based tests may request a printed final examination. For faster service, please call Enrollment Services at **1-800-443-1083** or fax this form to **417-862-0863**.

If preferred, mail this form to:
Berean School of the Bible, Global University
Attn: Enrollment Services
1211 South Glenstone
Springfield, MO 65804

Please allow 7–10 business days for delivery of your final examination. **You may only request an exam for the course or courses in which you are currently enrolled.**

Student Number

Name

Address

City, State, Zip Code

Phone

E-mail

Certified Minister	Licensed Minister	Ordained Minister
☐ BIB114 Christ in the Synoptic Gospels	☐ BIB212 New Testament Survey	☐ BIB313 Corinthian Correspondence
☐ BIB115 Acts: The Holy Spirit at Work in Believers	☐ BIB214 Old Testament Survey	☐ BIB318 Pentateuch
☐ BIB117 Prison Epistles: Colossians, Philemon, Ephesians, and Philippians	☐ BIB215 Romans: Justification by Faith	☐ BIB322 Poetic Books
	☐ THE211 Introduction to Theology: A Pentecostal Perspective	☐ THE311 Prayer and Worship
☐ BIB121 Introduction to Hermeneutics: How to Interpret the Bible	☐ THE245 Eschatology: A Study of Things to Come	☐ MIN325 Preaching in the Contemporary World
☐ THE114 Introduction to Pentecostal Doctrine	☐ MIN223 Introduction to Homiletics	☐ MIN327 Church Administration, Finance, and Law
☐ THE142 Assemblies of God History, Missions, and Governance	☐ MIN251 Effective Leadership	☐ MIN381 Pastoral Ministry
	☐ MIN261 Introduction to Assemblies of God Missions	☐ MIN391 Advanced Ministerial Internship
☐ MIN123 The Local Church in Evangelism	☐ MIN281 Conflict Management for Church Leaders	
☐ MIN181 Relationships and Ethics in Ministry	☐ MIN291 Intermediate Ministerial Internship	
☐ MIN191 Beginning Ministerial Internship		

Signature _____   Date_____